100 Surefire Improvements to Sell Your House Faster

R. Dodge Woodson

100 Surefire Improvements to Sell Your House Faster

R. Dodge Woodson

John Wiley & Sons, Inc.

New York • Chichester • Brisbane • Toronto • Singapore

Library of Congress Cataloging-in-Publication Data:

Woodson, R. Dodge (Roger Dodge).
   100 surefire improvements to sell your house faster / by R.
  Dodge Woodson.
     p. cm.
   Includes index.
   ISBN 0-471-59252-8   (cloth) —ISBN 0-471-59253-6 (pbk.)
    1. Dwellings—Maintenance and repair. 2. Dwellings—Remodeling.
3. House selling. I. Title. II. Title: One hundred improvements
guaranteed to sell your house faster.
TH4817.W66 1993
643'.7—dc20   93-6487

Printed in the United States of America
10 9 8 7 6 5 4 3 2 1

This book is dedicated to my wonderful daughter, Afton Amber Woodson. While only four years old, Afton is amazing. She understands the importance of my writing and allows me the indulgence.

For Kimberley, my wife, I must extend my thanks. During the many hours I devote to my book projects, Kimberley always holds the fort. We have just had our eleventh wedding anniversary, and I have no regrets; I would do it all over again.

Kimberley and Afton, I love you.

Acknowledgments

I would like to thank and acknowledge the following professionals, in order of appearance, for their contribution to this book.

Mr. Peter L. Chander, CPA—with the firm of KPMG Peat Marwick, of Portland, Maine.

Mrs. Jane L. Furbeck-Owen, Certified General Appraiser—General Partner of Brunswick Real Estate Services, Brunswick, Maine.

Further, I would like to acknowledge my parents, Maralou and Woody. Without them, I would not be here to write this book. Thanks, Mom and Dad.

Mr. Mike Hamilton, and others at John Wiley & Sons also deserve acknowledgment. Without their combined efforts, this book would not be in your hands. Mike, thank you and all of the people involved in the production of this book.

Contents

Introduction

This book is not like most books written to help you sell your home. When you read the following chapters you will discover simple, cost-effective home improvements that help to sell houses faster. These techniques are proven producers. The advice given comes from experience. You will get inside tips from a real estate broker, a real estate investor, a builder, a remodeling contractor, a master plumber, a certified public accountant, and a real estate appraiser. If you are serious about selling your home, this book will help you set your house apart from the crowd, and sell it fast.

The projects discussed in this book will be rated for ease of completion and financial feasibility. You will be given estimates for how long each project will take to complete. You can see examples of how much the improvement will cost if you do the work yourself and how much it will cost if you hire contractors. Tax consequences and advantages will be looked at and explained.

The author, R. Dodge Woodson, has been involved with real estate for nearly 20 years. He is licensed as a designated real estate broker, a general contractor, and a master plumber. His accomplishments have included selling and building as many as sixty single-family homes in a single year. This man knows what it takes to sell real estate, and he shares it with you in this unique book.

Chapter 1

Projects That Require Time, But Not Much Money

There is a multitude of home improvements you can do that require time, but not much money. Sprucing up your house doesn't have to be expensive. If you walk around your home and look, you will see potential for several simple projects.

Is your shrubbery neatly trimmed, or is it a little rough around the edges? When was the last time you inspected the caulking around your plumbing fixtures? Have you ever gone away for a few days and noticed unpleasant odors in your home upon returning? These questions are only a starting point to finding aspects of your home to improve upon.

When you live in a house, you begin to accept little annoyances. You might become so accustomed to minor flaws that you no longer notice them. However, when you attempt to sell your house, these little nuisances that you have come to accept may turn a buyer away.

Home buyers can be finicky. If buyers come to view your home and find two or three little problems, they may become suspicious about the rest of the property. For example, consider this scenario.

Your home is listed for sale, and prospective buyers come to inspect the property. When the buyers attempt to locate your house, they have trouble. Since you postponed replacing the old house numbers blown down in the last storm, the buyers have to guess which house is yours.

The buyers, after trying to determine which house is yours, pull into the driveway. Because of the lack of visible house numbers, they are slightly annoyed. As the buyers step out of their car, the first factor they notice is your unkempt hedge.

Moving toward the front door, the buyers start up the steps, and one of them notices that the handrail is loose and wiggles.

You answer the door, and the buyers step into the foyer. As usual, the first thing the buyers do after greeting you is look around. While looking up, the husband notices a hole around the light fixture in the foyer, the result of your replacing the old fixture with a new, more attractive light. You meant to repair the hole, but you just haven't gotten around to it.

The wife heads for the kitchen, but is repulsed at the brown ring around the kitchen sink. While the wife checks out the kitchen and the bathrooms, the husband heads into the basement, where he wants to set up his model-train collection.

When the man enters the basement, he is met with musty odors, mildew on the walls, and oil stains from the heating system on the floor. His eyes and nose tell him that this basement is not suitable for a hobby room.

Meanwhile, upstairs, the wife has found dripping faucets that won't shut off and plumbing fixtures with a buildup of crud around them. She has decided that this house is going to take some hard housecleaning to make it acceptable.

The rest of the house tour goes well, and the prospects leave, telling you they will discuss the home and get back to you. As the couple is driving away, they begin their discussion of all the flaws they found in your home. The good points about the house are not mentioned.

The immediate response of the husband and wife is to look for a home that doesn't need so much work. You lost a potential sale because you didn't prepare the house for sale properly. With a little time, and not much money, you could have corrected all the factors that caused the couple to strike your house off their list of possible purchases.

This example is not farfetched. As a real estate broker, I have seen people rule out properties for fewer reasons than were given in the example. It doesn't take much to turn hot buyers off. The right sales pitch might overcome the objections and rekindle the buyers, but it's a gamble.

When you want to sell your home, you should remove as much of the gamble as possible. By tending to small features you can improve your odds of a sale without putting a strain on your bank account. Now let's see what you can do to help sell your house without spending much money.

Trimming Shrubbery

Will trimming the shrubbery help sell your home? It can; unkempt shrubbery will send negative signals to prospective buyers. When buyers see shrubbery unattended to, they assume other areas of the property may be neglected.

Curb appeal is a term used to describe how your home will project its first impression on buyers. If a house has poor curb appeal, buyers may not be interested in looking beyond the exterior.

As a broker, I have pulled up to houses only to have my customers ask me to keep going. After seeing the outside of the homes, these buyers had no interest in wasting time with inside features.

You can't afford to alienate potential buyers. While nine out of ten buyers may not care if your shrubbery is neatly trimmed, the tenth prospect may be fickle enough to ignore further inspection of your home. Since you can never be sure which potential buyer will buy your home, you must make the house appealing to as many buyers as possible.

Trimming your shrubbery certainly isn't an expensive proposition. However, losing a buyer because you didn't groom the greenery is an expensive lesson. Now that you agree with the need to keep your bushes looking nice, let's look at some specifics to keep in mind with your shrubbery trimming.

Security

Shrubbery can create a security hazard. While most buyers will see your landscaping as an asset, some buyers will look upon your shrubbery as a place for criminals to hide.

When you trim your shrubbery, it will normally be best to keep the plants well-shaped and not too expansive. If your house is in a high-crime area, smaller shrubs will probably be more productive in the sale of your home than massive ones.

Foundation Cover

Many people use shrubbery as a foundation cover. These plants are meant to be low-growing and to conceal the home's foundation. When trimming this type of shrubbery, don't thin out between the shrubs too much. Keep the height in line with the bottom of the home's siding and allow the plants to grow out, not up.

Overpowering Size

The overpowering size of some shrubbery makes a negative impact on buyers. If you have shrubs growing close to your home that reach the roof, the house will look small. From inside the home, these monster plants may obstruct views from the windows. The security factor is another consideration with these big shrubs. You should plant and trim your shrubbery to compliment you home, not overpower it.

Cleaning up after Yourself

Cleaning up after yourself is important when trimming shrubbery. If you leave the cut trimmings on the ground, they will discolor and become an eyesore. Then you have a lawn littered with shrubbery clippings that show negligence. Remember, you never want buyers to assume that you are negligent in the maintenance of your home.

Trimming shrubbery is not difficult. On a rating scale of 1 to 10, with 10 being the most difficult, trimming shrubbery rates a 1. As for the cost of this home improvement, there is none, unless you use electric trimmers, and even then you are only paying for a little electricity. Your time investment in this task could range from about an hour to a full day. If you engage a professional to trim your shrubbery, expect to spend a minimum of $35. Rates for this work will range from $20 to $30 per hour.

Installing New House Numbers

Installing new house numbers can play a role in the sale of your home. Have you looked at your house numbers recently? Are they in good repair and easy to read from the street? If they aren't, you should replace them.

House numbers are a feature that homeowners take for granted. Since homeowners know where they live, they don't rely on their house numbers to get home. However, people who are not familiar with the home's location will depend on the house numbers for identification. If prospective buyers can't find your house, they can't buy it.

Take a walk outside and look at your house numbers. Don't just stand on your porch and inspect them, go out to the street and look back at your house. Remember, prospective buyers will be driving on the street in search of your home, not standing on your porch. Also keep in mind that the buyers may be trying to find your house in the dark. Do your house numbers show up well in low-light conditions?

If after inspecting your house numbers you find they are inadequate, replace them. This is a simple job, and the cost of new house numbers is minimal. There are, however, a few pointers you should keep in mind with this job.

If you are going to replace your house numbers, be aware of the potential need to do some touch-up painting or staining. When you replace the old numbers, try to use numbers of the same style and size. If you must use a different type of house number, try to buy numbers that are larger than the existing ones. Your goal is to eliminate the extra work of concealing the evidence of your number replacement.

The siding behind the old house numbers will not look the same as the rest of the house. Weather and exposure will have changed the color of the exposed siding. The siding behind the old numbers will be an obvious mismatch. By using larger house numbers you may be able to avoid repainting or staining the siding.

Don't be too cheap in the purchase of your house numbers. Remember, the house numbers are going to be the first item that prospective purchasers associate with your house. If you use peel-and-stick numbers, you will not make the same impression that you would with brass numbers.

The difficulty rating for changing house numbers is a 1. The cost for this type of project could easily be less than $10. Plan on spending between one and two hours on this project. Hiring a handyman to do the work will probably cost around $25.

Keeping Porch Rails in Good Repair

Keeping porch rails in good repair is not only good for safety, it may help to sell your house. Have you ever walked up to a friend's house and had the porch rail shake and wobble? Did you wonder why your friend didn't fix the darned thing? Well, home buyers might ask themselves the same question about your loose porch rail.

Loose porch railings are annoying and potentially dangerous. The railings can damage the steps they are attached to, increasing the cost of future repairs. To a home buyer loose railings indicate homeowners with little regard for their home. This is an impression you cannot afford to cast.

Fixing loose porch railings is usually a simple procedure. The job often requires no more than tightening a few bolts. If the procedure is so simple, why don't more homeowners correct their defective railings?

Railings are not repaired for many reasons, but the main reason is that they seem to be a trivial problem. Granted, most shaky rails are not a physical hazard, but they are annoying, and they can repel buyers.

Selling your home is a big job. There is competition you must beat and market conditions to be dealt with. If you are serious about selling your home, you cannot afford any chinks in your armor. You must make your house as salable as possible. This means not turning your back on little things like shaky railings.

Can you fix your own railings? Most homeowners have more than enough do-it-yourself skills to tackle the job of repairing loose railings. If you are lucky, all you will need is an adjustable wrench and about ten minutes of your time. The job could be more difficult, but if you are at all handy, you can do it yourself.

Many rails are held in place with lag bolts, which are essentially big screws with a bolt-type head. If the lag bolts become loose, turning them clockwise should tighten them and solve your problem.

Some metal railings are screwed into the walls of the home and into the steps. In the case of brick homes and concrete steps, the screws are screwed into a sheath. When these rails become loose, it may be necessary to remove them and reinstall them, but this is not a big job.

As time passes, the screws and anchors used to hold railings in place can become loose. Years of use will cause the holes for the anchors and screws to become enlarged. When this is the cause of your loose railings, you must replace the screws and anchors with larger ones.

When you remove the screws from your railings, the railings should come off. As a side note, this would be a good time to put a fresh coat of paint on your railings. With the railings off, remove the anchors. The anchors may be made of lead or plastic. In either case, a flat-bit screwdriver, driven into the anchor, should aid in its removal. Drive the screwdriver's bit into the anchor and pull it out. With this done, install a new sheath for the replacement screw.

The anchor or sheath you use could be plastic or lead. The sheath should be snug going into the hole. When the replacement screw is installed into the sheath, the sheath will expand, causing the connection to become tight.

Once all the anchors are in place, set your railing back in position. Install your new screws and the railing should be tight.

Lag bolts and the screw-and-anchor method are the two most common ways of attaching porch railings. However, it is possible your railings are nailed into place. If this is the case, and the nails come loose, replace the nails with screws.

None of the methods of tightening loose railings are very difficult.

On the rating scale of 1 to 10, this job rates a 2. As for expense, the cost could range from nothing, other than time, to a few bucks for screws and anchors. The time requirement for this type of work could range from a matter of minutes up to a few hours. A licensed contractor will likely charge between $30 and $100 for this job.

Patching Holes

Patching holes should be an obvious need in preparing your home for sale. However, it is surprising how many home sellers fail to notice or repair holes in their homes. While sellers may be oblivious to these holes, home buyers aren't. To a scrupulous buyer, holes will not go undetected. The visual impact of holes in your house will have a lasting effect on prospective purchasers. If you have holes, repair them.

There are many types of holes that you may have to deal with. These holes range from tiny penetrations that once supported pictures, to gaping holes caused by water damage or physical abuse. In all cases, the holes must be fixed.

Even if the holes in your house offer little challenge to correct and leave no doubt that they were only used to support picture frames, the impact they make on a buyer will be detrimental. While educated consumers don't expect lived-in homes to be impeccable, they do expect the basics to be intact. This includes walls and ceilings that are not riddled with holes.

Fortunately, patching holes is not particularly difficult, and it is generally not expensive. You can have all the holes around the house sealed up in a jiffy. Now let's talk about what's involved with most patch jobs.

Drywall

Holes in drywall are usually easy to fix. The only expense required for these repairs is a little joint compound, sandpaper, and some paint, assuming you have basic tools lying around the house.

Since most holes are not huge, you shouldn't need any additional drywall. Normally, filling the holes with ready-mixed joint compound is all that is required to plug the opening. To do this, put the joint compound on a putty knife and press it into the hole. If you don't have a putty knife, you can use a piece of stiff cardboard or similar tool.

Fill the hole and spread the joint compound out over the wall in a thin layer. The compound should be feathered back from the hole to allow it to blend in when the area is repainted. Once the hole is filled, let it set overnight.

When morning comes, take some light-grit sandpaper and sand the compound until it is flush with the finished wall surface. Then apply a second coat of joint compound. This coating should be applied thinner than the first. Feather the compound out and let it sit until it is dry.

When the second coat of compound is dry, sand it lightly. If you are a perfectionist, apply a third coat of compound. The third coat normally isn't needed in small patch jobs, but it doesn't hurt, and it may make the appearance of the job more appealing.

After the last coat of compound has been sanded, you are ready to paint. If the wall had enough holes to make it look like a shotgun went off in the room, be prepared to paint the entire wall. On the other hand, if you are only repairing a hole here and there, you can probably get by with a touch-up paint job.

After matching your new paint as closely as possible to the existing wall or ceiling color, apply it sparingly. A heavy coat of paint will show up as a patched area. You want a thin coat of paint that gradually feathers out into the existing paint. It may be necessary to apply two coats of paint, but one coat will often suffice for small patches.

If you have a large hole in your wall or ceiling, you may have to cut out a section of the drywall and replace it. This still is not a big job, but you will need some extra drywall and some drywall tape.

Using a keyhole saw or a utility knife, cut out the damaged section of drywall. Make the cut so that you will have wood to attach your new drywall to. This means splitting the cut of the drywall so that half of the old drywall is on a stud or joist and half of the new drywall will share the same wooden member.

Cut your repair piece of drywall and install it in the opening; you may use nails or screws, but the fasteners must countersink into the drywall.

Once the new drywall is in place, apply joint compound along the seams and over the fasteners. Then cut sections of the drywall tape to place over the seams, but not over the fasteners. Lay the tape into the compound and smooth it out with a putty knife or similar tool. From here on out, the rest of your drywall finishing will be the same as described earlier.

Plaster

Holes in plaster are a little more difficult to work with. Normally plaster is set into a wire lathe or attached to wooden strips. When a big hole is made in plaster, the surrounding plaster often cracks for long distances. However, small holes, like those used to hang pictures, rarely damage the surrounding plaster.

If you have a very small hole, you can probably repair it using the same techniques described for drywall. However, if you have a large hole, you will have to use different tactics.

A trip to your local building supply store will allow you to purchase a plaster repair kit. These kits contain all the elements you need to mix a concoction for the repair of your walls or ceilings. Follow the manufacturer's directions that come with your kit; not all repair kits are the same.

In general, mix the kit components into a substance to fill your hole. Apply the mixture and smooth it out. When the mixture dries, you are ready to paint.

The difficulty rating for repairing holes in your walls and ceilings is a 3. You will need some skill and patience to accomplish this work. The expense incurred in your project will range from less than $15 to a maximum of about $50. Your time spent on this type of project will range from about two hours to a maximum of about six hours, not counting drying time. A contractor will probably estimate the cost of this work at between $75 and $125.

Recaulking Fixtures

Recaulking fixtures will give your house a cleaner look. Fresh caulking is much more attractive than old caulking that has become stained with dirt and mildew. Consider this: would you prefer to bathe in a bathtub that has fresh, clean white caulking around it or a tub that is surrounded by a black and green stripe of cracked caulking? I would imagine you chose the tub with the fresh caulking. Well, home buyers look for just this type of thing in homes they are considering. It may seem silly, but fresh caulking could be a pivotal point in a home buyer's decision. If the buyer is looking at two nearly identical properties that are priced the same, little features like fresh caulking can make the difference in which home seller gets to hang the "sold" sign.

Not only will fresh caulking give your fixtures a better appearance, it will protect your walls and cabinets from water damage. If a home buyer sees cracked caulking, a close inspection for water damage is sure to follow. The same is true for grouting around the tile of your bathing unit. If the tile grout has discolored and turned to sand, water damage is imminent. Educated buyers know what to look for, and they will be looking for hidden water damage.

If there is no visible caulking around the faucets in your shower, buyers might wonder if water is entering around the escutcheon and collecting in the walls, floors, and ceilings of two-story homes. These picky buyers aren't being ridiculous; they have well-founded concerns. Water can cause extensive structural damage, and insufficient caulking and grouting are common causes of water infiltration.

So what are you to do? You must check around your fixtures for caulking or grouting that should be replaced. If you find unsuitable caulking or grouting, replace it; it won't be expensive, time consuming, or laborious.

Replacing caulking is nearly child's play. To begin with, remove the old caulking. You can do this with a knife, flat-bit screwdriver, putty knife, or other similar tool; be careful not to scratch your fixture or countertop.

Once the old caulking is out, clean all surfaces to remove grease, oil, and grime. Allow the surfaces to dry. If you are in a hurry, dry the surfaces with a hair dryer. Then install the new caulking. For small jobs you can purchase your caulking in easy-to-use squeeze tubes. If you have a big job, you might want to use a caulking gun and tubes of caulking, but this will rarely be needed for the average residential re-caulking job.

You can choose between clear and white caulking. There are other options available, but clear or white will be fine. When you open your tube of caulking, make the opening cut on about a 45° angle; this will give you more control in applying the caulking.

Before you begin your job, get a wet towel or several wet paper towels on hand. Begin the caulking process by placing the end of the caulking tube where you want the caulking applied and squeeze the tube of caulking or the trigger of the caulking gun.

As the caulking starts to come out, move the caulking tube around the fixture, filling the crack between the fixture and the wall or counter with caulking. Don't linger in one spot. If you keep the tube is one spot too long, you will get a large buildup of unwanted caulking.

Once you have a bead of caulking around the fixture, disengage the caulking gun or cap the caulking tube. Wet your index finger with water and pull your finger through the caulking. The pressure from your finger will force the caulking deep into the seam and spread the caulking, creating a desirable groove in the finished product. Use the wet towels to remove excess caulking.

Replacing the grout between your tiles is more difficult. To do this, you must first remove the existing grout material. A screwdriver or small chisel can be used to open the cracks between tiles. Remove as much of the old grout as possible.

When the old grout is gone, clean the surfaces around the cracks with bleach and a soft brush. Allow the surfaces to dry. Again, you can use a hair dryer to speed up the drying process.

When ready, mix new grout material to install between the tiles. This material can be purchased at any tile store, but tell the clerk you are using the material as a replacement grout. Follow the manufacturer's recommendations for mixing your grout material.

When the mixture is ready, spread the grout between the tiles. This is best done with a grout trowel, but a hard piece of flat rubber will work.

When the cracks are filled, remove excess grout from the face of the tiles. Don't procrastinate on this step; if the grouting dries, it will be very difficult to remove.

When your job is done, let it set for a week or two. Then apply a light coating of silicone sealer over the grouting. This silicone sealer will enhance the waterproofing qualities of the grouting.

Replacing the grouting and caulking around your fixtures can give a whole new look to your bathroom or kitchen. The work is easy and the expense is nominal. The results will be pleasing to the eye and protective to your wood surfaces.

Simple caulking will cost less than $5 and can be accomplished in less than 30 minutes. Full-scale regrouting may take several hours and cost as much as $25 to $50. On the difficulty scale, caulking rates a 1 and grouting rates a 3. Professionals will handle simple caulking for their minimum hourly rate, about $25 to $35. Having a pro replace your grouting could run up into the range of $150.

Cleaning Fixtures

Cleaning fixtures certainly doesn't require years of experience, but it can improve the odds of selling your house. Seeing bathtubs with soap rings, kitchen sinks with iron deposits, and toilets with black bowls is enough to discourage some buyers. Making the effort to get your fixtures squeaky clean will help in the showing of your house.

When you clean your fixtures, be careful not to scratch them. Normally, a soft-bristle brush and a nonabrasive cleaning compound will work best.

The difficulty rating of this type of cleaning is a 1. The time required is less than two hours. Outside cleaning companies will do the job for you, but expect to spend between $40 and $75. Doing the job yourself will cost less than $10.

Eliminating Plumbing Drips

Eliminating plumbing drips will save you money and make your house more desirable to the buying public. Drips can cause stains in your fixtures that will not allow easy removal. If you have modern plumbing and basic skills, you can tackle the job of stopping drips.

There are many types of plumbing faucets, and some of these faucets are best left to professionals when it comes to repairs. However, most modern faucets can be repaired, to stop drips, by an average homeowner in less than 30 minutes.

Faucets with Washers and Washerless Cartridges

Some faucets still use washers, but they are now a minority. Tub and shower faucets that use washers generally require the use of tub wrenches for access to their seats, stems, and washers.

The first step in stopping any drip is cutting off the water supply. Most lavatory and sink faucets will have cutoffs beneath them. Tubs and showers may not have individual cutoffs. These faucets might require you to shut off the main water supply to the house.

With the water cut off, start by removing the cap that conceals the screw in the faucet's handle. You can pry these caps off with a knife. Next remove the screw from the handle and pull the handle off the stem. There may be a trim piece covering the faucet stem. If there is, try pulling the trim piece off. If it doesn't slide off, turn it counterclockwise.

When the trim is removed, you will see the brass or plastic stem. There will normally be flat spots on the stem to accept a wrench. Make sure the water is off and then turn the stem counterclockwise. It will come out, exposing the washer, if it has one. Some stems are plastic and don't use washers. For this type, you must purchase and install a replacement stem.

If the stem is equipped with a washer, remove the screw from the bottom of the stem, where the washer is. Take the old washer to a hardware store or plumbing supplier and buy a replacement. It is wise to replace the screw, too. Screws that stay on stems indefinitely can become corroded from the water and next to impossible to remove.

If you have a washerless stem, take it to the store and buy a replacement. After acquiring and installing the stem or washer, put the faucet back together. Turn the water on and test your job. If you still have a leak, you probably need to replace the faucet seat.

The faucet seat is what the washer sits on. When these seats become pitted, the faucet drips. Cut the water off and remove the faucet stem. Get a piece of sandpaper and a pencil. Wrap the sandpaper around the end of the pencil, and use it to sand the seat. If this doesn't work, use a seat wrench to remove and replace the seat.

This type of repair job will take less than an hour and cost less than $10. However, a plumber will probably charge between $25 and $40, plus parts, to fix your drip. The difficulty rating for this job is a 2.

Cartridge-Style Faucets

Cartridge-style faucets are a breeze to fix. Cut the water off and remove the handle and trim from the stem. You will see a small brass clip holding the cartridge in place. Use needle-nose pliers to remove this clip. Then pull the cartridge out with your pliers.

Install the replacement cartridge in the faucet body and replace the clip. Don't forget the clip; if you do, and put the water back on, the cartridge can become a flying missile. Replace the trim and handle and turn the water on. Your problem should be solved.

These cartridges cost between $10 and $20 and can be installed in less than 30 minutes. A professional will normally charge a minimum of one hour's labor for this type of work. If you call a professional plumber, expect to pay between $25 and $40, plus the cost of the part. On the difficulty scale, this job rates a 1.

Ball-Assembly Faucets

Ball-assembly faucets can be frustrating. They contain numerous springs and parts that tend to get scattered all over the place. However, with patience and concentration, you can repair these faucets.

You can purchase complete repair kits for ball-assembly faucets. These kits come with instructions; follow them. I will give you a description of the basics now, but don't ignore the instructions packed with your repair kit.

Cut the water off. Loosen the set screw that you will find in the front at the base of the faucet handle. Your repair kit should include a wrench for this part of the job.

With the handle off, loosen the large knurled retainer that surrounds the piece the handle was mounted to. When you turn the retainer counterclockwise, it will come off, exposing the ball-assembly.

At this point, you can remove the entire ball-assembly by lifting it out of the faucet body. Install the new ball-assembly and put the faucet back together. As long as you don't drop the assembly, scattering the parts on your floor, you should be all set.

This job can be done in less than 30 minutes, and the parts will cost less than $15. To call in a pro, you are looking at a minimum charge of probably between $25 and $40, plus parts. The difficulty rating on this job, as long as you don't scatter your parts, is a 1.

Cleaning up Oil Spots and Odors around Your Heating System

Cleaning up oil spots around your heating system will improve the impression your home makes on a potential buyer. If a buyer sees oil surrounding your heating system, red flags will go up. Even if the leak is being caused by a loose flare-connection, the buyer will assume the worst.

It is not uncommon for oil-fired heating systems to stain the flooring around them. When the systems are serviced and bled, they leak oil. When connections work loose, oil is dripped on the floor. Oil spots around heating systems and oil storage tanks can cause the mechanical area to stink. If a prospective buyer smells the odor from the oil, you have offended a second sense. Not only can the prospect see the oil, he or she can smell it.

Before you put your house on the open real estate market, take a little time to tidy up around the heating system. If you have an oil leak, find and fix it. Most oil connections are made with either threaded joints or flare fittings. Both of these types of joints can be tightened.

If you are dealing with copper tubing and flare fittings, be careful not to crimp the copper tubing, cutting off the flow of fuel. To tighten a flare connection, use two wrenches. Put one on the body of the flare fitting and one on the nut that surrounds the tubing. Tighten the nut while supporting the body of the flare fitting with the second wrench. If tightening the nut doesn't stop the leak, call a professional.

For threaded fittings, you will normally need a set of pipe wrenches. With one pipe wrench on the fitting and one wrench on the threaded pipe, turn the pipe clockwise to tighten it. Again, if the leak persists, call in a professional.

When you are dealing with a flammable substance like oil, you cannot afford to take chances. If you break the supply tubing or pipe, your house could become flooded with fuel oil. Don't get overly aggressive in tightening these devices.

Once the leak is stopped, you have to get rid of the smell and the stain. Start by covering the oil puddle with an absorbent sand like the type used in kitty-litter boxes. When the oil has been soaked into the sand, remove the sand and dispose of it properly.

Use bleach on your concrete floor to reduce the visibility of the oil stain. After scrubbing the area, let it dry. If you really want to hide the stain, dust the area with some mortar mix. The gray dust in the mortar can be spread over the area and rubbed into the porous concrete, creating a more natural gray look.

Now for the smell. You can go to most stores that sell heating supplies and buy sprays that are designed to eliminate oil odors. These sprays go by different names, but your heating supply dealer will be able to help you.

This cleanup job should take less than two hours and cost less than $10. If you call in a pro, you could be looking at an expense of between $50 and $75. The difficulty rating on this job is a 1.

Cleaning Floor Registers

Cleaning floor registers may not seem like much, but it is advantageous in the sale of your home. You'd be surprised at what some home buyers look at.

This project is very simple. If you have a forced hot air heating system or a central air conditioning system, you probably have floor registers. Floor registers are the little grates in your floor that the hot and cold air are blown out of. Normally, these grates can be removed simply by lifting them up. This allows you to vacuum the dust out of the duct work and to clean the registers. While this might not sound like much of a sales tool, it couldn't hurt.

This project rates a 1 on the difficulty chart and will not cause you to come out of pocket with any cash. There is no need to call in a pro for this job.

Removing Mildew

Removing mildew may improve your respiratory system, and it will definitely improve your odds of a fast home sale. People don't want to buy a house that has mildew and moisture problems. There is almost nothing that will send a prospective buyer running quicker than an ugly green growth of mildew on the bathroom ceiling.

Since you live in your home on a daily basis, you might not notice small concentrations of mildew that a prospective buyer would. For this reason, you should inspect your home carefully for this unpleasant resident. If you find mildew, get rid of it. How do you get rid of mildew? What is mildew? Where does mildew accumulate? Let me answer these questions for you.

What Is Mildew?

What is mildew? Mildew is a fungal growth. It is most common in areas that are dark, damp, and warm. The odor given off by mildew is generally easy to detect. Some people are allergic to the spores associated with mildew.

Where Does Mildew Accumulate?

Where does mildew accumulate? Mildew concentrates its growth in warm, dark, damp areas. Basements are one common place to find mildew. Bathrooms are another favorite place for mildew to get a foothold.

How Do You Get Rid of Mildew?

How do you get rid of mildew? To eliminate mildew, you must eliminate all the mildew spores, both active and dormant. There are some special cleaning solutions available for this purpose. You should look for a cleaner that specifies its effectiveness against mildew.

If you want to make your own secret weapon for fighting mildew, you can do so with water, bleach, and laundry detergent. By mixing one quart of bleach with three quarts of warm water and one third cup of laundry detergent, you have an effective mildew cleaner. Don't use products that contain ammonia. The combination of ammonia and bleach can be hazardous to your health.

You can apply your homemade formula directly on the visible mildew. It may take up to 15 minutes, but this concoction should remove the mildew stains.

Once you win the mildew battle, you must take steps to win the war. To keep your mildew enemy from returning, provide the affected area with adequate ventilation and preferably some natural light. By keeping the area dry and well lighted, you will discourage the growth of mildew.

This project should take less than an hour to complete. The cost of the job will be less than $10, and the difficulty rating is a 1. Professionals should not be needed for this type of task.

Controlling Musty Odors

By controlling musty odors you can make your home a more pleasant place to live, visit, and buy. Nobody likes a house that stinks. If your house is damp and musty, you are sure to have some unpleasant odors. When you live with these smells on a regular basis, you may not notice them. Since you can't be sure if your house is emitting unwanted aromas, you should take steps to insure that it isn't.

What should you do? Well, if you have a damp basement, put a dehumidifier in it and keep it running. The dehumidifier will control the moisture that causes musty odors.

Proper ventilation is a key to correcting all moisture-related problems. If your house has a basement, open the basement windows and allow air to circulate. If your house sits on a crawlspace foundation, open the foundation vents and let the breeze blow thorough.

Bathrooms and kitchens are frequently filled with condensation. This steam can lead to moisture problems. Use ventilation fans and windows to keep these rooms free of moisture and odor problems.

There is a host of odor-hiding sprays and arrangements on the market. These sprays—powders, liquids, and so forth—are fine for short-term help, but they cannot win the battle alone. Most of these products only mask the odors. To remove the odors, you must reduce moisture and increase ventilation.

This project is not complicated; it rates a 1 on the difficulty chart. The costs involved to get rid of musty odors should be minimal, unless you need to buy a dehumidifier. Dehumidifier prices start under $100 and go up. You won't need pros to solve your odor problems, just less moisture and more ventilation.

Clean Out the Refrigerator

When you place your house on the market, you should clean out the refrigerator. Check the crisper for food that was tucked away and forgotten. Get rid of items that are out of date and taking up space unnecessarily. If your freezer has an ice buildup, defrost it. Sort through the contents of your refrigerator and reduce them to the essentials. A refrigerator that is stuffed with food looks small. You want yours to look spacious.

After the load in the refrigerator has been cut back, clean the interior of the appliance. Get rid of old juice stains and leftover lettuce. Wash the sidewalls and the shelves. By making the inside of your refrigerator spotless, you won't alienate buyers. People can lose their appetite quickly when they open the refrigerator and find unidentifiable objects lurking within. They cannot only lose their appetite for food, but for your house as well.

This project rates a 1 on the difficulty scale. There is no money involved, and you don't need professional help for the task.

Remove Clutter from Closets, Basements, and Attics

When you remove clutter from closets, basements, and attics, you are able to present buyers with much-needed storage room. Storage room is a big issue with buyers. A closet that is crammed with everything from the vacuum to last year's Christmas decorations indicates the home lacks sufficient storage space.

It is perfectly acceptable to leave coats, boots, and similar clothing in the closet. You don't want it to be empty, just uncluttered. When buyers look into your closets, you want them to envision their clothes hanging in the space. If they see you have been forced to use the closet for everything except clothes, they may question the suitability of your house for their needs.

The same principle applies to attics and basements. People expect these out-of-the-way places to store objects that see little use, but they also want to see that there is plenty of room to add to the collection of goods.

One way to make attics and basements appear larger is to eliminate the stuff you are storing in them. Since this isn't always feasible or desirable, there is another option. Arrange the items in an orderly fashion. Invest in boxes and pack the goods away. The boxes can be stacked neatly along one wall, and when you are ready to move, your stuff is already boxed and ready to go.

Many sellers fail to compress, eliminate, or organize their items in storage. This is a big mistake. Buyers will be assessing every part of your home. If they stick their head into the attic and can't see past the piles of stuffed animals and scattered boxes of old tax records, they will not be favorably impressed. If buyers were thinking of converting the attic into additional living space, the clutter may distort their mental picture, causing them to move on to another house.

Items stored in a basement can serve a useful purpose. People are often suspicious of basements. The common belief is that all basements leak and experience water problems. If a buyer sees the heating system and water heater set up on blocks or pallets, the suspicion is all but confirmed. However, when the buyer sees personal effects sitting on the concrete floor, the fear of water infiltration slowly subsides.

Storing some items on the basement floor is good strategy, but don't heap piles of unorganized stuff in the corner. Make the storage area neat. When buyers look at the cardboard boxes and don't see any water stains, they will breathe a little easier.

This job rates a 1 on the difficulty scale. The only cost involved is the possible expense incurred for boxes. As you might suspect, no professional help is needed for this job.

Move Furniture out of Traffic Patterns

Before you allow potential buyers to see your home, you should move furniture out of traffic patterns. Not only can furniture force an area to appear smaller than it is, it can impede the flow of traffic. Buyers are usually accompanied by at least one real estate broker, if not two. When you get three or four people moving through the same hallway, conditions can get cramped.

I remember one showing of a house I had listed as a broker that soured due to poor furniture placement. When I listed the house, I advised my clients to remove some of the furniture and to place it in storage. The clients were more than a little perturbed. I guess they felt I was insulting their taste or something. All I was trying to do was make the house show better, but the sellers wouldn't heed my advice.

On the day of the showing, I arrived with buyers interested in the house. As we approached the home, my buyers were excited. They loved the exterior of the home and couldn't wait to get inside. The homeowners were not in the house. I had instructed them to go for a walk until I was finished showing the home.

When I let the potential buyers in the home, they were taken with the vaulted ceiling and the decorative railing around the second story. The three of us stood in the foyer, somewhat constricted by an umbrella stand, a valet, and potted plants.

Knowing the house, I took the buyers up to the main level of the split-foyer home. The wife adored the kitchen and the dining area with the deck off the back. The husband was intrigued with the unique fireplace in the living room. The bathroom and upstairs bedrooms were acceptable—though small—and we began our descent into the lower area, where more bedrooms and the family room awaited inspection.

We negotiated the crowded foyer and started down the steps. There was a large antique water bench at the base of the stairs. It was beautiful, with its massive mirror, its bowl and pitcher, and its towel racks. However, when the three of us reached the bottom of the steps, there wasn't enough room for us to stand at the landing. Going through the door into the family room, we felt like cattle being prodded onto a livestock truck.

When we got into the family room, the feeling of cramped quarters didn't get any better. The furniture was massive and plentiful. What was actually a large room appeared tiny. We never got to the other bedrooms. When the buyers assessed the seemingly crowded foyer, the nearly impassible landing, and the awkward family room, they decided they had seen enough and wanted to continue their search with another house.

As it turned out I never was able to sell that couple a home. As for the house with poor furniture placement, the same scenario played out over and over, not just with me, but with other brokers. No one made an offer on the house in the 90 days I had it listed.

Furniture was not the only flaw of this home, but it did put up barriers that many buyers were not willing to look beyond. This was not the first time poor furniture placement had cost me a possible sale, and it wasn't the last time.

It is important to arrange your furniture to allow for an easy, free-flowing tour of your home. If your house is crowded with furniture, put some of it in storage. Don't allow your furnishings to create a maze or cattle-chute effect.

This job rates a 1 on the difficulty scale, and it doesn't require any cash, unless you have to pay to store your excess furniture. You shouldn't need any professional help for this job.

That completes our list of projects that can be done with time and not much money. Now we are ready to look ahead to Chapter 2 and explore projects that will cost $50 or less.

Projects You Can Do for Under $50

There are many projects you can do for under $50. A job as simple as replacing your mailbox can make a difference in the impression your home gives to a prospective purchaser. Mulching flower beds and shrubs will give your grounds a more finished and cared-for look. If you don't have flowers, planting them can serve as a beautiful invitation for visitors contemplating the purchase of your home. Installing a new door knocker and brass kickplate to your front door can transform your home from ordinary to unique. Such inexpensive outdoor improvements will enhance the curb appeal of your house.

What can you do with a ceiling that is discolored from an old water leak? You could repaint it or texture it. If the ceiling sags or has uneven seams, texturing can hide the minor imperfections. Adding accessories in the bathroom or kitchen can make a big difference. These inexpensive accessories are not only functional, they can be attractive.

While the improvements that will be discussed in this chapter are inexpensive, they are not without value. It is difficult to predict what will trigger a person's decision to buy your home. Every buyer will be a little different. For the handyman, hanging pegboard in your garage could be a decisive factor. A perfectionist might pick up on the fact that the baseboard heating units are in good shape. When preparing your home for sale, you should cover all the bases. Now let's look at what you can do for less than $50 that may make your house sell faster.

Mulching Flower Beds and Shrubs

Mulching flower beds and shrubs can be hard on the back, but it is easy on the pocketbook. This home improvement may not do much for the appraised value of your home, but it can be enough to capture the attention of a potential buyer.

If you set two nearly identical houses side by side, one with attractive landscaping and one without, which house do you think will pull more interest from buyers? Compare the grounds of your home to your clothes. Do you feel more comfortable wearing a suit or tattered jeans?

When you place your house on the open market, it will be scrutinized closely by serious househunters. Since buyers expect a house to look its best when being offered for sale, it is important to dress up the property. It is as if the house is looking for work and the potential buyers are the employers. The house will need to make a good impression to get the job of being the new buyers' home.

It will take more than attractive landscaping to close the deal, but you have to get buyers into the home before you can sell it. If buyers take a look at the outside and consider it shabby, they will have no interest in looking at the home's interior features and benefits. This is where landscaping can make a difference.

Consider this example of two homes competing for attention from buyers. The first home is well-kept in all areas except in its landscaping. This house has untrimmed shrubbery, weeds growing up through the neglected flower beds, and a dull outside appearance. Its competitor has a different look.

The second house is accented with manicured shrubbery. The flower beds are mulched with fresh wood chips. Because of the mulching, there are no weeds dotting the flower beds. Clean, colorful gravel forms a border between the mulch and the lawn. This house's landscaping projects a professional image.

If you were riding down the street and saw "For Sale" signs in each yard, which house would you want to look at first? If all other factors were equal, you would likely choose the house with the fresh landscaping.

In this example, the new landscaping caught your attention and beckoned you to come in for a closer look at the house. Getting you through the front door is the first step in selling you the house. Of course, there is no guarantee you are going to buy the house, but at least you are inside and are under the influence of the home and the efforts made to sell it.

Mulching is not a trivial waste of time. Even if your flower beds and shrubs already have mulch around them, a fresh layer of mulch will enhance the home's appearance. Now let's see what is involved in doing this job the right way.

There are two basic approaches to mulching. The first is mulching a single item, such as a tree or bush. The second is filling an enclosed area, such as a flower bed, with mulch. Let's start our work with mulching a single item.

Mulching a Tree

Mulching a tree is pretty simple. Essentially, mulch is placed around the tree and graded out toward the lawn. However, there are many types of mulch that can be used, and there is the issue of installing a ground cover.

Laying a piece of plastic around the tree as a ground cover will prevent grass and weeds from growing up through the mulch. If you decide to take this approach, limit the ground cover to a single seam, and make sure the plastic at the seam overlaps itself. If the two pieces of plastic merely butt together, grass can grow up between the seam.

With the plastic in place, you are ready to put down the mulch. The mulch might be wood chips, pine needles, gravel, or some other type of dressing. Wood chips seem to be the most accepted form of mulch, and pine bark is one of the most common forms of wood chip mulching.

When you install the mulch, don't just dump it out of the bag and let it land at will. Start the mulch pile near the base of the tree and gradually slope it down toward the lawn. This type of installation is as simple as it comes. On the difficulty scale, this job rates a 1. The cost for mulching a single item will be less than $10.

Bed-Mulching

Bed-mulching is a little different than single-item mulching. Bed-mulching techniques can be used for single items or groups of flowers and shrubs.

A retainer is usually installed to contain mulch in a bed. This retainer can be a roll of flexible edging or it could be landscape timbers. The retainer can have a low profile, as with rolled edging, or it can rise well above the ground, as with the use of timbers. In either design, the retainer prevents the mulch from becoming scattered on the lawn.

Laying a ground cover is more difficult in a bedding situation if more than one item occupies the bed. The easiest way to work around multiple items in a bed is to use strips of plastic. The strips are laid out between the plants with the edge of each strip overlapping the previous one.

When mulching multiple items, care must be taken not to damage individual plants. Rather than dumping mulch into the bed, lay it in place by hand or with a shovel. Spread the mulch evenly. This type of mulching rates a 1 on the difficulty scale. The cost for the job will depend on the extent of your mulching. The front of most homes can be mulched at costs of less than $50. If a contractor is hired for the job, expect labor rates of between $20 and $35 per hour.

Planting Flowers

Planting flowers can make any lawn more attractive. The beauty of flowers is enough to make people stop and take notice, and this is exactly what you want would-be buyers to do.

When choosing what types of flowers to plant, look for flowers that will give your home instant appeal. Planting flower bulbs and waiting for them to grow is fine for the gardening homeowner, but as a home seller, you want flowers that will be in bloom the minute you plant them.

Flowers can be used to dress up your walkway, mark the corners of your driveway, and add color to the front of your home. They can be planted in raw ground, in custom-built flower beds, pots, and window boxes. Hanging baskets of flowers can be installed on decorative posts, in the ceiling of a porch, or from the edges of decks.

Lattice can be used to support climbing plants. If you have a porch on a pier foundation, lattice will close in the porch foundation, giving a place for flowers to climb and hiding the often ugly underside of the porch.

Planting flowers is not hard work. On the difficulty scale, planting flowers rates a 1. As for cost, $25 will buy enough flowers to make a considerable difference in the front lawn of a home. Of course, larger and more complex flower arrangements will cost more. A trip to the local nursery will be all it takes to see firsthand what your flower expense will be.

Replacing Your Mailbox

Replacing your mailbox can have an effect on the sale of your home. Old, beat-up, and rusted mailboxes do not add much appeal to a property. However, a new mailbox, with a clear address, cannot only show a prospective buyer where your house is, it can implant a good first impression.

Some homes have mailboxes mounted to the siding or to porch posts. Other houses have their mailboxes set on posts near the street. Replacing either of these boxes will not be difficult; the job can be completed in less than an hour.

Surface-Mounted Mailboxes

Surface-mounted mailboxes are the easiest type of mailbox to replace. Normally these boxes can be removed by lifting them up and pulling them away from the mounting surface. The boxes generally just hang on the heads of two screws. In some cases the screws may have to be loosened or removed before the box will come off.

When replacing a surface-mounted mailbox, be sure the new mailbox is of equal size or larger. The surface behind the old mailbox will not be the same color as the rest of the siding. Since the mailbox protects the mounting surface from sun and weather, the mounting surface will not have aged in the same way as the rest of the siding. Replacing an old box with a smaller one will leave these awkward areas exposed.

Post-Type Mailboxes

Post-type mailboxes are very common in rural and suburban areas. These boxes range from small sizes to extra-large. They are available in various materials and designs. A post-type mailbox can take on the shape of a covered bridge, a barn, or one of many other available shapes. Colors and finishes range from dull gray to intricate artwork. The expanse of possibilities can cause considerable confusion in choosing just the right mailbox.

Post-mounted mailboxes are usually held in place with screws. Normally there will be a board that the box sits on and is screwed to. The board is attached to the post with nails or screws. When replacing a post-type mailbox it may also be necessary to replace the mounting board. The existing mounting board may have rotted, or it may be too small or too large to accommodate the new mailbox.

To remove the mounting board, you will first have to remove the mailbox. A quick look around the bottom edges of the box should reveal screws. Remove the screws by turning them counterclockwise. Once the screws are out, the box should lift off, exposing the mounting board.

If the mounting board is in good shape but is too large for the new box, it can be cut down to fit the new mailbox. If the mounting board has rotted, replace it. When the board is too small, remove it and install a new mounting board on the post. If you don't remove the old mounting board before installing a new one, the increased thickness of the mounting surface is likely to extend below the edges of the new mailbox, creating an unattractive protrusion.

Replacing a mailbox rates a 1 on the difficulty scale. The prices of mailboxes vary a great deal. A simple mailbox will cost less than $15, but a fancy one can cost well over $50. If you hire a contractor for this job, expect a labor charge of between $20 and $35.

Texture a Ceiling

There are many ways to texture a ceiling. Why would you want to texture a ceiling? Textured ceilings are common in new homes, and they can hide minor imperfections. If a ceiling has uneven seams, texturing the ceiling will hide the flaws. If a ceiling is stained from an old water leak, adding texture to the ceiling will conceal the problem. Ceilings are textured for looks as well as practical purposes. Can you texture your own ceiling? You should be able to; the job is not very difficult.

Choosing a Texture

There are many different types of texture to apply to your ceiling. There are also various materials that can be used to obtain the desired texture. Texture materials are available in small quantities and in ready-mixed form. Some textures will be little more than a pebble surface in a paint. Other textures will resemble small stalactites hanging from the ceiling. Joint compound, the same material used to finish drywall, is often used as a texture material, but there are many other texture materials to choose from. Choosing the right texture material will be easy once you know what type of texture you want.

What type of texture are you after? Do you want the ceiling to have a swirled texture? If you do, the texture material should be applied with a brush, like a paint brush. Would you prefer to have a ceiling textured with a pebble finish? Is so, a stipple-type paint roller will be the tool. How about a star-burst effect, would you like that? The star-burst effect is achieved by stomping the ceiling, usually with a stiff round brush. Perhaps you would prefer a crater-type texture; this type of texturing is done with a trowel. Let's look more closely at the various ways to texture your ceiling.

Rolling a Texture

Rolling a texture is simple; you merely use a paint roller to paint the ceiling with a texture material. However, any type of texturing can get messy. Before you begin applying texture, take the time to protect your floors, walls, windows, and furniture from accidental splatters and spills. If unwanted splatters occur, a putty knife will remove them.

To roll a texture you will need a texture material, a paint roller, a stipple-type head for the roller, a roller pan, and a ladder or roller extension handle.

Many texture materials are premixed; all you have to do is apply them. A stipple texture is usually done in thin layers, similar to painting. Most texture materials are available in quantities that cover between 200 and 400 square feet. A room with dimensions of 12' x 14' will have a ceiling with 168 square feet. If the ceiling is vaulted, it will contain more square footage.

Assuming your existing ceiling is white, a single coat of texture may be all that is needed. If the ceiling is badly stained or painted a dark color, a primer should be applied before texturing the ceiling. Without primer, the dark color or stains may bleed through the new application of texture.

Brushing a Texture

Swirls can be achieved by brushing a texture. All you need for this job is your texture material, a stiff paintbrush, a bucket, and a ladder.

To swirl a ceiling, pour the texture material into the bucket. Dip the brush into the texture and move the brush in a swirling motion on the ceiling. The arc of the swirls can be long or short; it's up to you. Some people even use sponges to create swirled ceilings. You can let your imagination create the design with this type of texturing.

Troweling a Texture

Troweling a texture will give a crater-like texture. A 10" trowel, texture material, bucket, ladder, and possibly a putty knife are all you need for this job.

This procedure involves using a thicker coat of texture material. The texture is loaded onto the trowel and spread over the ceiling. It is common to start in a corner and work out into the room. The more pressure you apply to the trowel, the thinner the texture will be. The trowel can be pulled in a straight line or it can be arced to create a swirl.

As the trowel is removed from the ceiling, the texture may tend to pull down at the separation point. Use the trowel or a putty knife to flatten out the pulled texture.

Stomping a Texture

Stomping a texture can be fun. Most people use a stiff round brush to stomp a ceiling, but a potato masher will also work. In addition to the stomper, you will need texture material, a paint roller, a roller head, a roller pan, and a ladder or paint roller handle extension.

The first step is applying a uniform coat of texture material with the paint roller. Once the ceiling is covered, use the stomping device to create your design. This is as simple as pushing the brush into the ceiling and pulling it back. Many designs are possible with a little experimentation.

A potato masher can give you the stalactite look. This requires a thicker coat of texture material. The thicker material is usually applied with a trowel rather than a roller. As the masher is pressed into the texture, the texture will push through the holes in the face of the masher. When the masher is pulled away from the ceiling, the texture compound will pull with it and remain hanging from the ceiling.

If you want to add color to your texture, you can usually mix paint right into the texture material. If you prefer to paint the ceiling after it is textured, you should let the texture dry for at least 48 hours—more for thick coats of texture.

The difficulty rating for this job is 2. The cost of the job, not counting tools, should be less than $20. A professional might charge between $150 and $300 for the job. The average homeowner can texture a normal ceiling in less than four hours.

Brass Kickplates

Brass kickplates can add a nice touch to your front door. Decorative kickplates will not be enough to sell your house, but they may help, and they aren't likely to hurt your chances for a sale.

Installing a kickplate is simple. The kickplate will be held in place by screws. To install a kickplate you should have a screwdriver, an electric drill, and a drill bit. The drill bit should be a little smaller than the screws that will be used in mounting the kickplate.

Position the kickplate on the door as desired and mark the hole locations. Drill small holes in these locations. Drilling starter holes will make installing the screws easier. With the holes drilled, mount the kickplate.

This job should take less than 30 minutes, and it rates a 1 on the difficulty chart. The cost of kickplates will vary, but you should be able to get an attractive one for less than $25. Even though this is a small job, most professionals will charge a minimum of one hour's labor to come out and install the kickplate.

New Door Knockers

Installing new door knockers is much the same as installing kickplates. The job is simple, but it adds a new look to the front of your home. There are many styles of door knockers to choose from, but avoid models where your name is engraved on the knocker. New owners will not want a door knocker with your name on it.

Mounting a new door knocker is as easy as screwing it to the door. As with kickplates, drilling starter holes will make the mounting easier. Prices on door knockers start around $12 and go up. The difficulty rating for this improvement is a 1.

Mirrors

Mirrors can make your home appear larger; they can also turn a dull wall into an attractive one. Large mirrored panels are often used in stores and homes to give the feeling of more expansive space. Wall mirrors are convenient for last-minute looks before you run out the door, and with the proper frames they make good wall decorations.

Many bathrooms are equipped with mirrors. Some of the mirrors are mounted on the doors of medicine cabinets. Mirrors hung over lavatories are often only slab mirrors supported by little plastic clips. These types of mirrors are functional but rarely attractive.

Mirrors that are surrounded by oak frames can warm a room. Frames made of decorative metal can make a statement about a room's decor; they can be ultra-modern or a period reproduction.

Prices for standard wall mirrors start at less than $10 and go up, sometimes way up. However, mirrors with price ranges from $20 to $50 can be quite attractive.

Mirrors can be heavy, and hanging them can be tricky. Ideally, the support for a mirror should be attached to a solid surface, such as a stud in the wall. Driving a nail into drywall and hanging a mirror is likely to result in a broken mirror. The nail will pull out and the mirror will come crashing down. If you must hang a mirror without the benefit of a wall stud, use expansion anchors and screws for the job.

Homeowners often have trouble locating the studs in their finished walls. Let me give you a little advice that may help. Look at the baseboard trim around your wall. A close inspection should reveal the locations of nails. These nails should be driven into studs. Measure the distance between the nails. If the distance is a constant 16", you can bet the nails are hitting studs. When this is the case, all you have to do is measure from a corner to the nail you found in the trim. Then, holding the tape measure at the desired mirror height, measure from the same corner to determine the location of your stud. Mark the location on your wall with a pencil.

Before making a big hole in your wall and discovering that the stud is not where you thought it was, test for the stud with a small nail. The nail should have a small diameter and be long enough to penetrate the wall and start into the stud. Once you have confirmed the stud's location, remove the test nail and secure the mirror's mounting hardware to the stud.

Many hardware stores and building supply centers sell devices that help to locate studs. These devices depend on a magnet to find the nails in the studs. While these units can work, they are not always dependable.

If you need a starting point for finding a stud, look for electrical outlets and switches. The boxes that hold these electrical devices are normally attached to studs. Door frames have studs running next to them and so do corners in the wall. Most residential studs will be set with a distance of 16" between them—measured from center to center.

Expansion anchors and screws can be used to support mirrors when wall studs seem to be nonexistent. The anchors will usually be made of plastic. Once you have determined the locations for your holes, make holes slightly smaller than the anchors. This can be done with a drill bit, a nail, or even the end of a Phillips-type screwdriver.

Place the tip of an anchor in one of the holes and tap it with a hammer. The anchor will sink into the wall. Now you are ready to install the screw. As the screw is screwed into the anchor, the anchor will expand. The expansion will make it difficult for the screw to pull loose from the wall.

For heavy mirrors, anchors may not be the best choice in hollow walls. Toggle bolts have better holding power. Toggle bolts fold up to be pushed through a hole and then open up once they are in the wall cavity. As the bolt is tightened with a screwdriver, the blades in the wall cavity grip the back of the wall and distribute the stress of weight over a large part of the wall.

For best results, always follow the manufacturer's suggestions for installing mirrors.

Hanging mirrors rates a 1 on the difficulty scale. The cost of mirrors varies greatly, but you will find a wide selection with prices below $50. Many good mirrors can be bought for less than $25. You should be able to hang a mirror in less than 30 minutes, but a pro will likely charge for a full hour's labor.

Adding Fixture Accessories

Adding fixture accessories will not only make your home more user friendly, it can add to the appearance of the home. What am I calling fixture accessories? Toilet paper holders, toothbrush holders, soap dishes, towel racks, magazine racks, and linen racks are all examples of fixture accessories. These items make a room more organized and easier to enjoy. They can also dress up the room and add to its charm.

Most of these accessories will be installed with screws. Since the accessories are light in weight and will not be holding heavy weight, plastic anchors and screws will be adequate for mounting them.

While tasteful accessories will add to a room, distasteful accessories will detract from the room's appearance. There are also people who don't want to see toothbrushes hanging on the wall no matter how attractive the holder is. Toilet paper holders and towel racks are almost always a safe bet, but don't jump in with soap dishes, toothbrush holders, cup holders, and the like until you have done some market research. You may be installing items that the current buying public doesn't want.

Accessories are sold individually and in kits. Prices for an individual accessory can be as low as $7, for a decent one. Kits will have prices starting around $20. It should take less than 15 minutes to install most accessories—they only require two screws. Hanging accessories rates a 1 on the difficulty scale. Contractors, however, will charge a minimum fee, generally 1 hour's labor, to come out and hang your accessories.

Controlling Banging Pipes

Controlling banging pipes can be frustrating. However, if a potential buyer decides to try out your plumbing and hears the pipes banging, you may lose a sale. Pipes that bang and rattle can be controlled, but finding and fixing the problem is not always easy.

What causes banging pipes? The banging of pipes can be caused by several factors. The most frequent cause of banging pipes is the operation of quick-closing plumbing valves. Examples of these valves are the ballcocks in toilets and the fill valves in automatic clothes washers. These valves cut off quickly when they close, and this quick-closing action puts pressure on the pipes, causing them to bang.

Pipes that run for a long distance in a straight line are susceptible to banging. As water is pushed down the long runs of pipe it builds with force. When the water is made to turn at an elbow fitting, the water may hit the back of the fitting with enough force to cause banging. When pipes are not supported properly, about every 6', they are likely to rattle and bang.

To control banging pipes you may have to add pipe supports, install offsets in the piping, or install air chambers near the plumbing fixtures. Adding supports is easy, if you can get to the pipes. However, installing air chambers or offsets is more difficult.

Adding Support

Adding support to pipes is easy. You can buy pipe supports at the local hardware or plumbing supply store. Most types of water pipes should be supported at 6' intervals. The supports must be attached solidly. Some supports are made to be driven into wood; others have holes on a mounting flange to accept nails or screws.

Adding support to water pipe rates a 1 on the difficulty scale. The cost of pipe supports will be between 10¢ and 15¢. Most plumbers charge between $25 and $40 per hour, and they normally charge for at least 1 hour's labor, even if they are only in your home for ten minutes.

Installing Offsets

Installing offsets in your water pipes will require some plumbing skills. This job involves cutting the water pipes and redirecting them. Before doing this, make sure the main water valve to your home is cut off. After cutting off the valve, open all the faucets in your home to allow air into the pipes. Open the lowest faucet in the house or an outside spigot to let water drain from the pipes.

When you are sure the water is off and the pipes have drained, cut them at each end of the long run. Hacksaws and roller-type cutters will cut water pipes, but roller-type cutters work best.

After cutting the pipes, you will install 45 fittings on the ends of the pipes. Then a section of pipe will be placed into the opposite end of the fitting. On the end of this pipe you will place another 45 fitting. Then another piece of pipe is inserted, and the procedure continues. The goal is to eliminate the long straight run of pipe by offsetting the new pipe back and forth in shorter sections, until the pipes are connected again.

Exact procedures for installing your new pipe will depend on the type of pipe you are working with. If you have copper pipe, you will have to solder the connections or use compression fittings. For CPVC plastic pipe, you will use a cleaner, a primer, and a glue to make your joints.

Installing offsets in water pipes is not difficult when you know how to make plumbing connections. However, since many people have trouble with plumbing, this job rates a 4 on the difficulty scale. The cost of installing offsets will range from less than $15 to about $25, depending upon how much pipe you are working with. Professional plumbers will probably charge between $105 and $150 for their labor to install the offsets.

Air Chambers

If you can't get to most of your water pipes, you can still take action where the pipes connect to your fixtures. Installing water-hammer arrestors or air chambers near the plumbing fixtures may solve your problem.

Air chambers can be made with pipe and a permanent cap. Normally an air chamber is about 12" long and has a diameter at least twice that of the supply pipe. These devices work best when they are installed at the same time as the rest of the plumbing. However, they can be installed as an afterthought.

To install an air chamber on a finished plumbing system, you will be working with the pipes under your fixtures. Most of the water supplies under a fixture will be equipped with cutoff valves. By cutting the supply pipe between where it protrudes from the wall or floor and where it connects with the cutoff, a tee fitting can be inserted. The main water supply must be cut off for this job.

A tee fitting is installed in the fixture's water supply, and the air chamber rises from the tee. The air chamber should rise vertically as high as possible, up to about 18". The air chamber can be purchased as a ready-to-go unit, or it can be made on the job. If you make it, use a piece of pipe that is about twice the diameter of the supply pipe. You will need a reducing fitting to mate the air chamber to the tee fitting in the supply pipe. One end of the chamber will be capped off.

Once air chambers are installed they provide a space for air to collect. This air cushions the force of rushing water and should reduce the banging of pipes.

The difficulty rating for installing air chambers is a 4. The cost per air chamber will be less than $5. Professional plumbers will probably charge between $35 and $70 for their labor to install an air chamber.

Painting Baseboard Heating Units

Painting baseboard heating units can change the look of a room. If your baseboard heat has been beat up and is losing its paint, you can repaint it. When the color of your heating units won't compliment a new wall or carpet color, you can change the color. However, not all paints are suitable for painting baseboard heating units.

Baseboard heating units can be subject to a lot of abuse. Furniture can scratch them, kids can bang them up, and moisture can cause them to rust. Since baseboard heat contributes to the appearance of your home, you should make sure it looks as good as the rest of your house. A good cleaning with a damp rag may be all it takes to bring your baseboard back to life. But when dusting or rubbing with a mild cleaning solution isn't enough, you may have to turn to new covers or paint to revitalize your heat.

Painting the covers of baseboard heating units is not the same as painting a wall or ceiling. These heating covers are made from metal and they are exposed to high temperatures. Since the heating units are mounted near floors and outside walls, they can be exposed to more moisture than most of the painted surfaces in your home. When you combine metal, high temperatures, and moisture, you have a painting problem. However, this problem is easily solved. The key is in buying the proper paint.

If the baseboard units have rusted, it may be necessary to use sandpaper to remove the rust. If the old paint is cracked and peeling, it should be removed. You can do this with a putty knife, steel wool, a wire brush, or sandpaper. The covers of baseboard heat are removable. Normally, removing the end-caps, the pieces of trim at each end of the heat, will allow you to lift the covers off their supports. The end-caps should pull right off, and the element covers will come off when lifted up. Taking the covers off will make the job easier and will reduce the risk of unwanted accidents around your finished floors. Once you have a clean, smooth surface, you are ready to paint.

When you are starting with bare metal, apply a coat of primer before painting. If you will be covering a dark color with a light color in your new paint job, primer should be used first. Once the painting surface is properly prepared, you can paint. Spraying the paint on the covers will give a better looking finish, but the paint can be applied with a brush. The important thing is getting the right kind of paint.

Where can you get the right kind of paint? Stores and suppliers that sell baseboard heat should have access to the paint you want. The paint often comes in spray cans and is easy to apply. When you use these spray cans, don't hold them too close to the painting surface. If the can is held too close to the cover, the paint will accumulate and run, leaving streaks in your paint job. Hold the can 6" to 10" from the cover and spray the paint in a waving motion. Apply the paint lightly and use more than one coat if necessary. As with all products, follow the manufacturer's recommendations for use.

When you are done painting, let the covers dry for a few hours. Keep the freshly painted covers in a place where dust and lint will not cling to the new paint. When the paint is dry, hang the covers back on the heating elements. You may be amazed at what a difference a new paint job will do for your tired old heating units.

This job rates a 2 on the difficulty chart. It takes a little patience to remove and reinstall the covers, but the job is not difficult. Spraying the paint without runs may take a little practice, but almost anyone can do it. The time you spend on this task will depend on the number of covers you have to paint and their condition. If you have to remove rust or peeling paint, the job will take longer than if all you have to do is paint. Under good conditions the heating covers in an average room should take less than three hours to remove, paint, and reinstall. One can of paint will be enough to paint the covers for a standard room. These cans of paint will cost around $10 on average. If you call in a professional, don't be surprised if the bill exceeds $100.

Replacing Electrical Wall Plates and Switch Covers

Replacing electrical wall plates and switch covers is not heavy work, but it can change the tone of your home. Wall plates and switch covers are generally a light color, and these white or ivory covers show dirt. Not only do they show dirt, they are common. Changing your wall plates and switch covers can make your house different.

When you live in a house for a while, you get used to it; you take things for granted. But when potential buyers inspect your home, they will notice the little defects you have learned to live with. The smudges, fingerprints, and minor defects you ignore may become a factor in the sale of your house.

Replacing a cheap plastic wall plate with an attractive brass or wood wall plate could help in converting your home from average to custom built. Buyers pick up on little nuances. A house that is appointed with special features will rate higher on a buyer's list than the house down the street that doesn't have the amenities. While wall plates and switch covers may not seem important, they do help in making a statement about your home.

If you don't think minor decorating touches can make a difference, consider this example. Have you ever been to a restaurant where the food was great, but something was missing? You couldn't put your finger on it, but there was something that detracted from your enjoyment. When the time came to eat out again, you went to a different restaurant. Even though the food was good at the last restaurant, you wanted something different—something you couldn't describe.

When you went to the second restaurant, you were enchanted. You walked through an antique wooden door and saw the past re-created. There was a pot-belly wood stove centered in the restaurant. Its radiant warmth not only took the chill off the damp, foggy evening, it gave the place character. Smelling the faint aroma of wood smoke took your mind off your troubles. The old captain's chairs had armrests, and the bench seating was provided with cushioned pews from an old church. The tables appeared handmade from wooden planks. While the tables were clean, smooth, and coated with a nonabsorbent coating, you could still see the carvings from years past. There were initials, hearts, and symbols of all types etched into the tabletops.

As you looked around the room, you saw old-fashioned oil lamps. Even though the lamps had been modified to provide safe electrical lighting, they still glowed with memories. In the corner was an open grill, with the flames flickering around prime cuts of steak. As you took your seat you couldn't help looking at the wall-hangings and decorations that gave subtle hints of the past.

You enjoyed your dinner because the food was fantastic, the service was good, but most of all, there was a unique atmosphere surrounding you. The restaurant engraved a memory in your mind that would not be forgotten. In fact, the restaurant became your favorite place to eat.

Your house can be compared to that country restaurant. When buyers tour homes, they often see a lot of houses. When they get home, buyers are frequently confused as to which houses had what features. If you can impress buyers with an unforgettable feature, you have a better chance of selling your home. Sure the buyers will probably have to come back for a second look, but they will remember your house as the one they want to see again.

Customized wall plates and switch covers may not be enough on their own to draw buyers back, but they can help in casting the right impression. When you consider the minimal cost and effort required to enhance your home with upgraded wall plates and switch covers, there is no reason not to take advantage of these selling tools.

Wall plates can usually be replaced by simply removing a single screw. Once the old plate is off, the new plate is set in place and the new screw is installed. Switch covers will normally have two screws, but the job of replacing them is simple. However, there are hot wires behind these plates. If you place a finger or screwdriver on these wires, a strong electrical shock could result. As long as you pay attention to what you are doing and don't get careless, you shouldn't have any problem replacing your wall plates and switch covers. Decorative covers can be found in hardware stores, department stores, and at suppliers of electrical goods.

This job rates a 1 on the difficulty scale. The cost of the job will depend upon what type of covers you use and how many of them you need. Plan on spending between $3 to $6 for custom covers. You could hire an electrician at between $25 and $40 an hour to do the job for you, but there is no reason you can't do it yourself.

Dimmer Switches

Dimmer switches are not only easy to install, they allow you to control the mood of a room with varying degrees of lighting. Being able to adjust the quantity of light in a room is a pleasant amenity. Rooms that are often equipped with dimmers include family rooms, dining rooms, and bedrooms. However, any room in the house is a possible candidate for this inexpensive, but desirable option.

Dimmer switches can be used to replace existing electrical switches. These universal switches are sold in hardware stores, department stores, and stores dealing in electrical supplies. The switches cost less than $10 apiece, and anyone can install them.

Before you install your dimmer switches, it is critical to confirm that the power to the wires you will be working with is off. These circuits can be turned off at the main electrical panel. An inexpensive electrical meter will keep you from putting your fingers into a box of hot wires.

Once the power is off, all you have to do is replace the existing switch with the dimmer switch. This involves removing the switch plate and disconnecting the wires from the existing switch, which is not a big job. Then you connect the wires to the screws on the dimmer switch and mount the new switch in the box. The last step is putting the cover plate over the dimmer and screwing it on. When you are done, turn the power on and check your installation.

This project is simple, but it rates a 2 on the difficulty chart because of having to work with electrical wiring. As for costs, you can replace several of your regular switches with dimmers for less than $50.

Installing Pegboard in Your Garage

Installing pegboard in your garage can serve multiple purposes. Pegboard provides the opportunity for you to organize the items in your garage. Instead of having tools lying around on the floor or workbench, you can have them hanging on the wall. This makes the items easier for you to find, and it makes the garage neater for the inspection of potential buyers. By keeping tools, toys, and whatever up on the walls, the garage will appear larger than if the items were sitting on the floor. This can be a big advantage when showing your property to interested buyers.

If your garage doesn't have finished interior walls, pegboard hides the wall studs, insulation, and siding from direct view. Pegboard is easy to install, relatively inexpensive, and offers many utilitarian purposes. As a word of caution, don't draw outlines of the objects stored on the pegboard. Some people draw the outline of a pipe wrench or hammer to indicate the tool that should be hanging in a particular space. While this is good for the present owner's organizational pleasure, it may conflict with the plans of a new owner. Leave the pegboard in its natural state. If the new owners want to draw outlines or paint the pegboard they can, but you shouldn't.

Installing pegboard is simple. The material is lightweight and easy to work with. It can be cut with any type of saw and it can be hung with nails or screws. All you have to do is locate the wall studs and hang the board.

Hanging pegboard rates a 1 on the difficulty scale. Pegboard comes in different sizes, but 4' x 8' sheets are the norm. These sheets can generally be found with prices of less than $10. A homeowner can hang a sheet of pegboard in less than five minutes. Pros will be happy to do the job for you, but you don't need professional help for this improvement. Now, let's move on to the next chapter and see what you can do for less than $100.

Chapter 3

Projects You Can Do
for Under $100

There are many projects you can do for under $100. You can add
lighting under your kitchen cabinets, fix cracked concrete floors,
replace light fixtures, and much more. The improvements in this chapter will cost, on average, between $50 and $100. Now let's see what they
are.

Replacing Exterior Light Fixtures

Replacing exterior light fixtures can improve the curb appeal of your
home. The outside of your house is the first feature prospective buyers
see, and you should make sure the exterior gives a pleasing invitation
to buyers.

If the exterior light fixtures on and around your home are in poor
condition, buyers might assume the rest of the house has also been
neglected. What light fixtures am I talking about? The list of lights
could include: floodlights, post lanterns, walkway lights, porch lights,
and any other lights visible outside your home.

Days are short during the winter months. Since most home buyers
have jobs, they are unable to view properties until after work and on

weekends. With this consideration in mind, it stands to reason that many buyers may see your home after dark. Of course, interested buyers will come back to see the property again during daylight hours, but their first visit could easily come in the twilight hours.

If visitors arrive after dark, lights will be very important. But even during the day light fixtures will be noticed, especially old, ugly ones. If a light fixture is crooked or has a broken globe, it will stand out like a red flag. A post lantern that is bent, rusted, or leaning will scream of neglect. Buyers notice these things, and if you want to maximize the sale of your home, you had better notice them too.

Take a walk around your house and inspect the exterior light fixtures. Are light bulbs burned out? Have birds built nests in the lights? Has the weather been unkind to the fixtures? If you were shopping for a home, what type of impression would the lights make on you? Be objective in your observations. If your exterior lighting is below par, consider replacing the fixtures.

Don't I need a licensed electrician to replace my exterior light fixtures? Not necessarily. Many homeowners have adequate do-it-yourself skills to handle fixture replacement. What's involved in this type of job? Won't I be taking my life into my own hands by messing with hot wires? When the job is done properly, you won't be working with hot wires; you will have cut the power off at the main power box. As for what's involved in the job, let's look at the step-by-step methods employed to replace an exterior light.

In our example, we are going to see what is involved in replacing a wall-mounted porch light. This light is held on the wall by two bolts, of a sort. Actually, there are two all-thread rods that protrude from the electrical box, through the fixture housing, and that are covered with color-coordinated nuts.

The first step in replacing this fixture is having a suitable fixture to replace it with. If you want to keep the job simple, measure the distance between the two retaining nuts on the outside of the fixture. Let's say there is a 4" spread between the two nuts. When you buy your new light fixture, find one in which the mounting holes are spread 4" apart. This way you will not have to alter the electrical box and mounting hardware.

Before working with the light fixture, cut the power off. You can do this with the switch on the wall that you normally use to operate the light, but it is safer to cut the power off at the main electrical box. By cutting the power off at the main box, you eliminate the possibility of someone turning on the wall switch by accident. If you don't know which breaker to throw or which fuse to pull, turn on the light and experiment. When you find the right fuse or circuit breaker the light will go off.

Make family members aware of what you are doing so that they will not cut the electricity back on before you are ready for it.

With the power off, you are ready to proceed. The retaining nuts will usually consist of knurled nuts. These nuts can be turned by hand without tools. Turn the nuts counterclockwise. When the nuts are removed, the light fixture should pull away from the wall. You will see wires connecting the fixture to the household wiring. These connections are frequently made with wire nuts. Wire nuts are plastic devices with metal springs in them. Electrical wiring is stripped of its insulation and placed in the wire nut. As the wire nut is turned clockwise over the wires, the bare wires are twisted together, forming a connection. To remove a wire nut, all you have to do is turn it counterclockwise; this can be done with your fingers.

Once you have removed the wire nuts, the fixture should be loose and able to be removed. Even though the power is turned off, it is wise not to touch the exposed ends of the household wiring. If you have an electrical meter, check the wires to be sure the power is off. If you handle the wires by their insulation and don't allow the bare ends to touch you or any other conductive surface, there shouldn't be any problem. As long as the power is off, there won't be any problems anyway, but it is always better to be safe than sorry.

Now you are ready to install the new light fixture. Assuming that the mounting holes line up, your job should move along quickly. Following the manufacturer's instructions for installing the new light, you will have to make the connections between the house wiring and the fixture. This shouldn't require much effort. Normally, all you have to do is match the color-coded wires to each other. For example, you would take the black wire from the house wiring and mate it with the black wire on the light fixture. The bare ends of the two wires would be held touching each other while a wire nut is screwed down on them.

Some electricians wrap their wire-nut connections with electrical tape and others don't. If the wire nuts are the proper size and screw on tightly, tape shouldn't be needed, but I don't see that it could hurt to tape the connection for added security.

Once the wires are joined, push the wires back into the electrical box. The light fixture should push over the threaded rods and come to rest on the exterior wall. At this point you can reinstall the mounting nuts, and the job is done. Cut the power back on and test your light. If the light doesn't come on, replace the bulb. If the light still doesn't come on, try another bulb; it is possible to have a couple of duds.

If the breaker is being tripped or the light isn't working, you probably made a mistake in matching up your wires. You can repeat the installation procedure again, trying to fix your problem, or you can call an electrician. In most cases the light will come on the first time, and you will not have any problems.

This job rates a 3 on the difficulty scale. The cost of the job is hard to predict, since light fixtures range greatly in price. Some exterior light fixtures can be bought for less than $10. Other fixtures can cost hundreds of dollars. On average, $25 to $50 will buy a decent exterior light fixture. This job can be accomplished in less than an hour, even by an inexperienced homeowner. Electricians will probably charge between $25 and $40 for their labor to replace a light fixture.

Replacing Interior Light Fixtures

Replacing interior light fixtures requires about the same type of techniques used to replace exterior fixtures. However, there are many more options available for interior lighting. Exterior lights are important, but interior lights have even greater impact on home buyers.

What can new interior light fixtures do for your home? A lot! They can cast interesting shadows and designs on the ceilings and walls. They can brighten up dark areas and make rooms appear larger. They can modernize your home. They can lift your house above the crowd of competition. In short, light fixtures can help sell your home.

Does your bedroom have a ceiling light? Many of today's bedrooms don't have overhead lights. These bedrooms rely on lamps and switched outlets for illumination. However, there are still a large number of bedrooms with ceiling lights. Further, the buying public tends to favor a bedroom with a ceiling light, if the light fixture is attractive. What buyers don't like are bug-catcher lights. You know the type, those lights where the shade hangs under the light bulbs and catches all the dead bugs.

If your bedroom has a bug-catcher light in it, replace it with a new light fixture. Choose a fixture that shows good taste and makes interesting use of the light. A fixture that provides sparkle or interesting detail on the ceiling, by way of shadows, will be much better received than the traditional bug-catcher.

Is your hallway dark? Dark halls are depressing and confining, but you can change this with new light fixtures.

Hall lights with frosted globes provide limited light. A fixture with clear glass will increase illumination and make the hall feel more spacious. The right light will beckon people into the hall.

Can you imagine the difference a new chandelier would make in your dining room? The days of those old lights hanging over the table on a retractable cord are gone. Ceiling lights will brighten the dining area, but a chandelier adds class. Granted, chandeliers can get expensive, but there are many models you can buy for under $100.

Take a look at the light fixtures in your bathroom. Do you have the old standard of fluorescent light tubes beside or over a metal, mirrored medicine cabinet? If you do, chances are the light tube is hidden only by a flimsy plastic cover. What is your opinion of this light fixture? Sure, it gives enough light for shaving or fixing your hair, but are you proud of the light? Consider replacing the old medicine cabinet with a modern unit, and while you are at it replace the old lights. An oak light strip with decorator bulbs will give the bathroom a new look. If you don't like the wood look, go with a brass or chrome light bar.

Have you ever wished your bathroom was a little warmer after a bath or shower? Replacing the ceiling exhaust fan with a fan/light combination can help. These units can combine a fan, an incandescent light, and a heat lamp, all in a single unit. Not only will you enjoy the extra light and warmth, you will be adding an option to your home that could help sway a buyer in your direction. Before buying this type of combination fixture, make sure it is compatible with your present wiring.

Is your family room too dark? Family rooms rarely have extensive overhead light. When you combine this with the fact that many family rooms have dark walls, you have the makings for a dungeon effect. Obviously, nobody wants to feel like their recreation room is a dungeon. Track lighting can change the way you look at your family room. Replacing surface-mounted and recessed lights with track lighting will provide a substantial increase in the light offered to your family room.

Track lighting gives the advantage of multiple lights on a single strip. The lights can be angled in various directions for different effects. Track lights not only give your room more light, they modernize it.

Kitchens are another place where replacing interior light fixtures can have a dramatic impact. If you have one of those old glass ceiling fixtures that resemble a beehive, get rid of it. If you have a bare fluorescent light tube over the kitchen sink, replace it with a more attractive fixture.

Replacing interior light fixtures rates a 3 on the difficulty scale. Light fixtures range in cost from less than $10 to well into the hundreds of dollars, but there is a wide selection of attractive light fixtures with prices below $100. If you have average handyman skills, you can install a light fixture in less than an hour. Licensed electricians will jump at the chance to do the job for you, but expect to pay hourly labor rates of $25 to $40 for their services. As long as you take your time, pay attention to what you are doing, and follow the manufacturer's installation suggestions, you shouldn't need professional help.

Adding Under-Cabinet Lighting

Adding under-cabinet lighting has become very popular. The various styles of under-cabinet lighting range from the very simple to some pretty extensive add-ons. These lights are most useful in the kitchen.

Why are under-cabinet lights so desirable? People like them because the lights brighten up counter areas that may not benefit from overhead lighting. From a practical point of view, having lights under the cabinets makes working in the kitchen more productive. But there is another reason for the popularity of these lights.

Under-cabinet lighting accents the decor of the kitchen. Colored light bulbs and shades can be used to create a mood. Ornate back splashes and stenciled borders can be highlighted. Countertops can be accentuated with the proper lighting. In general, under-cabinet lighting makes it possible to transform a kitchen into a showplace.

How hard is it to add under-cabinet lighting? Depending upon the type of light fixture you are adding, the job can be very simple. In less than five minutes, using two screws and a screwdriver, you can install an under-cabinet light. If your tastes lean to the more exotic, you may have to call in a licensed electrician, but in any event the job is not difficult.

For less than $15 you can buy a simple, plug-in light that will mount under your cabinets. The fluorescent bulb is covered by a plastic cover, and the light is hung on two screws. While these lights won't win any awards for their outstanding personal appearance, they do a fine job of brightening up a workspace. Since the lights are hung under the cabinets, their housings are not a focal point of the room's decor, so their simple appearance is not a deterrent. This type of light is equipped with a plug-in cord; all you have to do is plug the cord into an existing outlet.

If you opt for a type of lighting that requires more than simply plugging it in, you should contact licensed electricians. The electricians should be happy to give you free quotes for what the work will cost to install your lighting. As a guesstimate, I would say you are looking at between $100 and $150 to have a professional install a new circuit and electrical hook-up. Of course, this will depend upon the accessibility of your electrical panel and the difficulty of getting wires into the kitchen. The price could be less, or it could be much more.

If it were my house, I would go for the inexpensive, plug-in lights. If you choose this route, you can do the installation yourself and save money, while still achieving good results.

The difficulty rating for installing plug-in type lights is 1. For homeowners attempting to install hard-wired lights, and I don't think they should, the difficulty rating is a 7. The cost of under-cabinet lights start at less than $15 and goes up. Licensed electricians, depending upon geographic region, charge between $25 and $40 per hour.

Dealing with Oil Stains in Your Garage

Dealing with oil stains in your garage can be frustrating. The annoying black spots never seem to go away on their own. Should you be concerned about oil spots? You bet you should! Some people, like my father, detest oil spots on a garage floor. Personally, I don't care if the floor of a garage is blotched with dried oil spots, but I may be in a minority. When preparing your house for sale, you should attempt to cover all the bases. I can guarantee you that if someone like my father was inspecting a home where the garage floor was dotted with oil, he would not be in a buying mood. If the rest of the house was perfect, he would probably buy it, but not without some strong negotiating for restitution on the cost to refurbish the garage floor.

What difference does it make if a garage floor is speckled with oil? Cars occasionally leak oil and cars are what garages are intended to house, so what's the big deal? It's hard for me to answer this question on a personal basis, but I can give you input from my experience as a real estate broker. People like houses to be impeccable. Many buyers, especially men, seem to take the garage's condition personally.

Garages are not always used to shelter vehicles from adverse weather. It is not uncommon to see garages that have been converted to hobby rooms. These garages contain everything from photography studios to extensive layouts for model trains. Garages are often used as storage facilities for everything, except motor vehicles. This being the case, I suppose it is not unreasonable for buyers to want a clean floor. The point is, if you have oil stains in your garage, get rid of them.

How should you go about getting rid of oil stains? There are many home remedies you can try, but some work better than others. If you have a really tough stain, look to industrial-strength cleaners. There are various chemical companies that manufacture solutions to dissolve oil. These solutions can be hard for the average individual to get, and they can be expensive. As an alternative, you can use products that are closer to home.

How many soft drinks do you drink in a day? I know this question isn't relevant to cleaning up oil spots, but you may alter your drinking habits after hearing what I'm about to say. Cola products are said to be very good oil removers. Now think about it, if cola can destroy oil stains, when everything else you have tried has failed, what is it doing to your stomach? Well, I'm not trying to lobby against cola products, but they are reported to be capable of removing oil from concrete and corrosion from battery terminals; this is powerful stuff.

Now seriously, pouring cola on the oil and scrubbing with a strong brush may remove your oil stain. Laundry detergent and laundry bleach are other options you can employ. Persistence might be the key to this task. Repetitive action can be required to annihilate stubborn stains.

If you don't like the idea of exerting a lot of elbow grease on removing oil stains, consider cheating. Yes, cheating; you can make one pass at the stains, and if it doesn't work, paint the floor. A painted floor will help control moisture and dust, while hiding deep-seated oil stains. Choose a paint made for concrete and follow the manufacturer's suggestions.

Removing oil stains rates a 1 on the difficulty scale. The cost of the job is negligible—less than $10. If you decide to paint the garage floor, the difficulty rating remains at 1, but the cost could go up to around $60 or $75. Professionals will remove your oil stains, but they wont be cheap; expect to spend upward of $75 to have simple stains removed by pros.

Fixing Cracked Concrete Floors

Fixing cracked concrete floors can be an issue when dealing with basements, garages, or houses on slab foundations. It is not unusual for concrete to crack, but when it does, it can alienate home buyers. When buyers see cracks running through concrete floors, they fear water infiltration and structural damage. In many cases, the fear of water infiltration is justified. Concrete floors that crack can leak. While cracked floors may not have a substantial impact on the structural quality of a home, they certainly taint the opinion of prospective buyers. You should not ignore cracked concrete.

Okay, we know you shouldn't ignore cracked concrete, but what should you do about it? Cracked concrete is not always easy to fix. However, the job can be accomplished by average homeowners.

Fixing cracked concrete can involve various methods. Perhaps the simplest way to fill a crack in concrete is with a sand or mortar mix. This type of mix can be troweled into the crack, filling it nicely. If the patch is left at that, it will be visible. However, painting over the patch can conceal the discrepancy.

It is important to use a sand or mortar mix, rather than a concrete mix. Concrete mixes contain gravel. The pebbles make finishing the mix to a smooth consistency difficult for any but the most experienced professionals. Sand and mortar mixes don't use gravel, and they are easy for the average person to trowel into a smooth surface. Since the cracks being fixed are rarely a structural problem, there is no harm is using the easy-to-use sand and mortar mixes.

Many concrete floors develop hairline cracks. These cracks are not substantial, but they can give a discriminating buyer ammunition for driving a hard bargain. These cracks are easy to fix. A tube of caulking and a caulking gun are all it takes to fill these voids. Both latex and silicone caulking compounds are used to repair these cracks. However, painting will be required to hide the patches.

If water is seeping in through cracks, more extensive effort is required. There are commercial materials that say they will stop water. Some of these products do seem to work. It is well worth the cost of these products to try them. If they work, you have saved a lot of money. If you can't block the water with paint-on methods, you will have to turn to more expensive options, such as drain tile, sump pumps, jackhammers, and other expensive methods.

There are a host of products available for concrete repair. You will have to evaluate your needs and match the products available with your requirements. This can take some time, research, and trial-and-error experiments, but the results should pay for themselves. Fixing cracks in your concrete should be at the top of your priority list.

How does patching concrete rate on the difficulty scale? The rating depends on your personal circumstances. Repairing most minor cracks will rate only a 2 on the difficulty scale. If the cracks allow water to seep in, the difficulty rating will jump to a 3. As long as the cracks do not cause a structural problem, the rating will not exceed a 3. The cost for repairing a small crack will be less than $10. Floors with larger cracks or multiple cracks could run the cost up to about $25. If you decide to conceal the cracks with paint, the cost can range between $50 and $100. Patching a small crack should take less than an hour. Concrete professionals will make these repairs for you, but they are likely to charge between $20 and $35 per hour, plus the cost of materials.

Interior Window Shutters

Interior window shutters can give a room a novel look. Depending upon the design of the shutters, the room can take on the appearance of an old-time saloon or an elegant sitting room. Interior window shutters mount inside a window frame and provide privacy, beauty, or both. This type of window treatment is very popular in kitchens, but they may be used throughout a home.

One of the more common types of interior shutter is made from wood and has movable louvers. Not only can the shutters be opened or swung in to close, the louvers can also be opened and closed. Other types incorporate stained or etched glass. The decorative options are numerous.

Interior shutters are easy for most homeowners to install. They are typically hung in the window casing with small hinges. The hinges allow the shutters to be opened and closed freely. When a colored pattern is built into the shutters, the natural light entering the room brings the design to life. Wood shutters can be stained or painted to match the surrounding trim.

Hanging interior shutters rates a 1 on the difficulty scale. The shutter can be purchased for less than $25 per pair, but prices can reach much higher, depending upon material types and detail work. Professionals are not needed for this job.

Lattice Work

Lattice work can hide unsightly foundations and provide a climbing surface for flourishing plants. Pressure-treated lattice can be installed in direct contact with the ground. Many homeowners use lattice to enclose their porches, dress up pier foundations, hide exterior mechanical equipment, and so forth. Lattice is also very popular in flower gardens and landscaping.

Lattice panels are frequently 4′ wide and 8′ long. A single sheet of lattice work will provide a lot of coverage. The thin wood is easy to cut and simple to work with.

On the difficulty scale, installing lattice rates a 1. Obscuring mechanical equipment or stacks of wood waiting for the fireplace can be done easily for less than $100.

Shelves

Shelves are an often overlooked improvement that can make a home more usable. Whether the shelves are built to accommodate a library of books or to make use of an unused corner, they provide a function almost anyone will appreciate. Corner shelves are a particularly good use of space.

Any room in the house can benefit from the installation of shelves. Kitchen shelves can hold cookbooks, spices, and a myriad of other items. Shelves in the family room or living room can hold trophies, collections, and fresh-cut flowers. Bedrooms that are equipped with shelves can accommodate books, toys, and anything else the occupant desires.

If you decide to add shelves to your home, plan the installation carefully. Shelves that are just stuck on the wall will look tacky. It doesn't do any good to add shelves to attract a buyer's attention if the impression will be a poor one. Take your time and plan the shelf placement and installation. Refrain from using ugly metal brackets. Keep the job classy.

Metal brackets are all right, if they are decorative and distinctive. Supports made of wood are a fine option, but use a wood with good grain and quality. The wood can be painted or stained, whichever fits your decor best.

There are many ways to incorporate shelves into your existing space. Spanning a corner with shelves is one of the best ways to make use of wasted space. If you are adventuresome, you can recess the shelves in your interior partitions. The walls separating interior rooms often contain hollow space. However, there could be plumbing or electrical wiring in these interior walls. If you decide to open the wall for recessing shelves, don't take any chances. Open the wall with a hammer to avoid cutting into hot wires. Once you have knocked a hole in the drywall, you can see if the path is clear and finish making the hole with a saw. Small strips of wood can be nailed to the studs to act as ledgers for holding the shelves. Once the hole has been opened and the shelves installed, the rough opening can be trimmed with standard window casing.

The horizontal space between the wall studs will be about 13". The depth of the cavity should be at least 3$1/2$. This isn't a lot of space for shelves, but it is adequate for some collections and many other types of storage.

The difficulty rating for this job is a 2, and $75 will buy a lot of shelving, brackets, and stain.

Bird Feeders

Bird feeders tend to keep songbirds around a house. Since most people enjoying seeing birds and an occasional squirrel around their home, bird feeders are a good project for sellers on a budget. While the cost of this improvement is minimal, the benefits of singing birds and cute squirrels could go a long way in setting the stage for a quick sale. If buyers see the wildlife and feel close to nature in your home, it may soon become their home.

Bird feeders come in all shapes and sizes. Avoid the cheap plastic ones. If you are dressing your house for success, you don't want to hang a bunch of cheap plastic feeders in the trees. Opt for some of the bird feeders that are made like churches, covered bridges, and similar buildings. These feeders not only provide a place for birds and animals to feed, they decorate the landscape with their sculptural appearance.

Upscale bird feeders will cost between $35 and $75. The feeders can be attached to trees or mounted on poles. The difficulty rating for this job is a 1.

Birdbaths

If you are going to provide birds with a place to eat, you might as well give them a birdbath to wash up in. Birdbaths are effective in making an attractive backyard garden. When a birdbath is worked into the landscape naturally, it can be a real asset.

Choose your new birdbath wisely. Cheap plastic units will detract from your home. This is not to say that plastic birdbaths are useless. There are many types of plastic baths that will look fine. Heavy concrete baths are more expensive, but they may lend more of an air of good taste. The choice is yours, but stay away from the puny plastic ones.

The difficulty rating for setting up a birdbath is a 1. When you shop for a decorative birdbath, you should have many to choose from with prices under $100.

Park Bench

A park bench can continue to build the image of your backyard garden. While the bench may be as much for decoration as anything else, it will provide a functional place to sit and enjoy your parklike setting.

The combination of beautiful birds, playful squirrels, delicate landscaping, and a park bench can be an aphrodisiac to prospective buyers. The buyers may find themselves sitting in the bench and feeling at home. If you're lucky, the buyers will find your place too peaceful to pass up.

Prices on park benches start around $75. The difficulty level for installing these benches is a 1.

Moisture Barriers

If your home sits on a crawl space foundation, a moisture barrier might be in order. The barrier will protect the home from moisture damage and make it easier for prospective buyers to inspect the underside of your home. Even if buyers are not aware of the value moisture barriers bring to homes, the professional inspectors they are likely to hire will.

A moisture barrier is not a complicated or expensive improvement. Plastic works fine as a barrier. The plastic should be laid on the ground under the house, covering about 80 percent of the area. Most builders install the plastic so that it is in the center of the space, leaving a gap between the barrier and the foundation walls.

The difficulty rating for installing a moisture barrier is a 1. Even with a large house and the use of thick plastic, the price for the job won't be much more than $50, if that.

Closet Organizers

Closet organizers are great. These specialty units allow maximum utilization of available space. The complexity of the units can range from simple to intricate. There are models designed to hold shoes, models that hang on the backs of doors, and many others.

If you want, you can build an extensive organizing unit. The units can have pull-out drawers, fold-down shelves, and many other accessories. These organizers are generally sold in modules. You should be able to outfit the average closet with an enviable organizer for less than $100. The difficulty rating for this job is a 1.

Replace Damaged Screens

Replace damaged screens before you put your home on the market. Screens that have been torn or patched are not what buyers want to see. When buyers are prepared to pay top dollar for a home, they want the house to be in good repair. This extends right down to the window screens.

Window screens may seem petty, but buyers won't want to be bothered trying to find screens that will fit your windows. If you have screens that should be replaced, replace them.

This job rates a 2 on the difficulty scale. Screens vary in cost, but most of them sell for less than $15. You can afford to replace all of your bad screens. The chances are good you can do the job with much of your $100 left over.

Range Hoods

Range hoods play important roles in kitchens. These units vent unwanted smells and gases to the outside air. Most models provide light over the stove top. The color and style of range hoods can influence the overall appearance of kitchens. If a range hood is stained with grease buildup, it detracts from the looks of the kitchen. Old range hoods tell buyers that the house has been around for awhile. Replacing the range hood can modernize and spiff up the kitchen.

Homeowners can tackle this type of job without much fear of failure. Range hoods are typically easy to replace. A few screws, a duct connection, and an electrical connection are all that stand between you and a new range hood. Some hoods are not even connected to duct work. These models use special filters to avoid the need for ducting.

You can buy a nice range hood for less than $75. The difficulty rating for replacing your range hood is a modest 2.

As simple as this job is, it can add just the touch you need in your kitchen. Now let's move on to Chapter 4 and see what we can accomplish with less than $250. I think you will be pleased with the number of improvements that fall into this category.

Chapter 4

Projects You Can Do
for Under $250

There are a great number of projects you can do for under $250. As the amount of money you have to spend increases, so do your options. The improvements up to this point have been inexpensive enough to require little second thought. Spending $50 on a project that doesn't produce the results you had hoped for will not make most people lose any sleep. However, as the price of projects reaches the $250 level, you have to be a little more careful with your investment. While $250 usually isn't enough money to cause major distress when it is not spent wisely, it is a large enough sum to be taken seriously.

All home improvements should be considered carefully, but the more expensive options require the most thought. You must decide if your investment will be returned to you. There are two ways to look at the return on your improvement investment.

One way to rate your return is in terms of dollars. If you spend $250 to add landscape timbers to your lawn, you want to get that $250 back when you sell the home. Does adding landscape timbers mean you can increase the price of your house by $250? Probably not, but the new landscaping may help to sell your house faster. This brings us to the other way of judging the rate of return on your investment.

You can look at your home improvement costs in the same way you do advertising. When you place ads in the local paper to tell people your house is for sale, you don't raise the price of the house with each ad you place. You accept the cost of advertising as a necessity for the sale of your home. You can take the same approach with the landscape timbers. If spending $250 on landscaping will help sell your house faster, it is a wise investment. While you may never recover the money spent on the improvement, you have sold the house quicker.

Selling your house faster is valuable. When a house doesn't sell quickly, time and money are spent in advertising and showing the home. If a house lingers on the market, interest rates could go up, reducing the likelihood of a timely sale. Many market conditions could change while you are waiting to sell your home, so the faster you can sell it, the better off you will be.

When you are contemplating the improvements you are willing to make to your property, you must look at how the cost of the improvement justifies itself. Some improvements will pay for themselves in the increased value of the home, but many improvements are meant to sell the house faster, not for more money.

Once you understand the purpose of your improvement, you are better qualified to make the decision for taking action. When you have decided to invest your money, you want to invest it wisely. This chapter is going to show you several improvements that you can make with less than $250. These improvements have proven to be positive factors in the sale of homes. Now let's move on to the improvements and see how you can improve your odds for a quick sale.

Adding Landscape Timbers

Since we talked about adding landscape timbers in our example, I will begin the list of improvements with this project. Landscape timbers are very versatile; they can be used in many creative ways to make a property more desirable. Let me give you a few examples of how adding landscape timbers can make a difference in the sale of your home.

There are many times when the use of landscape timbers can make it possible to do things that you can't do without them. For example, in Maine, many house lots have very sandy soil. When a house is built, the builder usually hauls in some topsoil, but even so, it is hard to get plants to grow in the sand. The soil that is hauled in is sufficient for growing grass, most of the time, but it usually will not support shrubs and flowers. For this reason, many of the houses along coastal Maine are not well landscaped.

When buyers from other parts of the country see these houses, their first comments are often that the property looks barren. It is not unusual to see house after house with no foundation shrubbery or flowers. This is a real turnoff for people not accustomed to Maine's sandy house lots.

There is, however, a way that homeowners can overcome their sand problems. By staking landscape timbers on top of each other, the homeowner can build a retaining wall. When the landscaping box is complete, it can be filled with rich soil. Adding flowers and shrubs to the planting box sets a house apart from the crowd. Now when buyers cruise the area, they are taken by the house with the flowers and bushes.

The planting area created with landscape timbers provides a depth of good dirt for plants to grow in. The cost of building the planter is not extreme, and the results are effective.

Let me give you another example. When I lived in Virginia, there was a very nice house that would have sold quickly, except for its one major drawback. The front of the home was beautiful and the interior was elegant. But the backyard was a problem.

The backyard of this house ran level from the house for about 20 feet, then it turned into a mini-mountain. There was a mound of dirt that surrounded the back of the house. The mound rose to a height of about 10 feet. When you looked out the patio door in the back of the house, all you noticed was a mound of eroded dirt.

Due to the steepness of the mound, water ran off it and puddled in the backyard. During the runoff, mud was carried from the mound into the yard and covered the grass. Consequently, the back lawn was frequently soggy and muddy, practically unusable. As nice as the rest of the house was, this defect in the backyard was a sale-killer.

Landscape timbers were the answer. It took many timbers and a lot of hard labor, but that mound was transformed into a gorgeous showcase of flowers and shrubs. Landscape timbers were placed at staggered intervals along the hill. The presence of the lumber broke up the starkness of the mound. In addition, the timbers slowed the heavy runoff of rain. When plants were placed all across the mound, their root structures held the soil in place.

The end result of this improvement was amazing. The landscape timbers and plants solved the runoff water problem and eliminated the mini-mudslides. Additionally, the improvement made the backyard a focal point for the home. What had once been an eyesore was now a relaxing garden of peace and tranquility.

This was not a simple or inexpensive proposition, but it made all the difference in the world. When the landscaping was complete, buyers were anxious to vie for this desirable property. So you see, landscape timbers can do a lot for the sale of your home. Now let's see what's involved with installing landscape timbers at your place.

Landscape timbers come in different sizes; some are the size of railroad ties and others are smaller than fence posts. These timbers are sold at nurseries, lawn and garden stores, and other outlets. Most timbers have been treated to resist rotting and insect infestation.

Landscape timbers can be cut with any saw that cuts wood. Chain saws are fast, but they are also dangerous. Buck saws, the type used in camping, will make quick work of cutting heavy timbers, and they are safer and less expensive than chain saws. A regular carpenter's saw will cut the timbers, but the saw's teeth will be worn down quickly by the hard, treated wood.

To get your timbers level, you may have to do a little digging in the dirt. It is standard procedure to level landscaping timbers. By digging or scraping the ground under the first timber, you can level it without much trouble.

It is not uncommon to want to stack landscape timbers. The stacking process builds a deeper containment area and provides more decorative exposure. The best method for stacking timbers, without having them shift and fall over, requires drilling each timber. This can be done with any standard drill and wood-boring bit. Once the timbers are drilled and stacked, rods can be driven down through the holes to hold the timbers in place. This method works well, is easy to accomplish, and is not especially expensive.

Now that you know the basics of how to install landscape timbers, let's look at what you can do with them. You have seen from the previous examples how timbers can be used to stop erosion, divert water, and provide containment for rich soil. What else can you do with landscaping timbers? These timbers can be used to build boxes around trees, making it easier to mulch the trees and to cut the grass. Outlining walkways with decorative timbers is another possibility. Creative placement of the timbers can be used to improve the aesthetics for the entrance to your property. A quick look around your lawn should give you many ideas for what you can accomplish with a few landscape timbers.

Installing landscape timbers is not difficult. You will need a saw, shovel, hammer, level, and possibly some rods, but the job is easily mastered. On the difficulty scale, installing landscape timbers rates a 2. As for cost, timbers will cost between $6 and $10 apiece. The front of an average house can be landscaped with timbers for a cost of less than

$250. Professional landscapers will do the job for you, but their labor charges will be significant, probably around $25 an hour.

Sodding Bare Spots in the Lawn

Sodding bare spots in the lawn is a viable choice when you don't have time to wait for grass seed to grow. Bare spots in a lawn are very distracting. When a lawn is splotched with brown spots, it doesn't make a good impression. However, seeding these bare spots is not feasible when you are looking for a quick sale of your house. Sod is the answer.

Sod can give you an instant lawn of lush, green grass. Sod is expensive, but if you are only filling in a few bad spots, it is well worth the expense. You can't afford to have prospective buyers driving up in front of your house thinking that the lawn looks like an old checkerboard.

Sod is generally sold in rolled-up bundles. When you get the pregrown grass home, you will need to prepare your lawn. Use a spade to make even cuts in the turf as you remove the damaged grass from your brown or bare spots. Once you have a clean cut on the existing turf, lay the sod in place. When you are satisfied with the fit, remove the sod and water the spot. Next, put the sod in place and compress it.

Professionals use rollers to press the sod into place, but you can use items found around the home. If you can't find a suitable roller, lay a piece of plywood on the sod and jump up and down on it. The purpose of the pressure is to get the sod's roots and dirt pressed into your lawn.

When you have finished compacting the sod, water it. Make sure the edges of the sod are pressed into the lawn. If necessary, use the toe of your boot to work the sod down into the existing grass layer. In less than an hour you have instant grass.

Sod prices fluctuate a great deal, based on geographic locations and time of the year. However, almost any lawn can be repaired with sod for a cost of less than $250. A good, flat-point spade is the only tool you'll need to do your own sodding. This job rates a 1 on the difficulty scale. If you hire professional landscapers to do the job for you, expect to pay at least $25 an hour for their time.

Resealing Your Driveway

Resealing your driveway is not only a good way to maintain the pavement's condition, it is an effective improvement toward the sale of your home. Driveway sealants protect asphalt from the weather. These sealants work to keep water out of the porous asphalt, reducing the risk of cracking. If water gets into an asphalt driveway and freezes, it will damage the driving surface. There are enough potholes to contend with on the highway; nobody wants them in their driveway.

Once a driveway begins to deteriorate, the problems escalate. The cracks turn into holes, and the holes turn into craters. These holes present a safety hazard for people walking on the driveway, and the holes are hard on your vehicle's tires. Resealing your driveway can help prevent these problems, while making your parking area more appealing to the eye.

Pavement that goes unattended will become dull and lifeless. Adding a fresh coat of sealant can make the asphalt shine and look like new. This is precisely what you want to do when selling your home. If your driveway is not damaged, adding a new coat of sealant will be a breeze. However, if your pavement is cracked or has accumulated some holes, they should be fixed before recoating the asphalt.

Small cracks can be filled with butyl cement. Clean the cracks to remove existing debris and fill them with the cement. A putty knife is effective in smoothing out the left-over cement. For larger cracks you will have to use a patching compound. These compounds may not match the color of your existing asphalt, but they are about the best you can do.

Mix the compound, if necessary, according to the manufacturer's recommendations. Pour the compound into the hole and pack it down with the back of a shovel. When you have most of the filling packed into the hole, place a sheet of plywood over the patch. Drive your car over the plywood to complete the final packing.

Once you have a good surface to work with, you are ready to apply the sealant. Driveway sealant is commonly sold in 5-gallon buckets. The material is usually premixed and ready to apply. The application process is easier in warm temperatures. Application of the sealant can be done with a paintbrush, but a stiff-bristled push broom is usually the fastest way to get the job done. As always, follow the manufacturer's suggestions for application.

Adding a new coat of sealant to your driveway shouldn't take more than an hour or two. This job rates a 2 on the difficulty scale. Cost will depend upon the size of your driving surface, but most driveways can be resurfaced for less than $150. If you hire a professional for this job, expect to spend about twice what it would cost for you to do the job yourself.

Refinishing Your Deck

Have you thought of refinishing your deck? If you have, you probably should. If your deck looks to you like it needs attention, buyers will almost certainly agree. Since you live with your deck on a daily basis you may have come to accept its slow aging process. But prospective buyers will see a rundown deck as a liability. A defective deck can be worse than no deck at all.

Look out your window and see if your deck is dull gray or powdery white. Are there places on the deck or railing where you can easily stick a screwdriver into the wood? If there are, you've got some rotten wood to replace. Is there mold or mildew growing on the deck? When you look at the deck, do you see a haven that beckons you to come out and relax or a problem that needs fixing? Obviously, you want the deck to be an asset, not a deterrent. If you haven't let the wood go to the point of rotting, refinishing the deck may make a considerable difference in the speed with which you sell your home.

Before you start splashing stain or paint on your deck, check the wood for rot. Probe the wood with a knife or screwdriver to determine if it needs to be replaced. If the wood is spongy, replace it. Also check the rails that surround the deck and steps. Buyers frequently lean on these rails, and if they are loose, buyers will be quick to notice it. Once you have all your rails tight and rotted wood replaced, you are ready to refinish your deck.

You can choose from a wide variety of paints, stains, and clear sealants for coating your deck. Most of these products are available in 1-gallon cans, and many can be bought in larger quantities. Depending upon what you decide to use, you can expect to get between 200 and 400 square feet of coverage from a gallon can. The degree of coverage should be displayed on the can's label.

It is wise to reduce the advertised coverage by at least 10 percent. For example, if a can's label says it will cover 200 square feet, plan on its contents covering only 180 square feet. Depending on the nature and condition of your wood, it could soak stain or sealant up like a sponge.

Before using any paint, stain, or sealant, observe and obey the manufacturer's suggestions for use. Most deck finishings are applied with a paintbrush, but some people find that staining mitts and rags work best. If you use rags, mitts, or sponges, be careful not to get stuck with splinters.

Applying a fresh coat of paint, stain, or sealant to your deck can revitalize the wood and make the deck shine. This is not a tough job; it rates only a 2 on the difficulty scale. The cost of the project will depend on the size of your deck, but many decks can be refinished for less than $60. Even large decks can be improved for less than $150. You can plan to spend between $15 and $25 for most gallon cans of finishing materials. If you call in a pro for this job, expect to spend between $100 and $300 for labor, depending on the size and condition of your deck.

Adding Chair Rail and Crown Molding

Adding chair rail to a dining room can change it from a mediocre room to a striking example of your home's quality. Chair rail used to be commonplace, but now it is considered a luxury. A home adorned with chair rail is generally thought to be a cut above the competition. It is not just that the chair rail makes it special, it is the logic that if the builder installed chair rail, the rest of the house is probably of equal quality. Even when you install chair rail yourself, as an after-market add-on, the perception remains strong. Chair rail commands respect and stands for quality construction.

When you consider the relative simplicity of chair rail, you wonder why more builders don't make it standard equipment. For whatever reason, most modern builders make chair rail an option, and this is good news for you. When you add chair rail to your dining room, it will appear that you paid the long dollar for your molding, when in fact you did it yourself and for a fraction of the cost shown on a builder's option sheet.

Crown molding is similar to chair rail in its effect on buyers. Crown molding is the trim work that covers the seam where a wall meets a ceiling. When chair rail and crown molding are combined, the room takes on a very formal appearance. This formal look adds to the value of your home on an appraisal report and in the eyes of buyers. Let's take a few minutes to discuss the mechanics of installing chair rail and crown molding.

Molding is not heavy, and it is easy to cut. However, cutting the proper angles is not always easy. Learning to use a back saw and a miter box is the most difficult aspect of installing crown molding and chair rail. Once you know how to cut the proper angles, the job is easy and will go fast.

Both types of molding are sold by the linear foot. To determine how much molding you need, you simply measure the horizontal distance you want to travel with the molding. This type of molding is expensive, so don't buy much more than you need and try to avoid making mistakes in your cuts. Before you start cutting on the expensive stuff, practice on some cheap furring strips. The practice will allow you to get used to the miter box without the costly lesson of missing your cut on expensive molding.

Chair rail and crown molding can be painted or stained, depending on the decor of your home. In either case, it is wise to paint or stain the molding before installing it. This reduces the chances of getting the paint or stain on your finished walls. After the molding is installed you will have to go over it and touch up the cut marks with your paint or stain. But this can be done with a tiny brush, and you are unlikely to make a mess of your walls when dealing with such a small amount of conflicting paint or stain. You will use small finish nails to attach your molding to the walls. These nails should be countersunk into the molding, and the nail holes will be filled with a putty compound. Once you know how to cut your angles—and the miter box does most of the work for you—you can trim out a dining room in just a few hours. From start to finish, counting painting time, cutting time, hanging time, and touch-up time, allow the better part of a full day for your time investment.

Due to the cutting procedures, this job rates a 3 on the difficulty scale. A 10' x 12' dining room can be trimmed with chair rail and crown molding for less than $250. If you do a good job, the trim will increase the appraised value of your home. Hiring a trim carpenter to do the work for you gets expensive. Most trim carpenters would charge around $300 for the labor to do the job, and that wouldn't include the labor for painting or staining.

Area Rugs

Have you ever walked into a building and commented on how beautiful the area rug in the entryway was? Area rugs have the power to make strong impressions. Their colors and designs can compliment a room, while making a statement about the owner of the property.

Oriental rugs are associated with wealth. Most people who see fine workmanship in an Oriental rug assume the owner is well off and has an interest in art and an international flair.

Rugs that are woven with a country pattern can make a house a home. Seeing the warmth of a homespun rug adds a touch of personal attention to a home. The designs in the rug can speak clearly on the personality of the owner.

Area rugs serve many purposes, but decoration is the primary purpose. When coordinated with furniture and wall decorations, area rugs tie the decor of a house together. Their distinction attracts attention and sets a mood for visitors to assume. All of this can be beneficial in the sale of your home. Buying area rugs can be fun; you get to shop for just the right look.

When you have settled on the right rug, installation is little more than unrolling the rug. You might want to use some double-sided tape to keep the rug from sliding about, but there are no fancy tools or techniques required for its installation.

Laying an area rug rates a 1 on the difficulty scale. These rugs can run in price from under $100 to well over $1,000, but there will be plenty of tasteful choices in the $250 range. No professional installation is required for this project.

Steam Cleaning Carpets

Steam cleaning carpets can make them look new again. Carpets get dirty—dirty beyond the point where a normal vacuum cleaner can meet the challenge. When this happens, steam cleaning is the best solution.

Some carpet styles and colors show dirt badly; other types of carpeting are less obvious in their need for a good cleaning. Living with the carpet on a daily basis makes it difficult for you to assess the degree of change in the carpet's original color. A prospective buyer will have no way of knowing the difference between a dirty floor and a dull floor. All they will see is a floor covering with no appeal. But you can avoid this negative impression with the rental of a carpet cleaner and a few hours of your time.

Most rental centers offer carpet cleaners for rent on an hourly or daily basis. These machines do an incredible job of removing dirt from carpets. The store clerks will show you how to operate the machine and tell you what solutions you need to make the machine do its job. The rental stores sell the necessary solutions.

Carpet cleaners are easy to use. Most of them are filled with water and commercial cleaning solutions. Then the machine is plugged into an electrical outlet and used much like a vacuum cleaner. As the machine lays down the cleaning fluid and picks it back up again, you will see the dirt being sucked out of your floor covering. Most of these machines have see-through tanks that allow you to watch and be amazed at what is coming out of your carpet.

It will be necessary to empty the dirty water from time to time and repeat the initial steps. A house with 2,000 square feet of living space should take between four and six hours to clean. This job rates a 1 on the difficulty scale. Rental rates on the machines vary, but you should be able to rent a carpet cleaner for less than $85 a day. The cleaning solutions aren't cheap, but they are necessary. The solutions for a 2,000-square-foot house should cost around $30 or less. Hiring professional cleaners to do the job for you could cost upward of $250.

Cabinet Pulls and Hardware

Cabinet pulls and hardware often impress home buyers. When the kitchen cabinets have unusual pulls and hardware, buyers frequently make complimentary comments. Some examples would be white porcelain pulls and pulls with designs or etchings on them. These accessories add the look of value to cabinets, and buyers notice it.

Individual pulls and pieces of hardware have prices starting at less than $5. However, it is possible to spend considerably more for exotic pulls and hardware. All that is required for replacing cabinet pulls is a screwdriver.

When you open a drawer or cabinet door you should see a screw or screws on the back of the drawer front or door. These screws hold the pulls and hardware in place. Removing the screws will allow you to remove the pulls and hardware. As long as the new pulls and hardware have the same screw spacing as the old ones, replacement is simple.

Replacing cabinet hinges is also simple, as long as the new hinges have the same screw patterns as the old ones. Again, all you have to do is remove a few screws and replace the old hinges with the new ones.

Replacing cabinet pulls and hardware is easy, and it gives a kitchen a new look. Refurbishing a kitchen with new pulls and hardware can be done for less than $150. It may only be necessary to install new pulls; this cuts the cost considerably. On the difficulty scale, this job rates a 1. If you hire a pro to do the job, expect to pay around $125 for the labor.

Adding Wall Cabinets

You can increase storage space in your kitchen or bathrooms by adding wall cabinets. Organized storage areas are very important to a majority of house buyers. When buyers see a bathroom with only a vanity cabinet or medicine cabinet, they can be discouraged. The same goes for kitchens. Buyers like to have more storage space than they think they will need.

Since cabinetry is not cheap, many builders provide a minimum of it. Cabinet space can be a deciding factor in which house a buyer will select. You can improve the odds of your house being the one chosen by adding wall cabinets.

If your home is not too old, you should be able to find cabinets to match your existing ones. Never install new cabinets that conflict with the existing cabinets. Most cabinets will have their name on them at some location. Some cabinets have brass nameplates on the outside. Others have their name on the inside of a drawer or the back of a door. Look for the name, so that you can match the old with the new. If you can find markings that indicate the style and color of the existing cabinets, your job will be even easier.

There will be times when you can't locate the name, style, or color of your cabinets. Don't give up; there is another way to make a good match. Remove a drawer or a cabinet door and take it with you to showrooms to match against new product lines. Show your sample piece to the store clerk and ask if it can be matched. Even though your cabinets are no longer on display, there is a good chance a knowledgeable supplier can find a source for you.

An exact match is critical in a kitchen. Since kitchen cabinets hang next to each other, it is easy to spot a difference in grain or color. However, wall cabinets in a bathroom don't have to match the vanity base. It is perfectly acceptable to have different shades of wood and different grains in the wall cabinets of a bathroom.

When you consider adding wall cabinets, you will have a lot to choose from. The choices range from simple basics to the exotic. Special features can include doors with stained or leaded glass. Doors with frosted and etched glass are popular in bathrooms. There are wall cabinets with built-in dish holders, built-in cutlery racks, wine racks, and much more.

Don't limit your thinking to small wall cabinets. Pantry-type cabinets are very popular in kitchens, as are broom-closet cabinets. Linen cabinets are appreciated in the bathroom. There are dozens of possibilities for cabinets to accentuate your home.

Hanging wall cabinets is not too difficult, but it does take a little patience and a lot of attention to detail. The basics of hanging a cabinet are simple. You position the cabinet on the wall and screw it to the wall studs. In theory this is simple; in reality it can be tedious work.

Hanging a single wall cabinet is not bad, but hanging additional wall cabinets in the kitchen can be another story. The single cabinet only has to be hung level and securely. Adding to a group of cabinets requires the new addition to be at the same height as the other cabinets and close enough to its abutting cabinet not to leave a gap. This can take a little extra effort to achieve, but you can do it.

Wall cabinets generally have strips of wood on the inside for mounting screws to penetrate. It is a good idea to drill a hole in these mounting strips to get the screw started without damaging the strip.

It is very important that the mounting screws sink firmly into a solid support, like a wall stud. Since the cabinet will conceal the wall when it is hung, you can use a small nail to find your wall studs. Drive the nail through the wallboard until you hit wood. When you find the first stud, mark your spot and measure horizontally for 16". Drive another nail and you should be on your second stud.

With both studs located, you are ready to hang your cabinet. You can use a faint pencil line to mark the location of the studs, so they can be found with the cabinet in place. Put the cabinet in place and prop it up or have an assistant hold it. Use short screws to screw the side of the new cabinet to the side of the existing cabinet. Then screw the new cabinet to the studs. You may find that a little trial-and-error experience is required before obtaining the final fit, but you can do the job.

Hanging single wall cabinets rates a 2 on the difficulty scale; hanging abutting wall cabinets rates a 3. The cost of cabinetry varies, but a good wall cabinet can be purchased with a price in the range of $100. Carpenters and cabinet installers will probably charge between $25 and $35 per hour for their labor.

Replacing a Faucet

There are several good reasons for replacing a faucet. If you have a faucet that drips and is expensive or near impossible to repair, you should replace it. When your faucets have gotten old and date the house, they should be replaced. If you replace an old sink, you should also replace the old faucet.

Plumbing is an important part of your home. Since many people fear doing their own plumbing repairs and think that plumbers make more money than surgeons, it pays for you to have all of your plumbing in good working order.

Faucets come in all shapes and sizes. Some are easy to install and others will try the patience of even professional plumbers. The faucets that are easiest to install have all of their major parts contained in a single body. By this I mean that the two handles and the spout are made together in a single unit. More expensive faucets often have each handle and the spout as an individual part. This type of faucet is much more difficult to install. If you stick with a single-body faucet, you shouldn't have much trouble in your replacement endeavors.

Most faucets can be replaced with common tools, but there is one specialty tool you should have for the job, a basin wrench. This device allows you to loosen the supply and mounting nuts from under the sink, without having to be an extreme contortionist. Without a basin wrench, you are going to be in for a frustrating time. Inexpensive versions of these tools can be bought for less than $10.

New faucets are packaged with instructions for their installation. Since there are so many possibilities of different types of faucets, you should follow the packaged instructions carefully. I will give you a broadbrush picture of what you will have to do to replace your faucet, but don't substitute these suggestions for the manufacturer's instructions.

The first step in faucet replacement is cutting off the water supply. This can normally be done with the cutoff valves found under the sink. Turn the cutoff handles clockwise until they won't turn any further. Turn the faucet handles on and see that the cutoff valves are working properly. If the cutoffs are not holding back the water, find the main cutoff valve for your house and close it.

Once the water is off, take your basin wrench and get under the sink. It is a good idea to wear safety glasses for this part of the job. Faucet nuts frequently accumulate rust, and this rust can fall into your eyes as you work under the sink.

Looking up from under the sink, you will see the water supplies entering the stems of the faucet. There will be a large nut holding each supply to the faucet stem. Use the basin wrench to loosen these nuts. When the nuts are loose, they will slide down over the supply tubes.

The next step is to loosen the mounting nuts. These are the nuts further up the stem near the rim of the sink or counter. Mounting nuts can be difficult to loosen, but with enough pressure, they should come off. In some worst-case situations it is necessary to cut these nuts off with a hack-saw blade, but that is the exception rather than the rule.

When the mounting nuts are removed from the stems, the faucet can be lifted off the sink. If, however, you are working with a lavatory faucet or similar faucet that uses a pop-up drain, you will have to disconnect the pop-up arm. This is a rod that runs from the sink drain toward the back of the sink. It connects with the rod in the faucet that is used to open and close the drain. You can disconnect this piece by loosening a setscrew or by removing a small metal clip.

Lift the faucet off the sink and clean the area where the faucet was seated. Most new faucets are shipped with gaskets, but if your faucet doesn't have a gasket, you can make one from plumber's putty. You simply roll the putty in your hand and lay it around the perimeter of the faucet. When the faucet is installed, the putty will compress and spread, preventing water from seeping under the faucet.

After you have put the gasket on the faucet, set the faucet down on the sink. Now you are ready to go back under the sink and reverse the removal process. Install the stem washers and mounting nuts first. As you tighten the mounting nuts, check the faucet to see that it remains in the proper position. When the mounting nuts are tight, install the supply nuts. The last installation task is to connect the pop-up arm to the pop-up rod of the new faucet.

When you believe your installation is complete, turn the water on and check for leaks. Small leaks can be hard to see, so wipe your connections with toilet paper. If there is a leak present, it will show up on the toilet paper. If all has gone well, you're done with your installation.

Replacing a common faucet rates a 4 on the difficulty scale. The cost of faucets can range from under $20 to over $2,500, but a good, average faucet will run between $75 and $125. A professional plumber will likely charge between $30 and $50 for the labor to swap out a faucet. A pro can change a normal faucet in about 30 minutes, but the job could take a homeowner up to two hours.

Replacing a Sink

Like faucets, sinks can be replaced for many reasons. When sinks get old, they lose their luster; this is one good reason for replacement. If hard items are dropped in cast-iron sinks, the porcelain can be cracked or popped; this is another viable reason for replacement. When a home has a single-bowl kitchen sink, replacing it with a double-bowl sink can be advisable. With the many designer colors now available in plumbing fixtures, sink replacement can be considered a decorating move. Along these lines, there are even sinks and basins with ornate designs cast into them. If your bathroom has a wall-hung lavatory in it, replacing that lavatory with a pedestal lavatory will upgrade your bathroom considerably.

Most kitchen sinks are held in place with clips. Many bathroom basins simply drop into the countertop and are held in place by their weight and plumbing connections. Some kitchen sinks are of the drop-in type, and some basins are held in place with rings and clips. Some lavatories hang on a wall with the help of a wall bracket. More elaborate lavatories are supported both by a wall bracket and a pedestal. Each sink or basin must be examined to determine how it is secured. When you buy a new sink or basin, it will come with instructions for its installation.

Since you should follow the manufacturer's recommendations for installing your particular sink, I am not going to go into extreme detail on the process. However, I will give you examples of how the most popular sinks may be replaced.

Wall-Hung Lavatories

Wall-hung lavatories hang on a wall bracket and may be secured to the wall with additional lag bolts. In all sink replacements you must have the water turned off to the supply pipes. This type of sink is replaced by disconnecting the waste and water connections. With that done, any bolts or screws holding the lavatory to the wall should be removed. The next step is lifting the bowl off the wall bracket. A professional can remove a wall-hung lavatory in less than 15 minutes.

If you are replacing the old lavatory with the same type of bowl, you may be able to use the existing wall bracket. If not, remove the screws that hold the bracket to the wall and replace the old bracket with the new one. Make sure the bracket is level across its top edge.

Install your faucet and drain assembly on the new lavatory before hanging it on the wall. This is not only easier, there is less risk of knocking the lavatory off the bracket and breaking it. When the new lavatory is trimmed out, set it on the bracket and tap it into place using the heels of your hands. Lay a level across the top of the lavatory and tap the rim of the lavatory until it is level. All that is left is to connect the waste and water lines to the fixture.

Drop-in Sinks and Basins

Drop-in sinks and basins don't require clips or brackets. These units are merely set in a hole in the counter and connected to the plumbing. It is standard procedure to run a bead of caulking around the bottom of the fixture's edge. This caulking prevents water from seeping between the rim and the counter.

Getting an old drop-in sink out of its hole can be tricky. Over the years these fixtures get set in their ways, literally. It is sometimes possible to pull the sink out of the hole by gripping the faucet and pulling up, but don't count on it. More likely, you will have to get under the bowl and exert upward pressure. It helps to have an assistant for this type of job.

Clip-Held Sinks

There are a few different types of clip-held sinks and basins, but they all work on the same principle. Most stainless steel kitchen sinks fall into this category. If you look under the sink, you should see a channel that runs along each edge of the sink. In this channel will be clips that bite into the bottom of the countertop. The clips will have slotted heads that allow their threaded portions to be turned with a screwdriver.

After all the clips have been removed with a screwdriver, the sink should lift out of the mounting hole. The new sink is set into place, on a bed of caulking, and new clips are installed. Each sink of this type will provide instructions for the installation of its clips. Basically, the clips have a head that you slide into the channels. There will be a projection extending from the threaded shaft of the clip. This projection is what bears against the underside of the counter. As you tighten the shaft of the clip, the projection digs into the counter and pulls the sink tightly into the hole.

Before buying a replacement sink, take accurate measurements of the unit you are replacing. It is also a good idea to measure the size of the mounting hole. If you buy a replacement sink that will work in the existing hole, your job will go more smoothly. If the sink is larger than your hole, you will have to use the template supplied with the sink to cut a larger hole. Making a mistake on this cut could force you to replace your countertop. If you must cut a replacement hole, cut it a little small on your first attempt. It is easy to make the hole larger, but it is impossible to make it smaller.

Standard sink replacement rates a 4 on the difficulty scale. The costs of sinks, lavatories, and basins can range from less than $50 to well over $1,000. Good fixtures of this type can be bought regularly in the $100 to $150 range. Plumbers are likely to charge in the neighborhood of $125 for their labor in a simple sink replacement.

Replacing a Toilet

Replacing a toilet is normally not a big job, but it can make a big difference in how a buyer feels about your bathroom. Bathrooms and kitchens are two of the most important rooms in your house when you are trying to sell it. If these two rooms are dreary, buyers will be lethargic in acting. You can replace your toilet and lavatory without major expense, and the improvement should make a noticeable difference to buyers.

Toilet bowls can be difficult to clean, especially if your water is heavy with minerals. Acidic water will turn plumbing fixtures green. Water with a high iron content will leave black stains in a toilet bowl. There are many reasons why your toilet may become permanently stained, but there is no good reason for trying to sell your house with an ugly toilet bowl in it. A plumber can replace a toilet in less than an hour. It may take you two hours, but the results are worth the effort. Let me give you an idea of what's involved with this project.

If your toilet sits on the floor and is not attached to the wall, you should be able to replace it with minimal effort and few tools. Measure from the back wall to the center of the toilet's drain. This is usually where the bolts are that hold the toilet down on its flange. There are three standard options for this measurement: 10", 12", and 14". Most toilets will measure 12". This is referred to as a 12"-rough toilet. Once you know the rough-in measurement for your toilet, buying a replacement toilet is easy. All you have to do is go to the local plumbing supplier and ask for a 12"-rough toilet. Most residential toilets have rounded seats and are called round-front toilets. So you want a 12-rough, round-front toilet combination and a seat—seats are sold separately.

The toilet tank will be packed in one box and the toilet bowl will be in another box. Normally, everything you need will be packed with the toilet, with the exception of the wax ring that seals the connection between the toilet bowl and the closet flange. Ask the store clerk to sell you a wax ring—it should cost about $1 or less.

When you get home, gather a sponge, a towel, a screwdriver, and two adjustable wrenches; these will be about all you need to do the job. Cut off the water supply to the toilet. Flush the toilet and hold the drain in the tank open to let most of the water escape. Use your sponge to remove the remaining water from the toilet tank.

Now look to the left front corner of the bottom of your toilet tank. You should see a small water supply going up to the tank. Loosen the nut that holds that supply in place. You will probably spill a little water in doing this. Next pry the plastic covers up from the base of the toilet bowl. Use your adjustable wrench to loosen the nuts on the closet bolts. When the water supply is loose and the nuts are removed, stand over the toilet and lift it off the floor slightly. Allow the water in the bowl and integral trap to run down the drain. Finally, lift the toilet off the floor and sit it on a piece of cardboard or some newspaper—expect to spill a little water. If you don't want to lift the weight of the whole toilet combination, you can remove the bolts that hold the tank onto the bowl and remove the two pieces of the toilet individually.

With the old toilet gone, place your new wax ring on the closet flange: this is the ring that the toilet bolts down to. Take the new toilet bowl and set it on the wax, but make sure the holes line up with the bolts sticking out of the flange. When all is aligned, press down on the bowl and turn it gently in a left-to-right motion: this compresses the wax ring. When the bowl is sitting solidly on the floor, replace the nuts on the closet bolts. Be careful doing this; if you tighten the bolts too much, you may break the toilet. The bolts are tight enough when the bowl will no longer shift from side to side.

Now you are ready to install the tank. You will place a gasket over the flush valve, the threaded shaft sticking out of the bottom of the toilet. Next you will assemble and insert the tank-to-bowl bolts. Set the tank in place and bolt it down, being careful not to exert too much force.

The bolts in the tank are tight enough when the bowl doesn't sway back and forth and water doesn't leak around the bolts.

Installing the seat is as simple as putting the integral, threaded shafts of the seat through the holes in the bowl and applying the mounting nuts. At this point you are ready to connect the water supply. Put the closet supply under the inlet of the tank and tighten the retaining nut. Now, cross your fingers and turn the water on; hopefully, nothing will leak. If you have small leaks, tightening the nuts should stop them.

When all seems to be in order, flush the toilet. Look for water that may run out around the base of the toilet. If the wax seal is not properly seated, you may experience leaks around the base. If this happens, you can try to tighten the nuts on the closet bolts, but you will probably have to pull the toilet and replace the wax seal. Fortunately, this problem is not common and you shouldn't have to worry about it.

Replacing a toilet rates a 4 on the difficulty scale. New toilets can be quite expensive, but most common styles sell for less than $150. In fact, there are many acceptable toilets available for less than $75. Toilet seats go for between $15 and $25. Plumbers are likely to charge between $50 and $100 for their labor to replace a standard toilet.

Installing a Garbage Disposer

You can compliment your kitchen by installing a garbage disposer. Disposers have become a common kitchen appliance, and they are pretty simple to install. Home buyers often peek to see if the kitchen sink is equipped with a disposer.

The only part of a disposer installation that you may have trouble with is the electrical work. If the sink has never had a disposer, a new electrical circuit will be needed. Most homeowners should call in licensed electricians for this type of wiring. Other than the new circuit, you should be able to do the rest of the work yourself. There are lots of different kinds of disposers to choose from, but all can be installed in the same way.

Garbage disposers attach to the drain of the kitchen sink. They replace the normal basket-strainer drain. To install your new disposer, disconnect the drainage fittings under your sink. Remove the basket strainer from the hole in the bottom of the sink. Now you are ready to install the disposer.

There will be a metal ring that mounts in the sink hole. Put plumber's putty under the rim of the ring and push in through the hole. The rest of the work will take place under the sink. Normally, there will be a mounting device that is slid over the collar you have just pushed through the sink. The mounting device should be followed by a split ring that holds the device in place. The mounting device is tightened until the drain ring spreads the putty out in the sink. You should, of course, follow the instructions packed with your disposer—not all disposers mount exactly the same.

Once the mounting device is secured, you can hang the disposer on it. This entails pushing the disposer into place and turning the lock-ring on the mounting device. The ring should lock onto the disposer and support it. Then you will install the little plastic elbow that connects to the side of the disposer. There will be a rubber gasket that fits between the elbow and the disposer. This part of the drain assembly is held in place by two screws. The final step is the connection of the trap to the plastic elbow. When this is done, all of the plumbing work is complete. All that is left is the electrical connection.

Installing a disposer shouldn't take you more than 2 hours. The job rates a 3 on the difficulty chart. If an electrician is needed, the cost for labor may hit $125. It is possible to buy a disposer for less than $50; however, if you are willing to spend $100, you will get a better unit.

Hanging Wallpaper

Hanging wallpaper in a room is one way to change the appearance of your home. Wallpaper is thought of as an upgrade over paint. When buyers see wallpaper, they think money. If they were given the choice of two nearly identical homes, one with painted walls, the other with wallpaper, for the same price, most buyers would choose the home decorated in wallpaper.

Wallpaper is especially appropriate in kitchens and bathrooms. Since these are often considered the two most important rooms in the home, it stands to reason they should be covered with wallpaper. A combination of wainscotting, chair rail, and wallpaper can make a dining room very appealing.

Hanging wallpaper is not as messy as it used to be. There are many new types of paper and adhesive available. It is important to match your adhesive and paper carefully. For instance, using the wrong adhesive with a vinyl wallpaper, the type you might use in a kitchen or bathroom, can lead to mildew building up behind the paper and showing through as a black stain.

Most of today's wallpaper is prepasted. All you have to do is dampen the back of the paper and apply it. However, using too much water on the prepasted surface can render the paste useless. Use water sparingly and to the manufacturer's recommendations. Some professionals hedge their bets by applying paste to the paper even when it is prepasted.

Wallpaper is sold by the roll. The widths available vary, but most rolls contain enough paper to cover 36 square feet. However, you must allow for some waste and shouldn't count on getting more than 30 square feet of usable paper. Most estimators figure the full square footage of the walls to be covered, and then deduct half a roll of paper for each window and door opening. Always buy your paper with the same lot numbers for color, and buy enough to be sure you don't run out and have to mix color lots.

Vinyl wallpaper should be used in areas where moisture is present, like kitchens and bathrooms. Vinyl is also good for areas with high traffic and activity, such as a family room. Reserve delicate patterns for low-impact areas, like adult bedrooms and formal living rooms.

Proper wall preparation is critical to successful wallpapering. If the wall has holes or cracks in it, fill them with joint compound and smooth the wall surface with sandpaper, after the compound has dried. You can apply wallpaper to plaster or drywall directly, but it is best to paint the walls with an oil-based primer first. The primer will make the job of removing the wallpaper much easier. Since you will be working with lived-in walls, clean the walls thoroughly before applying your primer and paper.

The procedures used to hang wallpaper are too complicated to cover in a few brief paragraphs, but the job is not very difficult. It is, however, demanding of one's planning and patience. You will do well to read carefully about the proper procedures to use with the type of paper you select. There are many books and pamphlets available on the subject of wallpapering.

This job rates a 4 on the difficulty scale. Costs fluctuate due to room sizes and paper prices. A normal bathroom can be papered for less than $50. A kitchen shouldn't cost more than $125 to paper. These prices are based on inexpensive wallpaper; you could spend two or three times this much, with the blink of an eye. Professional help shouldn't be needed for this job. However, if it is, expect labor rates ranging from $20 to over $30 per hour.

This concludes our discussion on projects priced under $250. Let's move on to Chapter 5 and see what we can do for less than $400.

Projects You Can Do for Under $400

A s we move up in price range, we find a large number of projects you can do for under $400. It seems the more money you have to spend, the more improvements you can find to do. However, you should be cautious to undertake projects that will not help in your quest for a quick sale of your home. You want to find ideas for your home that will make it more marketable. This isn't hard to do, but you must be judicious in how you spend your money. Dumping large sums of cash into your house with the wrong improvements will be a bitter mistake. This chapter is going to show you more ways to improve your chances for a fast sale, while spending less than $400. Let's see what they are.

Adding a Walkway

Have you considered what adding a walkway to your home could do for its public appeal? How important is a structured walkway to the average buyer? Most buyers would agree that they prefer a house with a designated walkway. Concrete walks are very popular, but they are also expensive. Asphalt walks are often appropriate, but these paths tend to be expensive, and they are not feasible for homeowners to do themselves.

Some walkways are outlined with landscape timbers and filled with gravel. These walks can be done by do-it-yourselfers, but gravel isn't normally considered a great walkway material. Then there is slate; slate walks are attractive and can be installed by the average homeowner. The cost can be eye-opening, and the slate can become very slippery when wet or frozen, but slate has proved to be a long-lasting, tradition-al walkway material.

Stepping stones are a cost-effective alternative to slate, but they don't carry the prestige associated with slate. While these stones may have more texture and be less slippery, they are still not on the same level as slate. How about bricks? Bricks are an acceptable walkway material. They have been used for years to provide solid walkways. However, bricks can be twisted or upturned with a wrong step, and grass tries to grow between the joints of these walkways.

Wood planking is another possible option for a walkway. However, it takes a special kind of house to look right with a wooden walkway. Most traditional homes would not benefit from a wooden boardwalk. There are, of course, other potential materials to use for walkways, but this grouping covers the most commonly used materials.

Any type of tastefully done walkway is better than none. For most locations, concrete is the material of choice, with asphalt coming in second. The problem with both of these types of walkways is their cost. First there is the cost of the materials, and then there is the fact that most homeowners are not capable of doing the work themselves. Whenever a professional is engaged, the price of a job goes way up.

You could easily spend $1,000 to get a professionally prepared walkway. Can you recover this investment? Maybe, but it's doubtful. You would probably recover a portion of your investment, but not nearly all of it. Will adding a concrete walkway help sell your house faster? It could, but it probably isn't worth the expense of the gamble. So, should you just leave your lawn alone and not worry about a walkway? No, take one of the less expensive routes of giving your guests something other than grass to walk on.

Stepping-stones are about the fastest and least expensive way to achieve your walkway goal. Stepping-stones are frequently about one foot square and generally sell for less than $5 apiece. Since each stone will have space between it and its next partner, you can install a walkway of average length for less than $200. By the time you spend a little money to dress up the walkway with gravel, plants, or timbers, you may have $300 in it, but this is a far cry from the $1,000 you might spend on a concrete walk.

Slate is more expensive than standard stepping-stones, but slate is still much less expensive than concrete or asphalt. The hardest part about installing slate or stepping-stones is getting them seated firmly in the ground. You will have to do some digging, and after the installation, you will need to spend a little more money and energy on finishing touches, but this type of walk is acceptable and affordable.

It is possible for homeowners to build their own concrete walks, but the job is no small undertaking. You will have to grade the ground, build forms, place expansion joints, lay a vapor barrier, install wire or rebar, and pour and float the concrete. Don't attempt to do this job in a single day. You will probably need at least a day to prepare for your concrete. Then when the concrete is delivered, you will need several hours to pour and spread the concrete. Working the mixture into a suitable finish will take still more time.

Once you have your forms made the concrete company can estimate how much concrete you will need. You will have to tell them how deep the concrete will be and what the square footage of the surface area is. If you do this job yourself, you can probably build a walk of average length for less than $300 in concrete costs. You will still have the costs of your form materials and miscellaneous materials, but $400 will get the job done, if you can do it yourself.

You can decide for yourself what type of walk you are willing to invest in, but you should have some type of structured walk to your main entry door. The difficulty rating for stepping-stones is a 2; for concrete, the rating jumps to a 6. If you are willing and able to do the work yourself, you should be able to construct a 40' walkway for less than $400. Professionals will be happy to help you with this job, but they will charge you plenty for their time. Expect labor charges from $25 to $40 per hour.

Painting

Painting is a job anybody can do, right? Well, almost anyone can do it, but it takes some skill and knowledge to do the job right. Homeowners who rush to slap a coat of paint on their house often do more damage than good. Home buyers are not stupid; they can spot an amateurish paint job when they see it. If you are going to paint your house, take the time to do it right.

When should you paint your house? Technically speaking, you should paint in warm temperatures when moisture levels are low. From a marketing point of view, you should paint when the walls, ceilings, trim, or siding are dull and lifeless. Painting can be a touchy issue during the sale of a home.

Some people will tell you not to bother painting the home. They make the point that new owners will want to paint their own new home. This is a valid point, but a dull paint job can reduce the odds of a quick sale. Even if you are spending money on paint that will be covered over by new owners, if it sells your house faster, it's worth the investment.

Keep in mind that when you are painting to attract buyers, you shouldn't get radical. It is normally best to keep your colors on a generic level. For example, white and ivory are two favorite colors for interior walls and ceilings. Exterior colors will be influenced to some extent by the surrounding properties. However, pink, orange, lime green, and similar colors are relatively sure bets for failure. Browns, grays, blues, and the like are much more likely to appeal to prospective buyers.

Interior walls are normally painted with flat paint. Interior trim is generally painted with a high-gloss paint. Latex paint will take care of almost any painting need, and it is easier to work with and to clean up than oil-based paints. When you venture into painting, there are many questions you must ask and answer.

Painting is not as simple as picking up a brush and a can of paint and starting to work. You must learn when to prime the painting surface, what type of brush to use with different types of paint, and a whole lot more. I won't attempt to school you in all the proper painting techniques in this limited space, but I will give you a few pointers.

I've seen home sellers working with limited funds paint the front of their home, while ignoring the sides and back. This is not a good idea. If you aren't going to paint the entire exterior of your home, don't paint any of it. A little touch up here and there is okay, but don't paint a major section of the siding without following through to the completion of the house.

If you are going to do limited painting in the interior of your house, be careful how you do it. For example, it is okay to paint the foyer and hallway without painting the kitchen. This is all right because it is difficult to compare the difference between the hall walls and the kitchen walls. If, on the other hand, you paint the walls in a room that can easily be compared with unpainted walls, you have a problem. Don't put yourself in a position to have buyers see that you have started painting the house without finishing the job.

If you have a two-story home, it is acceptable to paint either just the upstairs or just the downstairs. However, if you paint the hall, don't neglect the walls enclosing your stairs. Since this is a flowing pattern of wall space—the stairway and the hall—it is important to paint the space uniformly.

If you have to choose between painting just the upstairs or just the downstairs, paint the downstairs. The downstairs is the first area buyers will see. It is also this area that is the most open to visitors. Obviously, it makes sense to paint the areas that the most people are going to see.

Interior painting is not particularly dangerous, and it is pretty simple, if you know what you are doing. A gallon of paint will usually cover up to 400 square feet of surface area. How much paint will you need? If you are repainting with a color similar to your existing color, you probably won't need a primer. If you will be using a light color over a darker color, you will need to prime the surface before painting.

If you are planning to paint the walls and ceiling in a 10' x 10' room, you might get by with one gallon of paint, but you will probably need more. In theory, the room will contain about 420 square feet of painted surface. If I were buying paint for this room, I would buy 2 gallons. You have to allow for some waste and excessive use.

Paint prices vary, but you can expect to pay between $10 and $25 per gallon. Paint in the $18 per gallon price range should do a fine job. How much will it cost to paint the inside of your home? The cost will depend on the size of your house, but a three-bedroom, 1,200-square-foot house will need about 10 or 12 gallons of paint, not counting the paint needed for trim. The exterior of this home will require about 4 or 5 gallons of paint, excluding paint for the trim. These are rough estimates; the conditions under which you are working and the painting surface can alter the estimate.

If you are willing to do a little research, painting is not a difficult project to accomplish. Given some basic knowledge from how-to-books and dealer advice, painting rates a 3 on the difficulty scale. Cost will depend on your residence, but many home interiors can be painted for around $300. These same homes can have their exteriors painted for less than $150. Larger homes will, of course, cost more to paint. Painters are not one of the more expensive trades you can employ, but their fees are still not cheap. Labor rates for painters will run from $15 to $30 per hour.

Installing Wainscotting

What will installing wainscotting do for you? Wainscotting will change the complexion of any room. Whether it is installed in a dining room, a living room, or a family room, wainscotting changes the atmosphere of a room. Wainscotting gives a look of elegance to formal settings like dining rooms and living rooms. In family rooms, wainscotting protects the lower half of the walls from the abuse of bouncing balls, and other mistreatments associated with active children.

There are some considerations to be aware of with wainscotting. First of all, it is expensive, but you won't need a lot of it. Second, wainscotting can darken a room to a point that is not desirable. Otherwise, wainscotting is generally considered to be a worthwhile upgrade.

Wainscotting is normally installed on the lower half of walls. The wood paneling ordinarily extends about 4' above the floor, and is trimmed out at its top edge. Can you install your own wainscotting? If you know how to use a saw and a hammer, you can.

Wainscotting comes in various forms. In its simplest form, wainscotting is a 4' x 8' sheet of paneling. It can be made from tongue-and-groove planks, old barn boards, or any number of other wood options. For the do-it-yourselfer, paneling is the easiest type of wainscotting to work with.

Installing wainscotting will require the removal of baseboard trim, but otherwise, you don't have to make alterations to existing conditions. You can install wainscotting over drywall and trim the top edge. If you want to undertake a real professional job, cut and remove the drywall where the wainscotting will go. This allows for a less obtrusive juncture between wainscotting and drywall.

The difficulty rating for installing wainscotting is a 4. Wainscotting in the paneling style will have prices beginning at about $18 per sheet. Each sheet will cover up to 32 square feet of surface area. You will need to purchase trim to finish around the edges of your wainscotting. If you are installing paneling-type wainscotting in a small dining room, expect to spend about $225. Larger rooms, like family rooms, can push the $400 mark. If you hire carpenters for this job, expect to pay between $25 and $35 per hour.

Stencil Borders

Home buyers like stenciled borders, but knowing what type of borders to stencil on your walls is a difficult quandary. One person may adore pineapples in the kitchen, while another individual will detest the decorating scheme. It is risky to take a strong stand with a hard-line item. However, a border of swirls and graphic lines, in a neutral color, is usually a safe bet.

Are you thinking that you don't have the artistic skills to paint a border around your room? If so, never fear, there are simple options available. You can purchase wallpaper-type stencils to decorate your home.

Wallpaper-type stencils come in many different designs. There are patterns for every taste. Whether you like birds, sports, or graphic lines, there are borders to fill your needs. These borders come in rolls and are applied like wallpaper. The job goes quickly and easily. However, take your time in measuring and cutting your material. Planning is the key to success with this project.

On our difficulty scale, applying wallpaper-type borders rates a 3. You should be able to stencil a large room for less than $275. Professional help is not needed for this job.

Storm Doors

Storm doors are not what they used to be. Not so many years ago storm doors were gray, metallic monsters. They were installed to save energy and money, but their drab looks did little for the appearance of a home. This is no longer the case. Storm doors are now available in many colors and with countless options. Since storm doors are no longer an eyesore, more people are willing to accept them; they want the benefits of energy conservation and financial savings.

The average homeowner will have little trouble installing a quality door. The job will go smoothly if the existing door frame is square and plumb. Following the instructions that are packed with your new door is the best way to install it. Most doors will require mounting a couple of hinges and the device that allows the door to close slowly. There isn't a lot of hardware to work with, and the job is fairly simple. If you have good working conditions, you should be able to install the door in less than two hours.

Installing a storm door rates a 3 on the difficulty scale. Quality doors will have prices starting in the $150 range. Doors with decorative options will cost more, and top-of-the-line doors could cost more than $250. If you hire a professional to do the job, expect a labor charge of between $75 and $100.

Replacing Hardware in the Home

You can give your house new zip by replacing hardware in the home. Doorknobs can live hard lives. They get bumped and banged, scratched, discolored, splattered with paint, and can become difficult to operate. When you have the rest of your home sparkling, you don't want abused door handles standing out like sore thumbs.

Hardware in the home is often overlooked as a sales factor. Most people never consider the fact that buyers will be going through their property with an inspection of the hardware, but some buyers do. When you want to sell your house fast, you should remove as many objections as possible.

Interior doorknobs can be bought for less than $10. These aren't top-quality products, but they will suffice. Units in the $15 to $20 price range should look and work a little better. Exterior hardware is more expensive. A good exterior lockset will cost upward of $25 and may run well over $50. The more decorative you get, the higher the price will be.

Replacing doorknobs is not difficult. Usually the only tool needed for the job is a screwdriver. You should be able to swap out a doorknob in less than 15 minutes. Instructions will come with your new hardware, but the procedure is so simple that you probably won't need the paperwork.

Hardware replacement rates a 1 on the difficulty scale. You can replace all of the doorknobs in an average house with good quality hardware for about $275. There is no need for professional help with this project.

Replacing Flat Luan Doors with Six-Panel Doors

Replacing flat luan doors with six-panel doors can get expensive, but the change will upgrade your home. Flat luan doors are about the cheapest interior doors available. Many builders use these hollow-core doors because they are inexpensive. In doing so, the builders label the house as being of lesser quality.

Luan doors can be painted or stained. They generally look better when they are stained along with the rest of the interior trim. However, there is no way to conceal the fact that they are cheap doors. Not only do the doors present a cheap image, they are bland looking. Six-panel doors, on the other hand, are classics and increase the value of a home.

There are two types of six-panel doors to consider. The first and most expensive type is a solid wood door. These doors are heavy and reduce the amount of noise coming through them. Solid wood doors can be stained or painted.

The second type of six-panel door is made from composite materials. Once these doors are painted they are hard to tell from their solid wood cousins. However, this type of door cannot be stained; it must be painted. These doors cost about half as much as solid-wood doors and about twice as much as flat luan doors.

As a builder, I have used the composite-type doors extensively. They have been durable and widely accepted. The only drawback to these doors is their inability to take stain.

When you want to replace an existing door with a new one, there isn't much work involved. Once you have bought the right replacement door you just mount the hinges and hang the door. This is not a perplexing chore, and the time spent should consume less than an hour.

On the difficulty scale this job rates a 2. A composite, prehung door should cost around $75. Solid-wood, prehung interior doors will run in the neighborhood of $135. Obviously you could replace a single door for much less than $400, but it will look odd to have only one six-panel door. This job is grouped in the $400 category on the assumption you will have a few doors to replace. Carpenters will be glad to hang the doors for you, but their labor rate will probably be between $25 and $35 per hour.

Installing Glass Shower Doors

Installing glass shower doors is a major upgrade from shower curtains. Buyers don't like shower curtains. Curtains are noted for their habit of developing mold and mildew. The fear of water getting past a curtain and causing structural damage is another justifiable reason for the uniform dislike. Glass doors are more efficient than curtains and they are easier to clean. They also present a better image for the home.

When you shop for shower doors, you will find dozens of options in the type of glass and designs. Simple doors will have chrome-colored frames and pebbled glass, but you can take the decorative look to any level you desire.

Installing glass shower enclosures can be extremely frustrating, especially if the mounting surface is not level. Getting the frame installed properly is crucial to the smooth operation of the doors. While most homeowners can handle the job, it may be wiser to hire a professional for this improvement. Even the pros get fed up with some installation problems.

If you decide to do the job yourself, your cost will be around $300. When you buy the doors from a glass company, they will often install them for less than $100. I've always considered this to be a bargain. In the best of conditions, the difficulty rating for this job is a full 4. In bad conditions, the difficulty escalates to a 6.

Refinishing Old Plumbing Fixtures

Refinishing old plumbing fixtures can give your bathroom the look of recent remodeling at a fraction of the cost. This is not a job for do-it-yourselfers, but in most cases, hiring a professional to refinish your fixtures is much less expensive than replacing them.

Refinishing experts can take a discolored or slightly damaged fixture and make it look new again. They can work their magic on fiberglass and porcelain fixtures. It may be worthwhile to replace a toilet or a lavatory, rather than having it refinished, but bathtubs make refinishing very worthwhile.

Since special skills and equipment are required for this task, homeowners should not attempt to do the work. Professional fees vary according to the size and type of fixture being refinished, but for less than $200 you should be able to get your bathtub touched up; $400 should take care of the whole bathroom, assuming your fixtures are not a total loss.

Adding a Ground-Fault Circuit

Adding a ground-fault circuit in your bathroom or kitchen won't do much for your home's appraised value, but it is a good safety feature and many buyers will notice the device. There are two ways to install a ground-fault circuit. You can use a ground-fault intercepter (GFI) outlet or a GFI circuit breaker.

Modern electrical codes require this type of circuit when there is a source of water near an outlet. If moisture is detected by the device, it shuts off the electricity, eliminating the risk of electrical shock.

I don't recommend that homeowners work with electricity. I believe the danger is too great for electrocution. However, if you have experience with electrical wiring, adding a GFI is not a big deal. For those who know what they are doing, this job rates a 4 on the difficulty scale. For those of you who are not familiar with electrical wiring, call a licensed electrician. If you manage to do the job yourself, the cost of materials shouldn't exceed $50. When you hire an electrician, expect to pay a total cost of at least $125.

Adding Exterior Lights

Good lighting is important in the sale of a home, and adding exterior lights can be well worth the cost. Installing new light fixtures on each side of your front door will provide good light and a well-balanced front exterior. Post lanterns are not as common as they once were, but they are still valued by buyers. In addition, a post lantern illuminates the front lawn and provides a place for hanging house numbers that can be seen easily.

Again, I don't recommend that inexperienced people work with electricity. These jobs require running new circuits from the main electrical panel, and the job is dangerous for untrained individuals.

If you know what you are doing, these jobs rate a 4 on the difficulty scale. Good exterior light fixtures will run at least $50 apiece. Post lanterns are available for less than $175. However, licensed electricians don't work cheap. The labor for adding porch lights could run as high as $200, and the labor for installing a post lantern, depending upon the circumstances, could hit $300.

Walkway Lights

Walkway lights are practical and pretty. Lining your walk with low-profile lights will make your house stand out at night. It will also make the walk easier to negotiate after dark. There are many styles of lights to choose from, and you can even opt for colored light bulbs.

The amount of electrical work needed for these lights will depend on the type of lights you buy. Some styles plug into an outlet, while others use solar power to produce light at night. Most require traditional wiring techniques and a new electrical circuit.

The difficulty rating for plug-in and solar lights is a 1. Hard-wired lights require working in the panel box and should not be connected by untrained hands. If you have the experience to make your own electrical connection, the difficulty rating is a 3. Walkway lights can cost as little as $80 and as much as $200. Electricians will probably charge at least $200 for their labor to install walkway lights.

Floodlights

Floodlights are very beneficial when you will be showing your home to prospective buyers after dark. Floodlights not only make it easier for buyers to walk around the exterior of your home, the lights allow them to see more about the house and its surroundings.

If you really want to impress buyers, consider installing floodlights that have motion sensors. These lights come on automatically when they sense movement. Not only are they convenient, many people see them as a security feature. Floodlights with motion sensors are not very expensive—usually less than $30 per pair.

Installing floodlights at the gable of your garage and at the corners of your home will provide a lot of light and some additional peace of mind. Floodlights are easy to mount and simple to wire, but you will probably need to run new circuits for the connections. As you know by now, this involves poking around in the panel box, where deadly electricity is present. I can't recommend that you do the final connection yourself, but you can mount the lights and run the wires to the panel box. Then an electrician can check your work and make the final connections.

Pairs of standard floodlights can be bought for as little as $15. However, plan on spending between $25 and $35 for most weatherproof floodlights. The wire used for running the circuit will probably be a 14-2 Romex wire. If you do all the work, except the hookup at the panel box, most electricians will probably charge less than $50 to make the connections. Given an unobstructed path to run your wiring, this job rates a 3 on the difficulty scale.

Track Lighting

Track lighting is very popular. This type of lighting provides good illumination and is very versatile. The lights can be angled in different directions to meet changing needs. As with other types of lighting, there are many choices to pick from with track lighting. The light housings come in different shapes, sizes, and designs. The strips holding the lights range from modest metal tracks to elaborate fixtures.

Adding track lights to your present lighting arrangements will require a new circuit. However, it is possible to replace existing fixtures with track lighting, and this does not require a new circuit.

Replacing existing lighting with track lighting rates only a 2 on the difficulty scale. Running a new circuit to add track lighting rates a 4. If you hire professionals to replace old lighting with track lighting, the labor cost should run about $70. Hiring them to run the new circuit could cost as much as $150.

Recessed Lights

Recessed lights are good for mood enhancement. These sunken lights can create an aura within a room. The use of colored bulbs and carefully aimed highlights can make a major difference in the way a room looks. While recessed lights are good for creating special effects, they are not the best type of lighting if you want strong, overall illumination. Due to their nature, recessed lights do not provide maximum illumination.

I frequently use recessed lighting in the new homes I build and the remodeling jobs that I do. If I am converting an unfinished basement into living space and have a beam to deal with, I box the beam and install recessed lighting. The lights give the box a purpose for being there. In addition, they add a different twist to the basement. You can use recessed lights in many places and for many reasons.

Replacing an existing ceiling light with a recessed light is not particularly difficult, but you should plan on having to repair the ceiling. Recessed lights install in joist bays and the holders usually attach from one joist to another. Because of this, you will have to cut a substantial hole in the ceiling to add recessed lighting.

If you are comfortable working with electricity, replacing an existing light with a recessed light is no big deal, electrically speaking. If you are installing recessed lights where there is no wiring present to connect to, you will have to run a new circuit. Again, I recommend contracting a licensed electrician for the electrical tie-in at the panel box.

Replacing existing lighting with recessed lighting rates only a 2 on the difficulty scale. Running a new circuit to add lighting rates a 4. Hiring professionals to replace old lighting with recessed lighting shouldn't cost more than about $70 in labor charges. Hiring them to run the new circuit could cost as much as $150. Recessed light fixtures can cost anywhere from around $40 on up.

Garage Door Openers

Should you install a garage door opener on your garage? Probably; having a garage without a garage door opener is very frustrating when the rain is pouring down on you or a cold wind is blowing snow into your face.

Garages serve many purposes. Some garages are used to store everything except the family car. Many garages are converted into hobby rooms or living space for teenagers. However, when a garage is used to shelter vehicles, it is nice to have an automatic door opener. The purpose of having a garage is somewhat defeated when you have to expose yourself to inclement weather to get the car in the garage.

Most buyers will assume the garage doors are equipped with an automatic opener. This assumption will be so strong that some purchasers will not even think to look for proof of the opener's existence. Then again, many buyers don't miss anything on their inspections. For these buyers the lack of a garage door opener could result in negative comments in their notebooks.

Home sellers share a common feeling on items such as garage door openers. Their sentiments are that if they have lived in the house for years without the convenience of automatic openers, why should they install them just as they are selling their homes. This is a reasonable resentment, but savvy sellers know they have to attract and please buyers. You may not like giving the new owners the benefit of options you never enjoyed, but if your effort sells the house faster, it's worthwhile.

Most garage door openers are not extremely difficult to install. In fact, many of them can be installed by inexperienced people in less than 4 hours. How much is an automatic opener going to cost? Some models can be found for less than $200, but expect to spend closer to $300 before you are done.

The difficulty rating for installing a common garage door opener is a 4. Hiring outside help to do the job could add up to more than $175 in labor. If you have basic tools and are reasonably handy, you shouldn't need to pay for professional help.

Building a Space-Saver Workbench

Building a space-saver workbench can help to capture the attention and desire of the home-buying handyperson. Many people have hobbies or part-time ventures that require space to spread out and work. However, these people can't justify using their entire garage or basement for their needs. This group of people will be impressed with built-in workbenches and similar amenities.

Whether you are selling your home to a woodworker, a model train enthusiast, a moonlighting plumber, or an aspiring floral designer, a good workbench can help to sell your house. Many people who have the need and desire for a good work area don't have the skills or the inclination to build their own work areas. When these people walk into your garage and see a fold-up, space-saving workbench, you have an edge on the competition in the real estate market.

Unlike the house down the street, your workbench is collapsible. It doesn't remain a permanent fixture that eats up much of the floor space in the garage. Your ingenious design thrills the happy handyperson. This type of personal impression can go a long way in making the sale of your house a reality.

There are numerous plans available to help you build space-saving workbenches. In the simplest form, you may be talking about only a piece of plywood, four hinges, and a 2" x 4" stud. These minimal materials allow you to construct a bench that folds against the wall, using less than 5" of your floor space. However, when folded out, this same setup can provide a 4' x 8' work space. The possibilities for sizes and designs are nearly endless.

To build the simple workbench that I've just described, the average person can complete the job in less than an hour. The difficulty rating for the job is a mere 2. More complicated designs can eat up most of the day in time and raise the difficulty level to a 4. The materials for my simple plan should cost less than $45. However, more aesthetically pleasing benches and benches with accessory pieces can run the material cost over the $250 mark. Full-time carpenters are likely to charge high prices for this type of work. Since this is specialty work, you might have to pay $40 per hour for a carpenter's labor.

Sealing Basement Floors

What is the purpose of sealing basement floors? One reason to seal these floors is to eliminate the dust that is often associated with concrete floors. Water infiltration is another valid reason for sealing basement floors. If you want your concrete floor to have a pleasing shine, seal it. You can use clear sealants or paints that are meant for concrete applications.

When water infiltration is your concern, you must look to one of the many water-barrier products available for basements. Depending upon your circumstances, these remedies-in-a-can may work, but don't be surprised if they don't. Serious water problems usually require extensive work to correct. The use of drain tile and pumps is normally the most effective way to control rising groundwater.

When you want to hide patched cracks and seal out dust, paint works well. There are enamel and latex paints available for concrete applications. Painting a concrete floor will make it more attractive, and the cost is much less than vinyl flooring or carpeting.

The difficulty rating for painting or sealing a concrete floor is only a 2. The materials for the job could cost as little as $125, but the cost is related to the size of the floor and the materials used. Professionals will do the job, but there is no need to call upon them; you can easily handle this job yourself.

Sealing Basement Walls

Sealing basement walls is very similar to sealing basement floors. Most walls are sealed in attempts to prevent moisture problems. Some walls are painted, but most are sealed and left in their natural color.

If your basement walls are growing mold and mildew, they should be cleaned and sealed. Mold and mildew can cause health problems for some people. Just the smell from these growths can be enough to push buyers away. If your walls are not clean and dry, spend some time and money on getting them into acceptable condition. Most buyers scrutinize basements for moisture problems. If your house is a candidate for these problems, it needs to be fixed.

Basement walls are not hard to seal. The job is very similar to painting. On the difficulty scale, the job rates a 1. As for cost, a small basement can be cleaned and sealed for less than $200. Larger basements run the cost up, but it is a worthwhile investment. You won't need any professional help for this chore.

Improving Your Basement Steps

Something as simple as improving your basement steps can influence the sale of your home. Basement steps are not normally required to meet the same standards as the stairs in the rest of a home. Many basement steps more closely resemble ladders than steps. Some basement steps have sloppy rails, no toe-kicks, and wobbly stringers. These conditions are not conducive to people wanting to see your basement.

Houses with dry basements offer the advantage of extra storage room. In addition, basements make good playrooms, hobby areas, and workrooms. However, if the stairs lend the impression that they are dangerous, nobody wants to go into the basement. As a home seller, you need to pitch every asset your home has to offer, and your basement may be a major asset. For this reason, you should spend some time taking care of your shaky basement steps.

Most building codes do not maintain the same standards of construction for basement steps that they do for household stairs. Money-saving builders are aware of these code differences, and they often capitalize on them, giving home buyers less than perfect basement steps. As a homeowner, you can improve these steps with minimal out-of-pocket expenses.

What are your options for improving basement steps? You could rip the existing steps out and start from scratch, but this would get expensive. It is usually not worth ripping out existing steps unless you are going to finish your basement into high-quality living space. However, this doesn't mean you should do nothing.

Most basement steps are made with two stringers, rough-cut treads, no toe-kicks, and one handrail. For this type of stairway, all you have to do is add to what you already have. Adding a third stringer between the two existing supports will make the steps more sturdy. Cutting strips of plywood or boards for toe-kicks will reduce the risk of tripping. An extra handrail will provide added security for negotiating the stairs. In general, this is all it takes to improve your basement steps.

The rise on the steps is sometimes very steep. This is done to conserve space in the basement. The stairs may be steep because there wasn't enough space to get a gentle rise in the staircase without the use of a winder. A winder is a landing that allows the stairs to make a turn in direction. Winders are frequently used in the normal living space of a house, but they are often ignored on basement steps.

If your basement steps seem to be nearly vertical, it may pay for you to rip them out and replace them with a winder system. This job requires expertise in carpentry and may be too much for the average homeowner to undertake.

Whenever feasible, it is worthwhile to make the access to a dry basement convenient. Buyers will appreciate the extra storage space and potential for finished living space, even if the living space is used only as a hobby or workroom.

The difficulty rating for improving existing basement stairs is a 3. However, the rating for replacing vertical stairs with a winder system jumps to a 6 on the difficulty scale. The cost for modifying an existing stairway should be less than $100. The expense involved in building a modest winder system could reach $250. If you have to hire professionals to build your winder system, and most homeowners will, the labor charges could hit $300 or more. Of course, the cost of this project will depend on existing conditions, and the cost could move up or down.

Ceiling Fans

Ceiling fans are both practical and decorative. A good ceiling fan can make an average ceiling noticeable. If the home has a vaulted ceiling, the fan can assist in making the most of your heating and cooling dollars. By adding a light kit, the fan-light combination serves multiple purposes. Even when all the fan does is hang there and look pretty, it is worthwhile.

Ceiling fans can be installed in any room, but they are at their best in rooms with high ceilings. If you are replacing an existing ceiling light with a fan or fan-light combo, the job will be easy and reasonably inexpensive. If you are installing a fan where there has never been a fixture, the job is a little more complicated. A new electrical circuit will be needed, and you will probably need a licensed electrician to do the job.

Replacing a light with a fan rates a difficulty score of 2. Installing a new fan will raise the difficulty rating to a 4, if you can do your own wiring. Standard ceiling fans have prices starting at under $100. However, good fans, with multiple speeds and reversible directions will up the ante. Adding a light kit will add some more to the price. A good, dependable fan with a light kit will run at least $200, and the price might reach closer to $350. If you call in an electrician to run a new circuit, expect a labor charge of at least $125.

Skylights

What would make a kitchen or bathroom brighter and happier than skylights? Skylights are very effective at making rooms look larger. Flooding a room with natural light is almost always welcomed by buyers. Skylights give you the means for making a radical difference in your bathroom, kitchen, bedroom, family room, or foyer.

Can you imagine lying in bed and looking skyward at the stars and moon? Well, if you install skylights in your bedroom, you can. Have you added artificial lights to your kitchen with lackluster results in the desired lighting? If so, a skylight might be your answer. There is no substitute for natural light. Skylights are no fad, they are here to stay.

Don't skylights have to be installed before the roof is put on? No; the job is easier when a roof is being built, but it is very possible to cut a new skylight into an existing roof. Won't add-on skylights leak around their edges? Not if they are installed properly. I've heard skylights are only able to be installed in vaulted ceilings. Is this true? No; you can install skylights in any top-floor ceiling; however, you may have to build a box in the ceiling. What do you mean by build a box? If you have attic space between your roof and your ceiling, a box will have to be framed to allow light from the skylight to enter the room directly. Typically, the box is framed and covered with drywall. The finished product can be quite attractive.

There are many different types of skylights. They also come in a variety of sizes. Some skylights are basically Plexiglas bubbles. More extravagant models have blinds built into the skylight and are equipped with screens and operable glass. Prices range from under $100 to well over $700. Bubble skylights are a good, economical choice for letting overhead light into a room with minimal expense.

Installing a skylight in an existing house can be a little tricky. It's very possible for homeowners to do the job, but many owners may need some assistance from a carpenter. For the homeowner, installing the average skylight in an existing ceiling rates a 6 on the difficulty chart. As for cost, the homeowner doing the whole job can get by with less than $300. If a carpenter is involved, the labor rate will likely be between $25 and $35 per hour.

Accent Fencing

Accent fencing can mark your property boundaries, identify your driveway, or just add to your landscaping. When we talk of accent fencing, we are not discussing fencing intended to provide privacy or security. Neither is it the type of fencing used to keep kids and animals confined to the property. Accent fencing is used as a decoration. One of the most common and effective types of accent fencing is split-rail fencing.

If you live outside the city, fencing can be a very good way to mark your driveway or property boundaries. Two sections of rail fencing on each side of your driveway will make the driveway easy to find while adding character to the land. Installing two perpendicular sections of fencing at each corner of your property will make it easy for buyers to establish your boundaries. If you have enough road frontage, and money, running rail fencing along the front of your property is a nice touch.

There are many types of fencing. chain-link fencing, picket fencing, palisade fencing, rail fencing, and many other types. When your aim is decorative accenting, rail fencing is hard to beat. Many of the other types of fencing don't look good in small sections.

The hardest part of installing rail fencing is digging the post holes. On the difficulty scale, installing rail fencing rates a 2. Four sections of fencing, enough to mark a driveway, should cost about $275.

Increasing Your Attic Insulation

Increasing your attic insulation can save you money on your heating bills and help sell your house. Educated home buyers are alert to the amount of insulation contained in homes. Disclosure reports given to buyers often detail the amount of insulation found in a house. A quick scan of the disclosure report is all that is needed for buyers to sum up the probable energy efficiency of a house.

If buyers don't see your new insulation reported on a disclosure, they will probably notice it when they stick their heads into your attic. At the least, they will discover the amount and type of insulation when they review the report of a professional home inspector. Since most buyers are using professional inspectors to confirm the condition of homes under consideration, you can almost count on the amount of insulation you have coming up at one point or another.

Adding insulation to your attic is not difficult. It may be a little itchy, but it's not hard work. You can roll in fiberglass insulation or you can blow it in. If you opt for blown-in insulation, you could use cellulose instead of glass fibers. Loose-fill insulation can be scattered in the attic by hand, but a blower makes the job easier. Many stores that sell loose-fill insulation will lend you a blower if you buy enough insulation to do an entire attic.

Insulation is not pretty, and it doesn't do much for making a house more usable, but it is a viable improvement. Everyone wants to save money, and most people are interested in conserving energy. Extra insulation meets both of these goals.

The difficulty rating for adding insulation to your attic is a 2. The cost of the job shouldn't exceed $400. In fact, a house with an attic of 1,000 square feet can probably have its insulation beefed up for around $300.

In Chapter 6, we are going to explore the improvements you can do for less than $600. These improvements will include jobs like adding island cabinets, installing disappearing attic stairs, refinishing wood floors, and so on. So let's turn the page and get into these more expensive improvement options.

Chapter 6

Projects You Can Do for Under $600

In this chapter we are going to look at projects you can do for under $600. These improvements don't deserve the classification of major improvements, but they can make major differences in the way prospective purchasers feel about your home. The list of improvements ranges from gutters to new floor coverings. Most of the projects can be accomplished without undue stress by average homeowners. Let's jump right into the ways you can make your house more appealing for less than $600.

Installing Gutters

Installing gutters can make your house more salable in multiple ways. Gutters can divert rainwater and dispose of it without destroying your well-kept lawn. When houses are not equipped with gutters, as many new houses aren't, water running off the roof can beat depressions in the ground around a home. These depressions are not only unappealing, they can cause damage to the home. If these depressions go unattended, they can retain water—water that has the ability to cause a number of problems.

Standing water is frequently a source of unwanted insects. Aside from biting insects, standing water can cause cosmetic and structural problems for your home. If the water seeps through the home's foundation, basements and crawl spaces become wet. This moisture can create mold and mildew, leading to health problems.

When water is absorbed by a home, the moisture content can break down the effectiveness of insulation, reducing the energy efficiency of a home. Added problems might include peeling paint. As moisture is conveyed upward in your home's walls, the paint on these walls may begin to crack and peel. Repainting the house, under these conditions, is only a temporary solution. If the moisture problem is not eliminated, the new paint will not last long. Gutters can do a lot to prevent this type of problem.

Water that is allowed to run wild off a roof can create erosion along the ground. As water pours off the roof, it beats into the ground and seeks a path of escape. Over time, these paths can become drainage ditches, destroying the appeal of your lawn. Again, gutters and underground drainage systems can arrest this type of situation.

Then there is the point of convenience. Have you ever stood in the rain while trying to unlock the door of a house without gutters? A hard rain can make standing on an open porch or landing feel like you are passing under a waterfall. Rain dumping off an unguttered roof will not only get you wet coming down, it will splash off the landing and get you wet from head to toe.

Many modern houses don't have gutters; if anything, they have rain diverters. Rain diverters are metal strips that are supposed to divert runoff water, but they are not always effective.

Builders prefer rain diverters because of their cost. These diverters cost a builder less than $15 installed. This is quite a saving over the price of a good gutter system. Many inexperienced home buyers also prefer rain diverters. Why would they prefer such an inadequate means of water control? These buyers feel gutters detract from a home's appearance. This feeling sticks with them until they experience the problems associated with not having gutters.

Appearance is not the only reason some homeowners detest gutters. Many first-time buyers remember the maintenance their parents had to perform on the gutters of the family home. They remember having to clean leaves and pine needles from the gutters. The pain of painting aging metal gutters remains fresh in their minds, and of course, there is the nagging of the extra expense of having gutters added on as an option to their first home. There are many reasons why new houses don't have gutters, but there are also many good reasons why you should consider adding gutters and a drainage system to your home.

Why do you need to worry about a drainage system when you have gutters? Chances are good you've seen gutters that terminate over a splash block. Splash blocks are found under the downspouts of gutters. Their purpose is to prevent the water coming out of the downspout from beating a hole into the ground. Splash blocks are effective in preventing holes at the bottom of the gutter, but they do little to remove the volume of water that sometimes comes out of a gutter system.

Drainage systems are much more efficient than splash blocks. The drainage system consists of pipes, usually flexible pipes, that connect to the gutter downspouts. These pipes are buried beneath the lawn and carry excess water away from the foundation of a home. The drainage pipes may terminate at a dry well, a gully, or a storm drain, but they get the water away from the house. The fact that they remove the water from the premises makes them superior to splash blocks.

Will buyers want your house to be fitted with gutters? First-time buyers may not care if your house has gutters, but seasoned home-owners, looking for a step-up home, will be impressed by the proper gutter system.

What type of gutters are best? The two types of gutters that are the most popular today are aluminum gutters and vinyl gutters. For do-it-yourselfers, vinyl gutters—or plastic gutters, as they are sometimes called—are best. This type of gutter is easy to assemble, hang, and maintain.

Vinyl gutters can be cut with standard hacksaws, and the joints between fittings and gutters are made with a gluelike mastic. For the most part, these gutters can be measured and put together on the ground. When the units are assembled, they can be hung on the house. Brackets can be nailed or screwed to the fascia boards of the home to support the gutters. Installation is simple, and the results are rewarding.

Vinyl gutters never need to be painted. Since the color is made into the gutter material, there is no reason for having to renew it. Some types of gutters allow themselves to be tipped, from ground level, for cleaning. Installing wire over standard gutter openings will prevent downspouts from clogging and will make cleaning easier. A few good blasts from a garden hose will blow leaves and debris off the screening, leaving the gutters open and ready for service. With all the modern technology that reduces maintenance needs, gutters are a better advantage than ever before.

Other than needing some help to hang them, vinyl gutters are easy to install. On our difficulty scale, fabricating and hanging vinyl gutters rates a 3. Gutters for an average home will cost about $150. This does not include the materials needed for a reasonable underground drainage system. To do the job right, you might spend in the neighborhood of $400. If you choose to hire professionals for the job, get many quotes before making a decision on which contractor to use. Prices in this field of home improvements vary greatly. Finding a company that does its own work will be far less expensive than a company that subcontracts the work out. A range for labor charges could be considered as $200 to $500, depending upon the extent of the job.

Adding Foyer Tile

Adding foyer tile can increase your home's appraised value. Tiled floors in an entryway are considered a high-dollar upgrade, but when you do the work yourself, the cost is not bad. Not only will you be adding to your home's value, you will be creating a great first impression for buyers. When they step into your foyer, they will notice and remember the tile.

A tiled foyer is pretty and practical. The nonabsorbent flooring is ideal during wet, muddy, and snowy conditions. People can step in on the tile and not worry about damaging the flooring. Unlike carpet or wood flooring, tile can take a lot of abuse and never show it.

Foyer tile comes in various sizes, shapes, colors, and designs. The flooring can be a modest earth tone, or it can have fancy designs and brilliant colors. Quarry tile is frequently used in foyers. This type of tile is large and thick, well suited for heavy traffic. When selecting your tile, pick a type that does not have a slick finish. Slick finishes increase the risk of falling when the tile is wet.

Can I install tile myself? Sure you can; laying tile in a foyer is fairly simple. If your existing floor covering is carpet or vinyl, you will have to cut out the area that will be tiled. Leave enough excess carpet or vinyl to work it back to the tile once the new flooring is installed.

When the subflooring is exposed, you are ready to begin your job. It is wise to start by installing a sheet of 1/4" underlayment over the existing subfloor. The underlayment will provide a smooth, even, and clean surface to set the tile on.

You could set the tile in a mortar mix, but most tile today is held in place with an adhesive compound. The compound is troweled onto the underlayment. Then the tile is set into place.

The most difficult part of installing tile is the planning of the design and borders. Before you put adhesive on the floor, lay the tile out and decide how you want it installed. Once you are satisfied with the pattern and spacing, draw a diagram of the layout. You can use the diagram to remind you of what order the tile will be installed in.

You will have to cut some of the tiles. The store that sells you the tile materials may lend you a tile cutter. If they don't, you can rent one at almost any rental center.

Begin laying your tile with the center tile. Work out from the center to each of the corners. Maintain uniform spacing between the tiles. Plastic spacers are sold to help keep the gaps even. Set the tiles in place and press them into the adhesive. It helps to have a rubber hammer or a block of wood and a regular hammer available to tap the tile into the holding compound. When all the tiles are set, you must wait for the compound to dry.

The next phase of the job is grouting. Grout is the material used to fill the cracks between the tiles. The grout material is wiped across the tiles, allowing it to fill all of the cracks. When the cracks are full, the excess grout is removed from the surface of the tiles with a sponge.

When the grout has dried, the carpet or vinyl can be cut to size and trimmed out. For carpet, tackless strips should be nailed around the border of the tile to hold the carpet in place. Metal borders are normally used to make the transition from tile to vinyl flooring.

For the handy homeowner, this job rates a 5 on the difficulty scale. The materials for a small entryway should cost less than $200. A professional will supply labor and material for this type of job for less than $500.

Refinish Your Wood Floors

Should you refinish your wood floors? Floors with a new finish shine and attract the attention of buyers. Wood floors that have become dull or dotted with black water spots are not conducive to quick sales. The visual effect of newly refinished floors is usually worth the effort of the job.

When thoughts of refinishing a wood floor run through the minds of most people, the image of big sanders, lots of dust, and hard work is conjured. This can be the case if the floors are in extremely bad shape, but in most cases the job is much easier than you might think.

Dull floors can often be brought back to life without the use of heavy-duty sanders. When the floors are covered with heavy accumulations of wax, they lose their luster. Steel wool and alcohol will remove wax buildups. The removal process requires some elbow grease, but it is manageable by untrained people. If needed, you can rent a small floor buffer and equip it with wire brushes. The buffer will be easy to operate, and it will reduce the amount of time you spend on your knees. Minor stains can be lightened or removed with the application of bleach.

Once the floor has been stripped down to bare wood, you are ready to refinish it. This may be as simple as waxing the floor. However, adding a coat or two of polyurethane might be your best course of action.

When wood floors are in extremely bad shape, they will have to be sanded. The sanders for this job are big and hard to handle. They can be rented from rental centers, but in the hands of inexperienced operators, these machines can do a lot of damage. The sanders may gouge the wood flooring, if not used properly, and they can swing about wildly, bumping into and damaging surrounding walls.

If you decide to rent sanding equipment, you will want two different types of sanders. The first is a drum sander. This machine is used for large open areas of flooring. The other machine is used for work close to walls; it is an edger or rotary sander. Before using these commercial sanders, get complete instructions on their use. It is very possible to do more harm than good when using such powerful equipment.

If major sanding is not required, this job rates a 3 on the difficulty scale. If you have to get into heavy sanding, the difficulty rating soars to a 6. When you are fortunate enough to get by without much sanding, this job won't cost much. Your materials for one or two rooms should run less than $100. When you have to rent sanding equipment, the cost for the same square footage might jump to $300, including a couple of days of equipment rental, stain, and sealant. Bringing in professionals to do the job will likely double the costs.

Replace Your Vinyl Flooring

How difficult is it to replace your vinyl flooring? In theory, vinyl flooring is not hard to replace. However, the job can get complicated by intricate cuts, heavy appliances, and poor subfloor conditions. All of these obstacles can be overcome, but they should not be overlooked.

Is it worthwhile to fool with replacing old vinyl flooring? If the flooring has discolored or become tattered, it should be replaced. If you have simply tired of the design, replacement may not be wise. New owners often replace the vinyl flooring in kitchens and bathrooms. Since you don't know what tastes your home's new owner will have, you shouldn't replace the flooring for its design, unless, of course, it is horrible. On the other hand, if the flooring has become a worn eyesore, you should replace it.

It is sometimes possible to install new vinyl flooring on top of existing vinyl. Most professionals prefer to strip the old vinyl from the subfloor, but it is possible to leave it in place. However, if the old vinyl is curled, torn, or bumpy, it should be removed. Some caution should be observed in removing old vinyl products. The material may contain asbestos. Since asbestos has become such an issue, you should consult professionals if your flooring is suspected of containing the potentially dangerous material.

Cutting vinyl flooring is easy and can be done best with a razor-type knife. Vinyl flooring is normally held in place with an adhesive. The adhesive is troweled onto the subfloor and the vinyl is laid in place. Rollers are used to smooth out the vinyl. The edges of the flooring are often held down by quarter-round molding. As I said earlier, in theory, this job is simple.

Working with vinyl requires some patience. If temperatures are low, the material may be stiff and hard to work with. Cutting the vinyl to fit around base cabinets, bathtubs, and other items that are difficult to move can be tedious. Seaming two pieces of vinyl together requires planning and care. If you are willing to take your time and read and follow the proper procedures for installing vinyl, you can do the job with minimal problems. If you get in a hurry and take shortcuts, you are likely to ruin the material.

Let's talk a little about the quality and prices of vinyl flooring. Vinyl is one product where you more or less get what you pay for. You can buy vinyl flooring at very low prices, some starting at less than $4 per square yard. A square yard of flooring will cover 9 square feet of floor space. Many bathrooms have less than 100 square feet in them. So, let's say your bathroom has about 80 square feet in it.

When you buy vinyl, you must allow for a little waste and the size should be large enough to roll up on all walls, allowing you to cut to the perfect size. When you buy flooring for your bathroom, you might get by with 10 square yards of material. But, to be safe, let's say you are going to buy 12 yards of material.

Okay, you know you want 12 square yards of vinyl. The least expensive vinyl you can find is $4 per yard. This amounts to a total cost of only $48. You've seen a better grade of vinyl for $13 a yard and the top of the line is going for about $22. In the small space of a bathroom, how much effect will these price differences have? On the surface, there is a considerable spread from the $4 vinyl to the $22 vinyl. However, when you work the math, the difference isn't so astronomical. The cheap vinyl will cost $48. The mid-range flooring will cost $156, and the best vinyl will run $264. Now, of course, there is still a good bit of difference in price, but the total cost is not startling for any of the vinyls. Which material are you going to buy?

The cheap vinyl isn't going to be as easy to install as the better, more pliable, grades of vinyl. The flexibility of the material is very important when working in a confined space like a bathroom. The least expensive vinyl will not hold its finish as well as the other grades, and it may puncture or tear easily.

The most expensive vinyl will be lovely, and it may last a very long time. However, you are selling your house. You don't need a floor that will last 15 years; you need a floor that will be easy to install and will be impressive to buyers. The expensive flooring will do all of this, but so will the mid-range version.

The mid-range flooring should be easy to work with, and it will make a good showing for itself. You will spend about $100 more than you would for the cheap stuff, and you will save about a $100 by not buying the best. The mid-range vinyl should be your best bet.

Replacing vinyl flooring, when things go well, rates a 4 on the difficulty scale. If working conditions are not too good, the difficulty rating might go up to a 6. The cost of this improvement will depend on the quality of flooring you choose and the amount of vinyl needed. Vinyl priced between $13 and $16 a yard should be adequate for your needs. Materials for an average kitchen, including underlayment, adhesive, vinyl, and molding should run less than $500. A bathroom floor should cost less than $300. Professional installers normally charge by the yard, but on small jobs like bathrooms may charge by the job. Expect to pay a professional at least $200 for the labor to install a bathroom. If the professional has to do the rip-out and install underlayment, the labor figure could more than double.

Replace Your Front Door

You can replace your front door and improve the exterior charisma of your home. The front door of your home is very important. If it is old, with peeling veneer, buyers will be turned off before they ever get inside the house. On the other hand, if the door radiates warmth and beauty, prospects will be anxious to tour your home.

While some buyers may never notice the extra layer of insulation you installed in the attic, they will observe your front door quickly. With this in mind, you might consider replacing your old door with a new, more enticing one.

The variety of doors to choose from is extensive. There are wood doors, fiberglass doors, and insulated metal doors. The doors may be solid or appointed with glass designs. Shopping for the right door could take some time. In fact, it will probably take longer to decide what door you want than it will to install it.

Replacing an exterior door is not hard work. It is simply a matter of removing the old door and hinges and installing the new one. If the replacement door is the proper fit, the job can be done in less than an hour, including the installation of new hardware.

Door prices vary tremendously. Some doors will cost less than $200, while others may ring the register at over $1,000. On average, a budget of $350 to $500—for door and hardware—will be adequate. The difficulty level of replacing a front door rates a 3. If you call in a pro, expect a labor charge of at least $75.

Install a Nine-Lite Door for More Light

You might want to install a nine-lite door for more light in your kitchen or dining area. The side or back door of a house is often in or near the kitchen. If the door doesn't have much glass in it, the room or hall can be dark. Dark rooms don't help sell houses. By replacing the old door with a new nine-lite door, you can have a new door and more light too. When decorated with the right window treatment, nine-lite doors can be very attractive.

The only drawback to nine-lite doors is their lack of security. Some people don't like doors with glass in them. These people fear a burglar will break the glass and gain entry to the home. While this is certainly possible, what is to keep a burglar from coming in through a window? If you suspect the buying public won't accept a door with glass near the handle, avoid this project. Otherwise, replace your old door and let the light shine in.

Prices for nine-light doors start at less than $250. The difficulty rating for replacing a door is a 3. Professionals will probably charge a minimum of $75 for their labor.

Storm Windows

Storm windows are loved by some and hated by others. Before installing storm windows, look around your neighborhood. If the surrounding houses don't have storm windows, think long and hard before installing them. While buyers might like the increased energy savings, they may detest the cosmetic appearance of add-on windows. Even with older houses, where adding storm windows was once common, replacement windows have become the preferred choice.

Replacement windows are much more expensive than storm windows, but they are considered more attractive. Storm windows are still used and accepted in many areas, so don't rule them out. It is possible to get storms with finishes that accent your home. Not all storm windows are battleship gray and ugly.

Good storm windows are a cinch to install. Professionals can mount a storm-window unit in less than 15 minutes. Basically, all that is involved is screwing the unit to the existing window trim. A good drill with a screwdriver attachment makes quick work of the task.

Hanging storm windows rates a 3 on the difficulty scale. As for cost, many storm windows cost less than $50. Professionals will generally charge a per-window price for installation. The labor charge could be as little $10 or as much as $20.

Replacing Countertops

Replacing countertops is a good way to make your house look new again. Counters take a lot of abuse, and they can become worn and tired looking. New counters can brighten a room and make strong impressions on buyers.

If you are not intimidated by minor plumbing work, replacing countertops in your bathroom or kitchen is not too difficult. In bathrooms the replacement procedure can often be accomplished in less than 3 hours. Kitchen counters are more complex and may take an entire day to replace, depending upon the size and design of the counter. Bathroom counters can usually be replaced by one person, but kitchen counters can be big and cumbersome. A second set of hands is most helpful when replacing kitchen counters.

Many suppliers of counters will send someone out to take measurements for your replacement counter. If you make your own measurements, do so carefully. Countertops generally are not returnable. A missed measurement can mean buying a counter you can't use.

Like most other home-improvement products, counters come in countless colors, styles, textures, and materials. A simple vanity top could cost as little as $75. A complex kitchen counter of superior quality might run in excess of $500. The difficulty rating for replacing vanity tops is a 3. The same rating for kitchen counters is a 5. Professionals will probably charge $125 in labor for replacing a simple vanity top. To replace a kitchen counter, the pros might charge upward of $400.

Add an Island Cabinet and Countertop

You can distinguish your kitchen from others when you add an island cabinet and countertop. Islands are very popular. They provide additional work space and storage along with being handsome. When your kitchen has enough open floor space to accommodate an island, you should give serious consideration to this add-on option.

In its simplest form, an island will consist of a base cabinet and a countertop. If you have the money and the motivation, you can install an island with a cooktop or indoor grill. Another common feature found in islands is a sink. Even if the sink is small, like a bar sink, it may improve the utility of the kitchen.

There are a few factors to keep in mind when adding an island. Depending upon local code requirements, you may have to install electrical outlets in the island. Most electrical codes determine the need for outlets of this type, based on the size of the countertop. If you will be installing a sink, the plumbing hookup could be complicated. In most states all plumbing fixtures must be vented. This is no easy task with an island sink. Since there is no wall into which to extend a vent, the plumber will have to use a combination waste and vent method or island venting. The cost for adding plumbing may be prohibitive.

When space limits the installation of a permanently affixed island, you might consider the use of an island on wheels. These units can be rolled to any location and offer great versatility. The base cabinet can be fitted with doors on both sides, allowing easy access regardless of where the unit is stationed.

What will a decent island arrangement cost? The base cabinet should cost around $250. The countertop will tack on another $150 to $200. These figures are based on a small island, one about 30" wide by 2' long. Cost goes up for larger units, but not drastically.

The installation of an island arrangement rates a 3 on the difficulty scale. If you hire a professional for the job, expect labor costs in the range of $300, excluding plumbing or electrical work.

Install a Prefab Broom Closet or Pantry

A lot of storage space is gained when you install a prefab broom closet or pantry. Storage space is a coveted asset in the kitchen. These prefab units allow you to provide additional space with minimal work.

Prefab broom closets are tall and easily hold brooms, mops, and other obtrusive items. Pantry cabinets are available in a wide range of choices. Many of these units include creative racks and shelves to maximize utilization. A pantry cabinet is a very good improvement for most kitchens.

These prefab units are easy to install. You set them in place and screw them to the wall. The difficulty rating for this job is a 3. Prices cover a broad spectrum, but a broom closet can be added for less than $300, and a pantry should cost less than $500, even with some super features. You shouldn't need professionals for this job, but if you do, expect labor prices to be between $75 and $150, depending upon the size and complexity of the job.

Replacing a Vanity

Replacing a vanity is not difficult, and it can increase the beauty of a bathroom. With bathrooms ranking number two in the list of rooms considered most important to buyers, preceded only by kitchens, it pays to direct your improvement money to the bathroom.

When you replace a vanity, you have the option of changing styles and colors. As you know, color makes a big difference in the way a room looks. A large, dark vanity cabinet may make the bathroom a bit depressing. Replacing it with a cabinet of a lighter color could brighten the whole room.

If you have enough space, you may wish to install a larger vanity. A vanity that offers both drawers and doors is more appealing to the public. Of course, increasing the size of the cabinet will also provide additional counter space, another sought-after amenity.

If you are able to perform minor plumbing duties, replacing a vanity is no big deal. The cabinet will be set into place and screwed to the wall. The top will be set on the cabinet and the plumbing will be connected. The whole job, including removal of the existing vanity, will take a plumber less than 3 hours. Most energetic, experienced plumbers can get the job done in 2 hours. If you allow half a day for doing the work, you should finish ahead of schedule.

The differences in quality among vanities and tops is notable. Cheap vanities are made of pressed wood. These vanities don't do well in areas with high moisture. Their construction soaks in the moisture, swelling and often times cracking the finish on the cabinet. Mid-range cabinets use some composition board and some solid wood in their construction. These units are much better than the economy versions. The best, and most expensive, cabinets are constructed of solid wood. Mid-range cabinets offer affordability and acceptability.

Vanity cabinets will have prices starting below $75, but they will be cheap and look it. A good vanity base, say 3' long, will run around $250. If you get into extra drawer bases and so forth, you could spend $400 on the unit.

Vanity tops may consist of kitchen-type counters where the lavatory bowl is cut into the top or cultured marble tops that have the bowl molded into the top. Cultured marble tops are easy to work with, usually less expensive, and almost always better accepted than counters with drop-in lavatories.

A molded top for a 36" vanity could cost less than $100. This type of top would be modest, to say the least. To get into the range of a good molded top, expect to spend at least $150. Using a counter and a drop-in bowl for this same vanity would cost at least $150 and probably closer to $200.

The combined cost for a reasonable vanity and top might average $375. A new faucet will add another $75 to the expense. The difficulty rating for replacing a vanity is a 4, mostly for the plumbing involved. If you hire a plumber to do the job for you, don't be surprised if the labor comes to $150.

Replace a Basin with a Pedestal Lavatory

When you replace a basin with a pedestal lavatory, your bathroom makes a strong statement. Pedestal lavatories are considered to be substantial upgrades over common basins. These regal lavatories are associated with success and wealth. A bathroom containing a pedestal lavatory commands attention and respect.

There are two faults with pedestal sinks. These units don't allow for any counter area or storage area. Of course, this flaw is also part of their charm. The temptation to leave a bottle of mouthwash or a roll of toothpaste on the counter is removed. Habits of sticking catalogs, dirty clothes, and other items under the vanity are broken. While this may be something of an inconvenience, it typically makes for a neater, better organized bathroom.

Pedestal lavatories may not have a major impact on the appraised value of a home, but as a sales tool, these specialty fixtures are hot. Since most homes don't have pedestal lavatories, the ones that do are distinctive.

Pedestal lavatories can be a bit of a pain to install; even professional plumbers will agree on this point. The basics of the installation are simple enough, but the reality of making the connections can call upon your patience. However, the job is easy enough for most homeowners to accomplish.

The bowls of pedestal lavatories hang on wall brackets. The brackets are mounted to walls with lag bolts. The bowls are then placed on the brackets, in the same way wall-hung lavatories are. The trick is hanging the bracket at just the right height. If the bracket is too high or too low, the pedestal will not fit properly.

Once the bowl is hung at the correct height, the plumbing connections are made. Typically, the plumbing pipes will be hidden once the pedestal is put into place. Some of these lavatories use 4"-center faucets and some use faucets with 8" centers. The 8"-center type is slightly more prestigious, but the faucets for them are considerably harder to work with. Most homeowners should stick with the 4"-center variety.

After all the plumbing connections are made, the pedestal is put in place. Ideally, the pedestal should conceal the plumbing pipes and fittings. When the bracket is hung perfectly, you will have to lift up on the lavatory bowl ever so slightly to slide the pedestal into place.

Some pedestals have a hole in their base that allows a lag bolt to be installed. The lag bolt aids in preventing the pedestal from being kicked out from under the bowl. Many types of pedestal lavatories, even good ones, don't provide this feature. These units depend on the weight of the bowl to maintain pressure on the pedestal. This is why proper placement of the wall bracket is critical.

If you will be replacing a vanity with a pedestal lavatory, you may have to repaint the bathroom walls. Removing the vanity might reveal a discolored section of wall. Since the pedestal will not conceal the odd wall color, new paint may be in order.

Pedestal lavatories come in many shapes, sizes, and colors. If you opt for high fashion colors, you will pay a premium price. Since pedestal lavatories have become popular again, there are many inexpensive types on the market. There was a time, not many years ago, when the average pedestal lavatory sold for at least $300. Now you can buy pedestal sinks for less than $175. The best brands sell for between $300 and $500, but there is a large selection at lower prices.

Faucets for 4"-center pedestal lavatories are the same type used on most other lavatories. These faucets typically cost around $75. If you go for the 8"-center version, the cost of a faucet could easily exceed $200. An economy setup of lavatory and faucet can be had for less than $225. However, better grades in the 4"-center variety will run around $350. Major brands with 8" centers will cost about $600 to set up.

The difficulty rating for replacing a basin with a pedestal lavatory is a 5. If you call a plumber for the job, expect labor fees of about $150.

Install Disappearing Attic Stairs

Install disappearing attic stairs and open a wealth of storage space. Today's buyers are starved for storage space. People always seem to want more storage room. If your house has an attic, you can tap into it for the strong selling feature of storage.

Many modern homes have nothing more than a scuttle hole for attic access. These plywood-covered holes in the closet ceiling are all but useless. Portly people can't use them, and climbing a stepladder and pulling one's self through a tiny hole is no one's idea of fun. Scuttle holes are nothing more than emergency maintenance entrances to attics. Disappearing stairs, however, are a different story.

When a house has a pull-down attic stairway, the attic becomes a viable storage area. Weight limits might need to be imposed, but the vast space above the ceilings can house a host of lightweight articles.

Some people don't like the look of disappearing stairways, but most buyers are willing to trade the unattractive ceiling appearance for the utility of more storage space.

Installing pull-down stairs is not a big job, not nearly as difficult as some would think. The stair units are made to fit between rafters. If your rafters are installed with standard spacing, putting in a pull-down stairway will not be a sizable chore.

In general, the installation of this type of attic access requires cutting a hole in the ceiling, between two ceiling joists or trusses. The stair unit is placed in the hole and nailed to the joists or trusses. A bit of finish trim is installed along the edges of the unit, and the job is done.

The difficulty rating of this job is a 5. The cost of a stair unit shouldn't exceed $200, even for a good one. With some mechanical ability and a helper, you should be able to complete the job is less than half a day, probably much less. If you call in carpenters for the job, their labor charges could hit $200.

Install New Stair Railing

When you install new stair railing, you can upgrade your home. Stair rails can be quite ornate and very expensive. Spending a ton of money on a fancy railing isn't wise. You won't see the money returned on an appraisal report, and most buyers will not appreciate the cost of your handiwork. However, installing new, semi-fancy railing could well be worth your while.

If your stairway is boring, a new railing can spark new life into it. Whether you are dealing with a bracket-mounted handrail or a roaming picketed rail, the woodwork can set your house apart from the crowd. Be advised, however: all components for stair rails tend to be expensive. Competitive shopping and a strong control over impulse urges are important for this improvement.

Bracket-type handrails are easy to install, but decorative rails, newel posts, and balusters can require the work of experienced trim carpenters. Like the work, the price for this type of improvement has a wide range. A simple handrail and accessory hardware can be bought for less than $50. An intricate railing system could cost more than $700. The difficulty rating for a bracket-type handrail is a mere 2, but complicated systems can drive the rating up to an 8. Good trim carpenters are hard to find, and they don't come cheap. Expect hourly rates from these tradespeople to range from $30 to $40.

Install Glass Fireplace Doors

If you want to add a nice touch to your living room or family room, install glass fireplace doors above your hearth. A fireplace lends character to a room. The addition of glass doors on a fireplace extends the depth of feeling. Fireplace screens are okay, but they don't always contain popping embers and they don't prevent household heat from going up the chimney. Glass doors are reasonably efficient at meeting both of these needs. Additionally, glass doors generally cast a better image of the home. Buyers love fireplaces with beautiful glass doors. Since this is a known soft spot with buyers, you might as well appeal to it.

Adding glass doors to your fireplace won't take a lot of your time, and the results may be a quicker sale of your house. Most glass doors are easy to install and come with good directions. You will need a masonry bit for your drill and some expanding anchors for the screws, but the job should go quickly and smoothly. As a result of your effort, you will have a more refined look at your home's hearth.

The difficulty rating for this improvement is a 4. Glass doors for fireplaces have starting prices of less than $200. Of course, if you get carried away with designs and finishes, you can spend much more. If all goes well, you can complete the project in less than 2 hours. If you elect to hire a professional, expect a labor charge in the neighborhood of $100.

Cut a Wall in Half

If your kitchen is confining, maybe you should cut one of the walls in half. What? Cut a wall in half? Yes; open up the wall into the dining area and create a pass-through. Some kitchens are just too darned small. When builders design houses, they sometimes make mistakes. If the wall between your kitchen and dining area was a mistake, get rid of it, or at least part of it.

Most interior partitions can be removed without structural damage. However, some interior walls do support the second floor or roof structure. Before you go hacking out a wall, check with experienced professionals to make sure the wall is not load bearing. Also, proceed with caution in the demolition work; you never know when you might find electrical wires or plumbing.

Assuming you are cleared for takeoff, getting rid of an interior partition is easy, and it can be a great way to relieve some stress. For safety sake's, open the wall with a hammer. Beating holes in the wall with a hammer will expose any wiring that would give you a jolt if you sawed through it.

When you can see that the wall cavity is empty, take a saw to the studs. You should remove all the wall covering before cutting studs. Once the studs are cut, you can pull them out of the top wall plate. The top plate can be removed with a pry bar or by pulling the nails out with your hammer and a nail puller.

If you plan to leave the bottom portion of the wall, nail a stud horizontally across the vertical studs. If you are removing the whole wall, pull the bottom studs off the sole plate and pry the sole plate off the subfloor.

You can now repair the damage to remaining walls and ceilings. If you are creating a pass-through, you might want to frame in a cased opening or install interior shutter-type doors. The end result will be a kitchen that is not cramped or confining. The openness gained from your remodeling will make your house look bigger. It will also add a new dimension to the utility of your kitchen and dining area.

The difficulty rating for removing a nonbearing interior partition is a 3. The rating for rebuilding the wall to make a pass-through is a 5. If all you are doing is removing the wall, the costs will be only what it takes to repair the walls, ceilings, and flooring. This could amount to less than $100. However, you will have to use some type of transitional trim to cover the gap left in the flooring if you plan to keep your costs down. If you will be adding a counter, shuttered doors, and replacing flooring for a flowing match, your costs could push up to $550.

Put a Fish Pond out Back

If you put a fish pond out back, you might attract buyers who would not otherwise give your place a second look. There is something about a fish pond that is captivating, even if it is only a few inches deep. Seeing colorful fish swimming among water lilies is enough to make anyone begin to relax. Reports claim that watching fish in an aquarium can be good for what ails you. If this is true, a fish pond must work wonders for your health.

Garden ponds have long been a theme of well-to-do estates. You can create this image in your own backyard. No, you don't need a running stream to make this type of pond, and you won't need a bulldozer to build the dam. The pond can be dug by hand, and the water can be circulated with an inexpensive pump.

The hard part of this job is digging the hole. The hole doesn't have to be deep, but it should have one area of extra depth. This will give the fish a place to escape from the summer heat and the winter cold. In climates with extreme temperatures, people often bring their fish inside to aquariums. However, if the pond has a decent surface area and a deep end, the fish should do fine without any special attention.

Once the hole is dug, it can be lined with a vinyl liner. This is much easier than the old procedure of pouring a concrete container for the water. If you don't use a liner, the water will seep into the earth and the water will tend to be muddy. You want the water to be clear enough to allow viewers to watch the fish.

If the pond is filled with water from a municipal supply, it will need to be treated with chemicals before fish are put in the pond. If you allow the pond to fill with rainwater, chemicals won't be necessary. Most well water can be used to fill a pond without chemicals. Once the pond is full, you are ready for your fish.

There are many kinds of beautiful fish that will thrive in small garden ponds. Some fish aren't cheap. Start with department-store fish. This will allow you to check the quality of your water, without the risk of losing expensive fish in the process.

To make your pond effective, you should add water plants. There are many types of plants that will add to the beauty of the pond and help to oxygenate the water. Some water plants spread quickly. It is necessary to check with your aqua-plant dealer to establish the types of plants that will do best in your pond and climate.

When the pond is complete, you will have an amenity almost everyone will enjoy. If you anticipate the buyers of your home will have small children, you might want to add a fence around your pond. It would be wise to check with local code regulations to see if a fence is required around the pond. Some jurisdictions do have rules that pertain to bodies of water, whether they are swimming pools or fish ponds.

The difficulty rating of this job is a 3. The pond construction can be accomplished for less than $150. However, by the time you are done buying plants, fish, and maybe pumps and fencing, your costs will range between $400 and $600.

This concludes our list of projects you can do for under $600. The next chapter takes you on a tour of projects you can do for under $700. Even though there is only $100 separating these two categories, you may be surprised at the number of options available in the next chapter.

Chapter 7

Projects You Can Do
for Under $700

This chapter deals with projects you can do for under $700. These projects cover everything from security systems to window treatments. You will explore how hanging drywall in your garage can help sell your house faster. The section on sump pumps will show you how to change a wet basement from a negative factor to a positive asset. All of the projects in this chapter still fall into an affordable range, and all of the suggestions can help sell your house faster.

Install a Dishwasher

When a home seller installs a dishwasher, the sales potential of the home rises. People today expect to have a kitchen equipped with a dishwasher. There was a time when this mechanical device was a luxury; now it is an expected feature. In today's market a home without an automatic dishwasher is like a home without indoor plumbing was several decades ago. Buyers not only want the convenience of a built-in dishwasher, they require it. If your house isn't equipped with a modern dishwasher, you had better consider installing one.

Fortunately, installing a dishwasher is not a major job, if you have the counter space to accommodate it. Modifying existing base cabinets could require the expertise of a skilled carpenter, but homeowners can do much of the work themselves. Running the electrical circuit should be done by a licensed electrician, but the plumbing is simple enough for the average person to handle. There are many facets to consider in adding a dishwasher to your kitchen.

You will need a new electrical circuit. An electrician can provide this, but it may not be easy. Look to see what obstacles will have to be overcome to get a wire from your panel box to the dishwasher's location. Since most kitchens are on the ground level, there is usually good access below them for running wires.

Modifications will need to be made in your plumbing. The water supply for the dishwasher can come from the hot water pipe supplying the kitchen sink. You can replace the cutoff under the sink with a cutoff designed to feed dishwashers. This new cutoff will have an outlet for the sink supply and the dishwasher tubing. The main water cutoff to the house will have to be closed before replacing the valve under the sink.

Drainage connections can be done in several ways. If your sink has a garbage disposer, the dishwasher's drain hose can connect to a special drainage port in the disposer. If you don't have a disposer, you can add a wye tailpiece to the drainage from your kitchen sink. A wye tailpiece is a piece of drainage tubing that has a branch coming off its side to accept the dishwasher hose.

Most plumbing codes require an airgap for the installation of a dishwasher. An airgap is a device that mounts on the rim of a sink or on the countertop. The airgap has a chrome cap that is not obtrusive on the counter or sink. The part of the airgap that is below the counter splits into a wye formation. The airgap has one arm that is smaller than the other. The small branch accepts the hose coming from the dishwasher drain and the large branch is used for the hose connecting the airgap to the sanitary drainage system. Airgaps prevent drain water from getting back into the dishwasher.

One of the main considerations will be the location of the dishwasher. If your cabinet layout was not designed for a dishwasher, space will have to be made for it. Cabinet work of this type is tricky and should be done by an experienced professional.

The last big decision will be what type of dishwasher to buy. You should buy a brand name that people will recognize. Buyers are more comfortable with appliances they know and trust. You shouldn't get a bare bones model, but you don't need all the bells and whistles either.

What is all of this going to cost? That depends on your personal circumstances. Assuming your cabinets are installed with future dishwasher plans in mind, the only work you will have to hire out will be the electrical work. If you are experienced with electrical work, you can even do that phase of the work yourself.

You can buy a dishwasher for less than $300, but spending $400 will allow you more options. The labor for an electrician will probably run around $125. Miscellaneous wiring and plumbing fittings might add another $50 to the cost. If you need to hire a plumber, the labor cost will probably be about $120. Carpenters capable of doing cabinet work are likely to charge $30 an hour. So you might get by for as little as $350, but $575 is more realistic, and $695 is very possible. The difficulty rating for installing a dishwasher, under average conditions, is a 5.

Hang Drywall in Your Garage

When you hang drywall in your garage, you make your house more desirable. A garage with bare studs and insulation visible doesn't look as good as one with covered walls. It is not necessary to finish and paint the drywall, but hanging and taping it will be beneficial in competing with the rest of the homes on the market.

There is another good reason for covering the walls and ceiling in your garage. If the crew building your house was a little sloppy, their poor workmanship will show in an unfinished garage. By hanging drywall, you conceal flaws that might influence a buyer in the wrong direction.

The hardest part about hanging drywall is handling the material. Drywall is heavy. Professionals frequently use 4' x 12' sheets to create fewer seams, but 4' x 8' sheets are lighter and much easier to work with.

Most fire codes have regulations affecting the installation of drywall in garages. It is common for the regulations to require all walls between the garage and living space to be covered with a fire-resistant drywall. Normally, this only involves the one common wall between the garage and house. However, if there is habitable space above the garage, the garage ceiling would have to be covered with fire-rated drywall.

You can hang drywall with nails or screws. Most pros use screws, but nails work well, if they are the right nails and are driven in tight. There are special nails used for drywall. Any supplier of drywall should be able to provide you with the proper nails or screws.

Covering the ceiling can be a challenge. Unless you have two helpers willing to hold the drywall while you attach it to the ceiling joists, you will need some braces. A tee brace can be made from 2" x 4" studs. Cut one stud in half and attach the half at the top of another stud. Measure from the ceiling to the floor to determine how long your brace should be. Remember to allow for the thickness of the drywall. Cut the length of the long stud in a way that will allow it to stand on the floor and support the drywall on the ceiling.

One person can hang drywall on a ceiling. It is not an easy job for an individual, but it can be done. If you are working alone, use two ladders to get the drywall close to the ceiling. With the sheet of drywall lying across the ladders, slide a brace under one end and push the drywall up to the ceiling. When the brace is wedged into place, it will hold the drywall. You can then climb the second ladder and hang the other end of the sheet.

Once the drywall is hung, you should tape the seams. Buy a bucket of premixed joint compound and a roll of drywall tape. Use a 4" putty knife to spread joint compound along your first seam. Then tear off a piece of tape and press it into the compound, covering the seam. Run the putty knife over the tape, seating the tape into the compound. Continue this process for all of your seams. If you were going to finish and paint the drywall, you would have more work to do, but for a garage a single coat of compound is all that is required.

The difficulty rating for this job is a 4. An average two-car garage will require about 45 sheets of drywall. The cost for this material should be under $300. The tape, compound, and nails or screws should cost less than $50. If you do the work yourself, you can get by with a total cost of less than $400. If you hire professional hangers, the additional labor costs might run several hundred dollars.

Install a Garden-Style Window

Have you ever thought how nice it would be to install a garden-style window? These windows are very popular, especially in kitchens. What is a garden-style window? They are windows that bow out, away from the house. They allow flowers and plants to be placed on their sills and provide something of a mini-greenhouse, not to mention letting a lot of light into the room. Garden-style windows have become quite fashionable.

Garden windows come in various sizes. Replacing an existing window with a garden window is not extremely difficult, but it does require some carpentry skills. The molding from the exterior of the existing window must be removed. Then when the old window is out, the new window is secured in place. This may require cutting some siding to allow the new window to be mounted. Once the window is secured, the exterior molding is replaced. While this sounds simple, it can become difficult. You shouldn't attempt this project unless you are prepared to hire professionals to bail you out if you get in over your head.

The difficulty rating for installing a garden window is a 7. These windows don't come cheap, but $700 will allow you several choices in style and size. Professionals, if you need them, will probably charge between $25 and $30 an hour.

Add New Gravel to Your Driveway

You can add new gravel to your driveway to dress up the exterior of your home. Exterior appearance is important, and a neat driveway is one of the first things a home seeker sees. If the driveway is not in good shape, buyers will use the rundown driveway as a bargaining chip to lower the asking price of the house.

As gravel drives are used, they begin to lose their shape. Loose gravel spreads out, and remaining gravel becomes packed down. Hard rains can beat holes in the driving surface. Old oil leaks begin to build up, and the driveway shows neglect. Adding a new layer of gravel solves this problem.

Once you have a solid base of stone, you can use small stone or pebbles for the finished surface of your drive. Adding a layer of brown pebbles will put a splash of color in your landscape. Whether you choose gray stone, brown pebbles, or some other option, keep your driveway in good shape.

This is not a job for the do-it-yourselfer. Therefore, there is no difficulty rating assigned to this project. All you have to do is shop for a good price and order the driveway topping. Prices will depend on the size of the drive and the surface materials selected, but $700 should be enough to dress up your driveway.

Install Shutters

The face of a house changes when you install shutters. Shutters don't compliment all styles of homes, but they fit in nicely with most types of houses. Adding shutters to your house will give the home more character. Shutters are effective in breaking up the bleak look of an expansive, naked house. Instead of looking like a big box, a house with shutters looks like a home.

Shutters in the old days were made of wood. These shutters required frequent painting. Today's shutters are made with the color molded into them; there is never a need for painting. This is a big advantage.

Few people enjoy removing shutters, painting them, and then replacing them. If you install shutters on your house, be sure to use the no-maintenance type.

Shutters come in different widths and lengths. There are also numerous styles to choose from. Once you have selected your shutters, all you have to do is screw them onto the house.

The difficulty rating for this job is a 2. Shutters rarely cost more than $25 per pair. Most homeowners install shutters only on the front of their homes, but some owners install them around all windows. You can buy about 28 pairs of shutters, more than enough for most houses, for $700. You won't need professional assistance for this job. If you need a tall ladder, you can rent one from the local rental center.

Window Treatments

Window treatments can make a miraculous difference in the way people perceive your property. Curtains and drapes play a big role in the overall impression of a home. Envision a house where the windows are covered with roll-up window shades that have yellowed with age. Imagine that the shades are set off by dingy gray curtains that used to be white. Now draw a different mental picture. Look at the same windows, but imagine they are adorned with mini-blinds and silky white curtains. Which set of windows would you prefer to spend the next five years looking at? Which windows would make you feel at home? I would have to guess the windows with the blinds and clean curtains would be your choice.

I'm sure you have been in many homes and commercial establishments where you noticed the window treatments. There have probably been times when you wished your windows looked as good as others you have seen. You might also have looked at the windows of others and wondered how they could put up with such disgusting curtains. Let me tell you a quick story about how window treatments changed a house.

I was in a house once that made me feel as if there should have been a coffin sitting on the coffee table. As I sat in the room, I couldn't help but notice the drapes. They were dark and heavy. The valances matched the drapes and extended the funeral home effect. Even the poles supporting the ghastly green drapes gave me an eerie feeling. I don't spook easily, and I'm used to seeing a lot of houses, in a lot of different conditions, but this house made me uncomfortable. If I had been a prospective purchaser, I would not have been able to concentrate on anything but the drapes.

The owners of that house replaced the grim drapes with light, flowing white window treatments. The next time I entered the house I couldn't believe the difference. The minute I stepped into the foyer I was shocked. What had been a house with a dungeon-like darkness was now a beautiful home. Not only was the house pretty, it appeared much larger.

As I took a seat on the couch I didn't have the old urge to find an excuse to leave. The change in the window treatments had made a tremendous difference in the home. I noticed features that I had never seen before. The house was alive with light. This experience convinced me of the power window treatments have.

As for your house, you have a wide array of window treatments to consider. If you favor blinds, you can go for vertical or horizontal types. The blinds can be wide or narrow, thick or thin. They can be made from metal, cloth, or wood. Drapes and curtains present endless opportunities. The possibilities for window treatments are limited only by your imagination.

Since you will be selling your house, there is a point about window treatments we should discuss. Window treatments are considered chattel—personal property. They are not a part of the real estate, and therefore don't have to be conveyed to the buyers in the sale of your home. Some buyers will ask if the curtains and drapes go with the house. Others will draw their own assumptions and let it go at that. However, if you want to avoid hard feelings, make the ownership of the window treatments clear in your listing agreement and sales contract.

If you are willing to let the window treatments go with the house, make sure your broker and the buyers are aware of your position. If, on the other hand, you plan to take your window dressings with you, also make that point clear. By putting your plans in writing you will avoid confrontations at a later date, and you might get a better offer for your house when the buyers know the lovely curtains come with it.

The difficulty rating for installing window treatments is only a 2. Prices for these items vary a great deal. I suppose you could spend $700 dressing up one large window. However, $700 will give you plenty of options for improving the appearance of your windows and your home. Professional assistance is not required for this improvement.

Replace a Bathtub

The work required to replace a bathtub is extensive. This is not a simple job but the results can be well worth the effort. When bathtubs become cracked or discolored, you need to do something. You can either have the fixture refinished or you can replace it. If a tub can be refinished satisfactorily, it is wiser to refinish than it is to replace. We have already talked about refinishing fixtures, so we will concentrate on replacement in this section.

Bathtubs may be made of fiberglass, plastic, steel, or cast iron. Cast iron bathtubs can weigh as much as 400 pounds. The other types of tubs are much lighter. Prices for these various tubs start at under $150, for a steel tub, and go well over $400. Most average tubs will cost in the neighborhood of $300.

Once a house is built, it is rarely possible to install a one-piece tub/shower combination unit. There are, however, many sectional units that can be used to replace bath/shower combinations in existing homes.

When you decide to replace a bathtub, you are making several commitments, whether you know it or not. When a tub comes out, the surrounding walls are damaged. The floor covering may also be damaged. If the new tub is not shaped like the old tub, the flooring may have to be cut or it may not reach and meet up with the edge of the new tub. All of these factors result in extra work and money. If your tub is surrounded by ceramic tile, the extent of repairs expands. See why refinishing is such a good idea?

The instructions needed for replacing a tub and repairing the damage are too extensive to cover in this section. If you are serious about replacing your own tub, there are many books available to show you what you are getting into and how to do the job. Most homeowners will be able to complete their own tub replacement with satisfactory results. However, don't go into the project uninformed.

The difficulty rating for replacing a bathtub is a 7. If you can do the job yourself, the cost of the tub, new faucet, new tub waste, and repair materials should be less than $700. It is conceivable you could do the job with less than $400. If you call a plumber or remodeling contractor to do the work, expect the labor charges to be at least $400. If the job is filled with problems, the labor cost could more than double.

Replace a Shower

The work involved to replace a shower is very similar to what's involved in replacing a tub. The job carries the same difficulty rating, and the costs will be about the same, maybe slightly higher.

Add a Security Lamp

In some neighborhoods your house might sell better if you add a security lamp. These are the lights perched high atop a pole that brighten up the grounds and parking area around your home. Some people will see these lights as being ugly. Other people will appreciate the security and convenience the lights provide. Installing a security lamp is a judgment call. They are helpful in the dark, but they are also unattractive lawn decorations. If other houses in the area don't have these lights, you probably shouldn't install one.

If you have a backyard pool, tennis court, or similar reason to install lighting, these lights are a good choice. If you are in a high crime area, pole lights are appreciated. There are pros and cons both ways for the installation of pole lights.

If you decide to install a pole light, you should hire professionals to do the job. Electrical wiring will need to be run and the pole will have to be set. These are jobs most homeowners are not prepared to handle.

For the few homeowners who can handle the job, the difficulty rating is a 7, mostly because of setting the pole. The cost for a pole and light should check in at under $250. The labor charge for a professional will probably be extensive. This job requires trenching for wires, setting the pole, and making the electrical connections. You should be able to get the job done for $100, but it might be cutting it close.

Install a Sump Pump

Some people never need to install a sump pump. But people with wet basements or crawl spaces have little choice but to install a pump. There is no question that seeing a sump pump will raise alarm in a prospective buyer. Buyers aren't stupid. When they see a pump, they assume the property has water problems. Some owners think it is better to avoid installing a pump and hope that buyers will see their property under dry conditions. This line of thinking can backfire.

If a house sits above a foundation with water problems, many buyers will find out about it, even if they don't see a sump pump. Consumers rarely buy a house today without first having it inspected by professionals. Even when the buyers are ignorant of the telltale signs of water problems, a professional will seldom be fooled. Buyers rely on professionals to assess and report the condition of the homes they are contemplating. When professional inspectors do their job, they don't miss much.

If your house has seasonal water problems, inspectors will find the evidence they need to disclose the defect. Mold and mildew might be growing on the foundation walls or floor joists. The joists may be rotting from moisture damage. Chalky white lines on the foundation wall will indicate the presence of water. There are many signs to signal a professional of water problems.

When an inspector files a report with buyers that indicates water problems, the buyers assume the worst. Their minds begin calculating the cost of preventing the water infiltration. Before you know it, the buyer either makes a ridiculously low offer or walks away from the deal entirely.

You don't have to let this happen. If you have water problems, correct them. Sure, buyers won't be happy to see a sump pump in the basement, but if they know the water is under control, they won't be intimidated by the problem. Inspectors cannot only find hidden problems, they can recognize sensible solutions to problems. If inspectors see the sump pump and drainage system, they can file their report with the information that the water problems seem to be under control. This will ease the mind of your buyers and improve the odds of a closed sale.

Installing a sump pump is a job almost any homeowner can accomplish. Some installations are harder than others, but all of them are within the grasp of average people.

Sump pumps are most common in basements. Good builders lay slotted drain tile around the perimeter of a basement when they are building a home, just in case there are future water problems. Drainage pipes lead to a sump in the basement floor. If water penetrates the foundation, it is collected in the slotted pipe and delivered to the sump. When this happens, a pump is installed to remove the ground water.

The discharge of sump pumps should not be piped into the sanitary drainage system. It should be routed to a storm sewer or an outside drainage location. As long as there is an electrical outlet in the vicinity of the sump, no professional help is required to install a pump.

Residential sump pumps are equipped with cords that plug into standard household outlets. All a homeowner has to do is set the pump in the sump, run the flexible drainpipe to a suitable location, and plug the pump's cord into an outlet.

If draintile was never installed around the basement floor, it may be necessary to install some. This will require renting a jackhammer and breaking up some concrete. Typically, a trench about 10" wide is made all the way around the basement. Slotted draintile is laid in the trench and covered with gravel. The drains converge on a common sump. Then the concrete is patched. This type of work runs the cost up and takes some time, but it is still very much within the capabilities of most homeowners.

The difficulty rating of installing a sump pump in an existing sump is a mere 2. If you are forced to break concrete and install draintile, the difficulty rating goes up to a 4. The low-end cost for this project will be less than $200. The high-end cost, if you do the job yourself, will be around $400. There is, of course, some middle ground, depending on how much help you need and how big the foundation is. An electrician will probably charge at least $100 to add an outlet if you don't already have one close by. If you hire professionals, the cost could exceed $1,000.

Install a Security System

Many buyers will be impressed if you install a security system. More and more people are afraid even in their own homes. It wasn't enough that it became risky to go out on the streets, now people come into your home and commit unspeakable acts. Homes are broken into every day. How safe are you or your child sleeping in the next room? Fear is here, and it is here to stay.

Crime is one of the highest concerns on the minds of many people. It makes sense, then, that security systems are in more demand than ever before. As much as people want to feel secure, as much as they are willing to pay for peace of mind, most people have no idea what type of security is most effective.

Home security breaks down into many different levels. Do you remember when devices first became popular for jamming sliding doors, so they couldn't be lifted above their latch and opened? How about the screws used to hold window sashes together, do you recall those? Deadbolt locks are still very popular. All of these devices offer limited security. They might keep pranksters and timid criminals out, but they won't stop professionals. At best, these devices buy a little time. If a window can't be raised, what is to keep a criminal from breaking the glass? Deadbolts are more effective than the average lockset, but serious criminals will either pick the lock or find another means of ingress.

Crime rises, and the number of police officers doesn't keep up with the increase in illegal activities. Do you think the police will get to you before a determined kidnapper can make off with your child? The chances are good you won't know the child is gone before morning. Professional criminals are good at what they do. To stop them, you must make your home more difficult to attack than the next house.

Any security system you choose can be breached. But some systems are more effective and more of a deterrent than others. This is about the best you can hope for. However, if you are about to sell your home, how much should you invest in a security system? Since most buyers don't know the effectiveness of any given system, there is little justification in going for the most expensive system on the market. Really paranoid people will probably replace your system once the house is theirs. They won't trust you or the other people that may know the ins and outs of your security setup.

Aside from locks and retention bars, there are many types of security systems to study. The one most people are familiar with is the type that uses tape and contacts on windows and doors. The most effective aspect of these systems is the hope that a bad guy will see the tape and look for a different house to hit. This type of system can be fooled with a jumper wire. The perpetrator can reroute the circuit and be in the house without breaking a sweat. The fact that the system is visible allows the burglar to know what type of system is being used. While these systems aren't very secure, they do make a good show for prospective purchasers, and they are relatively inexpensive.

Another common type of security system involves electronic eyes. These eyes monitor the premises and signal if their beam is broken. Professionals will use special optics to locate the beams and avoid them. However, most home buyers will be impressed with the high-tech security.

Sound-sensitive alarms are one of the best options available to homeowners. These systems monitor an area and set off an alarm if any programmed noise is detected. This type of alarm is troublesome for criminals, but it is also a bit of a pain for the homeowner. Due to the nature and sensitivity of these alarms, the systems often go off when it is not wanted to.

There are, of course, other security options, but these three may be the best known. When you consider costs and the purpose you are installing this alarm, the tape or electronic eye types are the best choices. If you were trying to protect your home, I would recommend the sound-sensitive alarms, but since they are low-profile systems, buyers won't notice them. If you are installing a system to help sell you house, you want one buyers will notice.

The difficulty rating for installing common household security systems is a 5, less for some models. Prices will be in the hundreds of dollars, but $700 should get you enough security to excite buyers. Common systems won't require professional installation. If you turn to pros, expect to pay dearly for their services.

Add an Intercom

Intercoms are not as popular in homes as they once were, but you can still gain a sales advantage when you add an intercom. Intercoms provide some security, a lot of convenience, and are not hard to install. When you couple the intercom with a sound system, you can have wall-to-wall music. Buyers with young children will enjoy the ability to monitor the rooms of their children. If you place an intercom at the front door, you never have to open the door to a stranger again. When dad is working in the basement, mom can call him to dinner without ever leaving the kitchen. Intercoms do have their advantages.

If your house has only one level of living space, an intercom system will be easy to install. You can run the wires under the house and snake them up the walls to the intercom locations.

Two-story houses are a little more difficult to work with. Getting the wires into various rooms may take some doing. However, with patience, persistence, and a creative mind, you can find a way. You can use closets to conceal wiring, or you might use electrical outlets as openings to snake the wire up. Another trick you can employ is removing the baseboard trim to gain access to a wall. When the trim is replaced, the hole will be hidden.

The difficulty rating for installing an intercom system is a 5. The cost of the system will depend on what you buy, but you can get a pretty good system for well under $700. Professional help might be needed for this job. If you engage an electrician, expect a labor rate of at least $25 an hour and don't be surprised if the rate is $35.

Upgrading Your Electrical Service

If your house still has a fuse box, you should consider upgrading your electrical service. Many older homes depend of a 60-amp fuse box to control their electrical system. These old fuse boxes are not only a telltale sign of a home's age, they are inadequate for today's electrical demands. When buyers tour houses and see undersized fuse boxes, they immediately think of the expense they will incur to modernize the home. The negative impact of buying a house and having to turn around and invest more money in electrical upgrades may be enough to send buyers looking for another house.

Electrical services should consist of circuit breakers, not fuses. There are many reasons why buyers want adequate circuit breaker panels. They don't want to be blowing fuses every time they dry their hair or turn on the dryer and the range at the same time. Buyers won't fancy the idea of replacing fuses in the dark. They would much rather flip a circuit breaker, if need be, than screw in a fuse.

Replacing your electrical service is a job for professionals. This is one project you should definitely not attempt. A licensed electrician will take care of obtaining the proper permits and inspections for the work. All you have to do is commit to making the improvement and paying the bill.

What size service should you have installed? If you are operating with a 60-amp fuse box now, a 100-amp circuit breaker system may be adequate. If you want to be safe and impress buyers, go for a 200-amp service. This will allow plenty of expansion opportunities for the new owners of your home.

Homeowners should not attempt this project. Therefore, there is no difficulty rating for this job; it goes right off the scale. The cost of a replacement service will depend on who does the work and where you live. However, if you are willing to shop for bids, you should be able to get the job done for around $700. It might be stretching your luck to stay under the $700 ceiling, but with enough shopping, it should be possible.

Replacing Appliances

Replacing appliances before you sell your house may seem silly. Why would you want to install new appliances in a house that you are selling? Well, the installation of new appliances could make your house sell faster. If your range or refrigerator is old and temperamental, it is a liability in the sale of your home. Today's buyers are smart, and they will be looking for overall value in a home. New appliances will not go unnoticed.

Most appliances can be bought for under $700. Ranges, dishwashers, trash compactors, garbage disposers, washing machines, and dryers are all available below the price limit. Refrigerators are often more than $700, but there are models that fall under that price.

The difficulty rating for replacing most appliances is a 2. Appliances that require plumbing connections and hard-wire electrical connections rate a 3 on the difficulty scale.

Building a Breakfast Bar

If you have enough space, building a breakfast bar can be a good idea. This is especially true with eat-in kitchens that don't have quite enough space to make a table-and-chair set-up comfortable. Not only will the breakfast bar be convenient and enjoyable, getting rid of the table and chairs will open up the breakfast nook. This will make your house more spacious and desirable.

Assuming you have a free-flowing kitchen that runs into the breakfast area, adding a breakfast bar is not a big job. There are two ways to approach this improvement. You can go the economy route or the more expensive, but also more desirable, way. The economy route will involve nothing more than a countertop, a few braces, and some stools. The more expensive way involves the use of base cabinets as a counter support. The cabinets serve double duty; they support the counter and provide additional storage.

Let's look at the least expensive alternative first. In this mode the key element is the countertop. Normally, the counter will begin at a wall and terminate somewhere in the open space. One end is supported by a ledger strip on the wall and the other end is held up by support columns. To complete the job all that is required are the stools to sit on.

Using a prefab counter, this job rates a 3 on the difficulty scale. As for costs, the total expense for the counter, supports, and stools should not exceed $400.

Looking for salability, the more expensive route is probably better, due to the increased storage area offered. In this plan you must decide on what type of cabinets to use as a base. You might choose cabinets with doors, drawers, or both. The good thing is that either way, you are creating attractive, unobtrusive storage space in the kitchen area. This is a need that never seems to be satisfied totally.

Once the base cabinets are installed, the countertop is set into place. The last element is the placement of stools. What will this type of breakfast bar cost? If you are conservative in your cabinet and counter selection, you can get by with a total investment of just under $700. The difficulty rating for this procedure is a 4.

Build a Storage Shed

Maybe you should build a storage shed. If your house lacks a basement, garage, or attic for storage, a storage shed can remove objections buyers might have. Storage sheds provide a place to park the lawn mower, store garden tools, and keep other items dry that are not wanted in the home. Buyers might turn their nose up at cheap-looking metal sheds, but they will appreciate storage space that is well-built and that blends well with the home.

Attractive storage sheds can be built by homeowners, and they don't require major money to build. The sheds may be built as free-standing units, or they may be attached to the home. The attached variety is less expensive to construct, and they blend in well with the home. Detached sheds are a little more expensive, and they tend to stick out more than attached sheds.

If you are going to build an attached shed, you should build it on a solid foundation. Since the shed will be attached to your home, you don't want frost heaves to raise it, damaging the side of your home. Independent sheds don't have to be on a foundation; they can be built on skids. This fact offsets some of the extra cost associated with detached sheds. If you build the shed on skids, it will not cost much, if any, more than an attached shed.

Building a shed requires a little knowledge of a lot of things, but the job is not out of range for average homeowners. The difficulty rating for building a shed is a 7. The cost of the shed will depend largely on its size and construction materials. A small shed can be built for less than $500. If you want to spend your full $700, you can construct a very nice storage shed.

Build a Gazebo in Your Backyard

You can build a gazebo in your backyard. Not only are these independent outdoor structures complimentary to your grounds, they are very nice for spending an evening sipping iced tea out of doors. If you add some screening, the gazebo becomes a bug-free retreat.

Like storage sheds, gazebos can be built on skids. Eliminating the cost of a foundation is a big savings. Since the gazebo is not attached to the home, it can float up and down with frost heaves, receiving no damage. If you extend the gazebo off your home, install a solid foundation beneath the structure.

Gazebos don't have to be big to be enjoyable. The difficulty rating for this project is a 7. The price of the structure could go over $1,000, but you can build a decent gazebo for less than $700.

We have completed our list of improvements that fall under $700. Now we are ready to move on to the big improvements—the ones that cost over $1,000.

Chapter 8

Projects You Can Do
for More Than $1,000

Let's talk about projects you can do for more than $1,000. These major-league projects require a lot of consideration. If you choose the wrong project, you may see most of your improvement dollar go up in smoke. You'll have the improvement, but it may not help sell your home. Even if it does enable you to sell your house faster, you may not recover the lion's share of your investment. When you step into the arena of big-money improvements, you had better know what you are doing.

This chapter is going to show you some safe improvements to consider. We will, of course, discuss the pros and cons of expensive improvements. These projects offer a great opportunity for handy homeowners. If you have the ability and willingness to tackle these jobs, you can realize equity gains of substantial value. Now let's get on with the program.

Reface Your Cabinets

If you reface your kitchen cabinets, you can gain the look of a remodeled kitchen at a fraction of the cost. The kitchen is said to be the most important room in the house when it comes to making a sale. This evidence leads savvy sellers to invest their money in kitchens and bathrooms. As a rule, this path is fruitful.

What is the most prominent feature in your kitchen? Your cabinets are more than likely the dominant feature. The countertop and sink are important, as are the appliances, but the cabinets capture most of the attention. If the cabinets are equipped with special doors, finishes, and accessories, they take on even more importance.

Cabinets are a focal point in the kitchen, but replacing old cabinets is expensive. There is, however, a cost-effective compromise. The compromise involves refacing your old cabinets. When the work is done, people will be hard pressed to tell whether you replaced your cabinets or refaced them. Refacing procedures have come a long way, and they are not only effective, they are cost effective.

The best way to obtain quality results in your refacing is to use new doors and cabinet fronts. The doors and cabinet fronts are wood and look great. The ends of the cabinets and the strips between doors can be covered with thin wood strips and panels or in some instances stick-on paper. This method produces results that resemble complete cabinet replacement.

The difficulty rating for refacing your own kitchen cabinets is a 5. You can reface an average kitchen with real wood for between $1,000 and $1,500. If you call in professionals, the labor charges could range from $450 to $900.

Add a Central Vacuum System

Add a central vacuum system to your home and watch the interest of buyers perk up. Central vacuum systems are desirable attributes for any home. They are especially appreciated in houses with multiple floor levels. Lugging a heavy vacuum up and down stairs is not a pleasant task. The chore of house cleaning is much easier if all you have to carry is a hose and attachments. Some people assume a central system is not needed in one-level houses. Well, they may not be needed, but they are convenient, and buyers know it.

Installing a central vacuum system involves gluing some pipe and fittings together. If there is access for installing the pipes, the job is not too tough. Trying to install this type of system in multi-story homes is a challenge. Finding ways to route the pipes with minimal damage takes some thought. If you are willing to look for creative ways to get your pipes upstairs, you can find a way.

The heart of a central vacuum system is the power plant. Typically, the power plant is mounted in a basement or a downstairs closet. The thin-walled gray piping is run in the walls and outlet plates are installed. There is, of course, some electrical wiring involved; you may need an electrician for this part of the job.

The difficulty rating for installing a central vacuum system in a one-story house is a 5. Doing the job in a multi-story house will increase the rating to a 7. Basic systems can be purchased for less than $800. By the time you are done with the accessories usually associated with the system, you will probably have at least $1,000 invested. If you hire an electrician, the labor could cost you an extra $300.

Replace Kitchen Cabinets

We've already talked about refacing cabinets; now we are going to talk about what to expect when you replace kitchen cabinets. The replacement of kitchen cabinets is an expensive proposition. This job could cost more than $3,000, but you can do the job yourself for about half the cost.

You already know how important the kitchen is in the sale of your home. But how important are the kitchen cabinets? They are very important. As we discussed earlier, cabinets are one of the most important elements of a successful kitchen.

Why should you spend big bucks to replace your cabinets when you could just reface them? There are times when cabinets have deteriorated to a point where refacing just won't cut it. If the cabinets are suffering from moisture damage or severe abuse, replacement is the only reasonable solution.

Removing existing cabinets is not a big job. However, removing the countertop will require some basic plumbing skills. The plumbing work is minimal, but it does intimidate some folks.

Installing new cabinets is nowhere near as simple as removing the old ones. Cabinet installation is a precise job. If you take your time, follow instructions well, and pay attention to what you are doing, you can do the job. If you don't, you will wind up with a job you won't be proud of.

Walls, floors, and ceilings are not always plumb. When this is the case, the installation of new cabinets takes on a new dimension. Adding shims and making cabinets fit perfectly in an imperfect space is an art: an art many professionals have not mastered.

When you look for replacement cabinets, you can look to production cabinets or custom cabinets. Prices in each category vary, but custom cabinets can cost a small fortune. If you put your mind to it, you could spend $10,000 on custom cabinets. However, you could outfit the same kitchen with production cabinets for less than $2,000. If you opt for the economy line of cabinets, you could get everything you need for about $1,300. As you can see, there is a broad spectrum of prices in cabinets.

Replacing kitchen cabinets rates a 6 on the difficulty scale. If you are dependent upon professionals for the labor involved in this type of job, don't be surprised to get a bill for $900 or more just for the labor.

Build a Deck

If you build a deck, you can build equity. Decks are very popular home improvements. Decks are also one form of home improvement on which you are likely to recover your investment. The key to building a cost-effective deck is to keep it moderate in size. Decks that are very small are not worth much. Large decks are expensive, and the expense is usually not justified in an appraisal of the real estate. Decks of moderate size are wanted and will carry their own weight on an appraisal. Decks with more than 80 square feet and less than 200 square feet are generally considered to be moderate in size.

Decks are normally built with pressure-treated lumber. This type of wood is used to avoid premature rot and deterioration. Pressure-treated wood is more expensive than regular wood, but the extra cost is justified. Most pressure-treated wood has a greenish color to it. This wood will not take paint right away. After the wood has aged for a while, it can be painted successfully.

Most decks are built on pier foundations. Pier foundations are holes dug into the ground and filled with concrete. The depth of the hole should be below the frostline—the point below which the ground does not freeze. Most decks have at least one edge connected to the home. When a deck is attached to a house, there should be flashing installed to keep water from running behind the ledger board, damaging the interior structure.

There are many good books available to instruct you in the proper procedures to use in constructing a deck. If you plan to build your own deck, you owe it to yourself to consult how-to books and pamphlets for instructions. Deck construction is not particularly difficult, but you should do your homework.

When you design your deck, don't get too fancy. It is fine to build in deck benches, flower boxes, and such, but don't get carried away. A simple, attractive deck will pull as much on most appraisals as an ornate deck. If you want to recover your cash investment, keep it simple and of moderate size.

The difficulty rating for building a deck is a 6. A moderate deck can be built by a homeowner for about $1,000. Having the same deck built for you might run $1,600. Most contractors charge so much per square foot for building decks. The price varies with the size of the deck, but $10 per square foot for labor and materials is a good guess for many areas.

Add a Porch

Like a deck, you can add a porch to improve the image and desirability of your home. It is, however, important to keep from building a grandiose porch. Covering a stoop or a small deck can be very effective, with most of the construction cost coming back to you when the house is sold. But building a full, wrap-around porch will be very expensive, and it will not return your investment at the time of a sale.

Covering a stoop with a roof provides a homeowner with a shelter to stand under while opening the door. The roof breaks up the front of a large house and adds charm to many types of homes. This type of mini-porch is not going to do a lot for your home's appraised value, but it may help pull in a hot prospect to buy your house.

Large porches are coveted by many and enjoyed by few. The old days of full-length and wrap-around porches are all but gone. The cost of these appurtenances prevents most buyers and builders from installing them. While big porches may invoke old childhood memories of Grandma's house, they are usually not cost effective in today's building trends.

Enclosed porches are quite popular, and they will sometimes pay for themselves. Screened porches are one possibility, and porches enclosed with glass are usually well accepted. If you want to invest enough money, a porch enclosed with large casement windows can provide the best of both worlds. The windows keep out the cold, the rain, and the wind. Yet, when cranked open, casement windows allow maximum circulation of air through their screens.

Enclosed porches range from the very simple to the exotic. The porch can exist to allow the enjoyment of fresh air, without the biting of pesky insects. Glass-enclosed porches can be used as additional living space for the home. A sunroom might house a spa, a dining room, a family room, or an office.

If you want to build your own porch, you will need good carpentry skills, among other things. It is possible for homeowners to build their own porches, but most owners will hire contractors to do the work. If you act as your own general contractor, you might shave 20 percent off the retail value of your improvement. This savings is instant equity in your home. Adding a $10,000 sunroom could give you a $2,000 equity gain—not bad for a month of part-time supervisory work.

The difficulty rating for building a porch is a 9. This job entails many facets of construction. Prices for porches will vary depending upon size, existing conditions, and the materials used. A screen porch built by contractors might cost you $25 per square foot. A porch enclosed with glass could go for around $60 a square foot.

Pave Your Driveway

After assessing the neighborhood, you might find you should pave your driveway. If you are one of the only houses in the area to have a gravel drive, you should consider paving it. Buyers like paved drives, and they will generally pay extra for a house that has one.

Homeowners will not be able to do this project without the help of professionals. Paving is a job that requires special equipment and skills. The contractors that do this type of work should be happy to provide written quotes for their work. When an average driveway has a strong base and is in good shape, having it paved should cost less than $2,000.

Complete Bathroom Remodeling

Complete bathroom remodeling is a big job, but it is one of the best ways to spend your improvement dollars. Statistics indicate that from a buyer's perspective, bathrooms are the second most important rooms in a house—second only to kitchens. Most people will agree that they like a bathroom to be bright and beautiful.

So far we have talked about various aspects of bathroom remodeling. We discussed replacing tubs, toilets, showers, and lavatories. Floor coverings have been explained, and light fixtures have been covered. Now we are going to look at combining all of these improvements, and more, to remodel your bathroom completely.

Assuming your subfloor and walls are in good shape, remodeling your bathroom is a project you can handle. However, the diversity of skills and knowledge needed will be more intense than it would for a small job. You may decide it's best to call upon professionals for some aspects of the work.

Let's take a look at what will be involved in the total renovation of your bathroom. You will have to remove the plumbing fixtures and light fixtures. The floor covering will be removed and so will any cabinetry. If the room is in good shape, this may be the extent of your demolition work. Otherwise, there could be rotted flooring to remove, damaged tile to come down, and drywall to be removed.

Once the demolition work is done, you are ready to start rebuilding the room. You should start with the bathing unit. Since tubs and showers are big and go in before the walls can be finished, they are the logical place to start. Normally, the next step will be to repair the damaged walls around the bathing unit. This generally entails some drywall work, including taping and finishing.

Once the walls and ceiling are ready for paint, they should be painted or covered with wallpaper. The material chosen as the finished wall covering should be designed for use in bathrooms. The material must be able to stand up to heavy moisture.

Typically, the floor covering is installed next. This job is easier to do when the vanity cabinet and toilet are not in the way.

After the flooring is in, the cabinets and plumbing fixtures are installed. This part of the job is followed by the installation of light fixtures and mirrors. Then, finish molding is placed around the baseboards to trim the edges of the new flooring.

How long will this type of project take to complete? The drywall work can take between three to five days. Even though the amount of work is small, time must be taken to allow the joint compound to dry. The compound is usually applied and sanded three times, and each time can take up to a full day to dry.

The demo work should be completed in a day or less. Depending upon your organizational skills and your trade skills, the job could be finished in ten days, or it could drag out for a month. Most professionals would allow at least two weeks for the job, and probably wouldn't commit to having it done in less than three weeks. However, since you will be living in the house and available to work long hours if you choose to, you can get the job done quickly.

The difficulty rating for complete bathroom remodeling is an 8. If you do the work yourself and use average materials, the project should cost around $1,500. If you call in professionals, the cost might range from $2,500 to over $5,000, depending on product choices.

Complete Kitchen Remodeling

Complete kitchen remodeling ranks high on the list of best home improvements to do. In fact, kitchens are seen to be the most important room in the house when it comes to selling your home. As far as recovering your investment goes, remodeling the kitchen is one of your safest bets for large-scale improvements.

There are two primary reasons for remodeling a kitchen. The first reason is to replace worn and outdated materials with fresh new ones. The other reason is to improve the utility of the kitchen with a new design. Handy homeowners can generally handle updating their kitchens, but when it comes to full-scale changes in the placement of cabinets, appliances, and plumbing, professional help may be needed.

We have talked, in various specifics, about remodeling parts of a kitchen. Here we are going to look at the job on a whole. Kitchen remodeling is a big job and it will inconvenience you for a while.

Demolition, or rip-out as the pros call it, will take at least a day of your time, maybe more. There will be wires and plumbing to contend with and a lot of dust and dirt.

Once the rip-out is done, you will do your wall repairs and painting. Next you will install the new flooring. Then the cabinets and counters will go in. Plumbing and electrical work will follow the cabinets. Appliances will go in near the end of the job. From start to finish, this work could consume weeks of your time. Experienced professionals can get the job done in two weeks, but it will probably take you longer.

The difficulty rating for complete kitchen remodeling is an 8. The do-it-yourself cost for this job will be at least $3,000. Professionals are likely to charge between $7,500 and $10,000 for the job.

Finishing a Basement

A lot of homeowners think that finishing a basement into living space is a great idea. They like the idea because they feel they can do most, if not all, of the work themselves. Some people assume that adding 1,000 square feet of living space to their home in the basement will increase the home's value in leaps and bounds. Are these people right? Not usually. Finishing a basement into living space is a risky proposition. Let me tell you why.

There are three basic types of basements: buried basements, daylight basements, and walk-out basements. Of these three, walk-out basements are the most valuable and buried basements are of the least value.

If you have a walk-out basement, finishing it into living space may be a good move. Since the basement has its own door to the outside and is likely to have windows in it, it can become good, usable living space.

Putting a family room in the basement is a common use of the space. Converting the basement into use for in-laws and teenagers is another frequent reason for finishing the basement. These are good reasons to convert the basement if you will be living in the house and using the space. But will a new buyer care about the basement improvements? You don't know; you don't have any way of knowing. If the basement isn't damp and musty, and if it has windows and doors, there is a good chance buyers will use the space. However, there is the question of how much extra they will pay for the habitable space. We will come back to the question of how much buyers are willing to pay after we cover the two other types of basements.

Daylight basements are basements that have full-size windows, but no exterior doors. Since these basements do have large windows, the space can be used for bedrooms and recreational purposes. Having the basement raised partly out of the ground reduces moisture problems, and the windows help control musty odors. This type of basement lends itself to viable conversion into living space, but it is not as good as a walk-out basement.

Buried basements are what most houses with basements have. These basements are sunken into the earth and have tiny windows around the top edges of their walls. Buried basements are valuable. They offer homeowners extensive storage space, and they can be used to house laundry facilities, oil tanks, furnaces, water heaters, and a host of other stuff. They can also be a good place for the kids to play on rainy days.

As desirable as dry, buried basements are in their unfinished state, a buried basement finished into living space is not ideal. Since the basement has no real windows or doors, it generally smells like a basement. Moisture on the walls and floors is common, and this can be a real problem when the basement is finished. The moisture can also cause problems for computer equipment, pool tables, and the like, so putting a rec room or an office in a buried basement may not be wise.

Light is another problem with buried basements. There is no good way to fill rooms with natural light. Therefore, the rooms feel like basement rooms, not normal living space. Finishing a buried basement for your own use and enjoyment is fine, but finishing one with the hope of making more money on the improvement from the sale of your home is not a good idea.

Now let's go back to the issue of how much buyers will be willing to pay for a finished basement. There are all types of buyers out there. Some of them are model train enthusiasts, some are photographers, a few are writers, and many have children. Every buyer in any of these groups could have a lot of use for a finished basement.

Then there are the people that can't stand the idea of going into a basement. This group would never spend much time in a buried basement, finished or not. You might get them to use a daylight or walk-out basement, but you can forget buried basements.

Some people will have little feeling one way or the other for the finished basement. They will see it as an advantage, but may not consider it worth any extra money. This type of person might buy your house faster because of the finished space, but you would lose considerable money in the exchange.

The size of your house can have a lot to do with the value of a finished basement. If you live in a neighborhood of small, box-type ranch homes, a finished basement might be the catalyst needed to make a quick and profitable sale. However, if your home has four bedrooms and two-and-a-half bathrooms, a finished basement may not be as important. In a large house, the basement might be used only for storage.

The gamble of finishing a buried basement is too great to take. If you have a daylight or walk-out basement, you might do all right with the project. How will you know if you should pursue the project? Check comparable values of homes sold in your area. Find out how much more the houses with finished basements sold for. This is a good way to evaluate any major improvement.

What kind of costs are involved in finishing a basement? The cost per square foot for finishing a basement is relatively low. This again is why the project is so appealing to many homeowners. Much of the final cost will depend on the type and quality of materials used.

Commercial-grade carpeting is normally installed in basements. Paneling is frequently used on the walls, but this can make the basement very dark. If you use paneling, use a light-colored wood. Acoustical ceilings are often used to compensate for pipes, wires, and other overhead obstructions. A basement with 1,000 square feet can normally be converted into habitable space for around $10,000, and that's about all it will be worth, at best, on an appraisal. If you spend big bucks on plush carpeting and finishes, you will lose your shirt on the project. The exception could be a walk-out basement; the appraised value might be much higher for this type of basement.

The difficulty rating for finishing a basement into living space is a 7. Homeowners doing the work themselves can finish an average basement for less than $10,000. The same work done by professionals could easily hit $15,000.

Converting an Attic

Converting an attic into living space cannot only help sell your house faster, it can put thousands of dollars of extra equity in your pocket. Attic expansion is one way of cost effectively increasing the size of your house and recovering your investment. By doing much of the work yourself, you should see a nice profit for your efforts. Unlike as with basements, most buyers will consider converted attic space to be real living space. The space is above ground, has windows, and feels like normal living space.

If you are contemplating spending a sizable sum of money on a major improvement, an attic conversion may be your best choice. This type of work can be complex and extensive, but it can also yield a high rate of return on your investment. We are going to talk about appraisal methods in Chapter 10, but let me give you a preview here.

In Maine, habitable living space in a normal house works out to be worth around $60 per square foot, not counting land and site improvements. This means that a house with 1,500 square feet is worth about $90,000. By the time the land and site improvements are thrown in, the total price might be $130,000.

If my attic wasn't already converted into living space, I could convert it and see a substantial gain in the value of the property. Would I realize a gain of $60 per livable square foot? Maybe not, but the gain would be sizable. Since my cost for doing the work would be less than $30 per square foot, I would be building a nice bundle of equity in the home. I might earn $10,000 in equity for my trouble.

Would a buyer pay this much for my improved home? Probably so, since it would be conventional living space. Now this deal could go sour on some people. If you overimprove your house, you can't recover your investment. Looking back at the box ranches we discussed in the basement section, they would probably not do well to extend their attics into second stories. If all the houses on the street, except yours, are ranches, a two-story is going to look strange and will not be worth as much as it would in another neighborhood. Additionally, if you have the most expensive home in the neighborhood, buyers will be skeptical about buying it.

Before you do any major home improvement, you should do a market study of the other houses on the market and of the houses that have sold recently. This research will guide you in making sound decisions.

Attic conversions have proved to be good improvements. The cost per square foot is lower than that of building an addition on the home, and the utility of the space is good. However, attic expansion and conversion gets expensive—sometimes very expensive.

If you have a Cape Cod or similar home where the attic lends itself to easy conversion, consider yourself lucky. Even if you don't do the conversion, you can impress buyers with the expansion potential. When your home has a truss roof system, unless they are room trusses, you will have to spend a lot of money to create overhead living space. In all cases, attic conversions are major jobs. It is unlikely you can do the whole job yourself, but there are many phases of the work you can accomplish. Just acting as your own general contractor could save you 20 percent of the retail value for the improvement.

The difficulty rating for an attic conversion is a full 10. The cost of this type of work depends greatly on existing conditions, materials used, and the amount of space converted. Some attics can be converted for around $10,000; others will run into $20,000 or more. Professionals won't be cheap for this type of work. Expect to pay between 20 and 35 percent more for the job if professionals do it.

Converting Your Garage

Converting your garage, or a part of it, into living space can help sell your home. This project is most effective when the garage is attached to the home. If the attic of the garage can be reached from an upstairs hallway with a little remodeling, the project takes on even more appeal. Garage conversions are not as common as attic and basement conversions, but they can be very effective, both in helping to sell your home and in realizing some extra value.

What do you see when you look at your garage? Do you see a structure that protects your vehicle from the weather? Is the garage little more than a handy storage area? Can you envision the garage as an in-law apartment or a teenager's private retreat? If you were an artist, would you enjoy having the attic of your garage turned into a studio? As a business owner working from home, would the garage offer ideal office space? As you can see from these questions, garages can be thought of as much more than a house for cars.

Garages provide good opportunity for conversion. They have a floor, roof, and walls already in place. Most of the structural aspects of the job are done. This makes it easy for homeowners to finish the garage into living space. The lower level can be left as a garage and the attic can be converted to living space, or the entire structure can be turned into living space.

Should you make a change in the use of your garage? It is impossible to make a blanket statement on the issue that would be correct. You must look at the current market, surrounding properties, and closed sales to come to a conclusion.

If your garage is detached from the home, converting it to living space may not be cost-effective. A detached garage might fare no better than a buried basement when it is finished and appraised. But if the garage is attached to the home, you have the chance of making a profitable conversion.

There will, of course, be a lot of work involved in converting your garage. There will be electrical and heating work. Plumbing might need to be added. Insulation and drywall will be a factor, and so will painting and trim carpentry work. This job is not only extensive, it is expensive.

The difficulty rating for a garage conversion is a 9. The cost for the do-it-yourselfer might be between $10,000 and $15,000, depending up the space being converted, and how it is being converted. Professionals will tack another 20 to 35 percent onto the do-it-yourself cost.

Adding a Bathroom

If your home has only one bathroom, you might consider adding a bathroom. Houses with one bathroom are quickly becoming things of the past. Even most modern small homes have at least one-and-a-half bathrooms.

Since so many families today depend on both spouses working, the need for multiple bathrooms is increasing. If both the husband and wife have to prepare for work at about the same time, a single bathroom is a liability. When you factor in children who will need to use the facilities, a one-bath house just isn't practical.

If you can find existing space within your home to convert into a bathroom, you should seriously consider the option. It may not be cost effective to build a new bathroom from scratch, but if you can convert a closet or enclose some unneeded space, an extra bathroom should pay for itself and then some.

You don't have to get fancy with the bathroom, and you probably shouldn't. Even a half bath is a major asset to a home with less than two bathrooms. Finding extra space for a full bath can be a problem, but there are usually places a half bath can be tucked into without much trouble.

A half bath can be put in a space that is 30" wide by about 5' long. Most full baths will require a space with dimensions of at least 5' x 7'. Closets and voids under stairways often provide adequate space for half baths. Walk-in closets can sometimes be used to house full bathrooms. Framing in a corner of a large bedroom is another way to generate space for a bathroom.

Adding a bathroom is not a big job for professionals, but it can be intimidating for homeowners. The difficulty rating for this type of project is an 8. A homeowner converting a closet into a half bath will need to spend around $1,000. Adding a bathing unit and a faucet will push the cost up by about $450. Hiring professionals will likely double the cost.

Adding a Room

Adding a room is a major commitment. This type of improvement is usually too risky to justify when your only intent is to sell your house. Buyers might recognize the value of the addition and pay the extra price, but they may not. Unless your present home is not functional without an addition or is not competitive, avoid this improvement.

Room additions are very expensive and recovering their cost is not easy, unless you do the work yourself. Even then, you may be at risk. However, there are times when building an addition is justified.

If your kitchen is extremely small, expanding it with an addition can be worthwhile. If you have only one bathroom, adding a dormer or building a small addition can be sensible. You must look at your personal circumstances and evaluate the market conditions to decide on the viability of building an addition.

Building an addition rates a 10 on the difficulty scale. Costs can range from under $6,000 to over $30,000. The new space should appraise well, but you may not be able to convince buyers to pay full price for the improvement. Use your head and do your homework before dumping a lot of money into an addition.

Building a Garage

Building a garage is not as hard as some people think. If you are only one of the few houses in the neighborhood not having a garage, this improvement could pay big dividends.

Buyers love garages. They desire them for storage, vehicle protection, and convenience. The most sought-after garages are the ones attached to homes. The second most popular type is connected to the home with a breezeway or at least a canopy. Detached garages are still very acceptable, but they don't allow their owners to get from the garage to the house without getting wet or cold.

Buyers will appreciate a one-car garage, but they generally expect a two-car garage. The extra cost for building the larger garage is minimal when you consider the advantages it gives. Two-car garages cost more to build, but they are worth more. Buyers will have to pay a little extra for the larger garage, but they will be paying for what they want, not a compromise. If you have the space and money to build a 24' x 24' garage, don't skimp by building a smaller one. The only exception to this rule might be if all the other houses in the area have single-car garages.

What's involved in building a garage? There is a lot of work involved in a garage, but the job can go quickly and easily. Some of the work will probably be subcontracted out to professionals. If you hire professionals to do the whole job, you can have a garage built in about a week.

The first step is to prepare for pouring concrete. In most areas this will require digging footings. Footings are trenches that are dug deeper than the frostline. When the footings are dug, they usually have to be inspected by the local code enforcement officer. With the footings dug and the pad area leveled and prepared, concrete is poured into the footings. Many contractors use a monolithic slab for the floor. This is when the concrete from the footings extends upward and covers the pad with 4" to 6" of concrete. Some contractors use floating slabs. This is when the footing is poured and allowed to dry. Then a short wall, either block, brick, or concrete, is built on the footing. Once the pad is surrounded by the short wall, concrete is poured over the pad. The short wall contains the concrete.

After the floor is poured, the exterior walls are built. When the walls are in place, the roof structure goes on. Many builders use trusses for the roof structure. Trusses are prefabbed, engineered roof structures. They are sometimes set in place with cranes, but with garages, most crews pull them up and set them in place by hand.

The plywood is placed on the roof structure. Next the roof is covered with roofing paper and shingles. Windows and doors are installed after the roofing. Then the siding is installed and painted or stained, if necessary. Electrical wiring is usually installed in the garage at some point. Sometimes the wiring is roughed-in before the floor is poured and sometimes it is installed near the end of the job.

As you can see, there is a lot of work involved in a garage, and you would probably agree that some of the work should be contracted out to others. Now let's see what we are looking at in terms of cost.

A two-car garage, in Maine, will appraise for around $7,500. The cost to build this garage, if you act as your own general contractor, will be about $6,000. If you do a lot of the work yourself, the cost might be as low as $4,000. You can see there is enough spread between the cost and value to make this project well worth considering. These numbers will change, depending upon where you live, but the principle remains the same. The difficulty rating for building a garage is a 9.

Special Considerations

Let's take a moment to look at some special considerations. When you get into some of the projects we have discussed, you will be required to obtain permits and to have the work inspected by the local code enforcement officer. The rules and regulations on permits and inspections vary from jurisdiction to jurisdiction. Before you undertake any major job, check with your local code enforcement office for details on what is required of you.

Permits

What will you be likely to need permits for? Any major construction, like adding a garage, an addition, a dormer, or converting an attic will require a permit and inspection. Some small jobs also require permits and inspections. For example, installing a dishwasher, garbage disposer, or water heater will require a plumbing permit. Adding light fixtures will typically require a permit. If you are replacing your heating system you will need a permit. On big jobs, you will need several permits—one for each trade.

As a homeowner, you will generally be able to obtain your own permits, as long as you will be doing the work yourself. It is generally illegal for a homeowner to obtain a permit and then have an unlicensed handyman or friend do the work. If you won't be doing the work yourself, you will need to contract professionals who are properly licensed and approved for pulling permits.

Zoning

Zoning is another factor you must take into consideration with some improvements. For example, you can't just convert your large house into a duplex and not worry about it. First of all, this work would likely require permits and inspections. But even if you did the work under the table, so to speak, and the conversion didn't comply with zoning regulations, you would more than likely get caught before the sale of your home was closed.

After your house went under contract and an appraisal was called for, the appraiser would make notes regarding the duplex. After checking for comparable sales, the appraiser would discover the nonconforming use of the property. This point would be exposed to the buyers and the sale would go bad. The same type of problem could occur with an addition or a newly constructed garage.

If you build an addition or garage too close to your property lines, you may have to tear it down. There are generally zoning regulations that prevent structures from being placed within a certain distance of the property lines. These no-man-lands are called setbacks, and if you build in them, the sale of your house and your financial investment can really get set back. Before you make a change in the use of your house or build a deck, addition, garage, or fence, check with the local zoning regulations.

Contractors

Since there will be times when you must rely on contractors to complete your projects, let's talk briefly about what you should look for in contractors.

The first two items to check about your contractors are licensing and insurance. All contractors should be licensed to do business, and they should all have liability insurance.

Some trades, like plumbing, electrical, and heating, require additional licensing. These trades require a trade license. For example, in order for a plumbing business to operate, there must be a master plumber involved in the business. The master plumber is not required to be on each job, but it is required that the master oversee all plumbing work. This is a loose regulation, but it basically requires a master plumber to work in the office and occasionally supervise and inspect the field work.

Before you commit to contractors, be sure they are properly licensed and adequately insured. Don't overlook the insurance issue. A plumber's torch is very capable of reducing your house to a pile of ashes. Accidents in electrical wiring can be fatal. Removing the wrong beam can cause major damage—both property and personal. If the contractors are not insured, you or your insurance company might be left holding the bag.

Get all of your agreements in writing. Contracts are essential when you are hiring others to perform work for you. Make the written agreements comprehensive and clear. Don't leave anything out. If you have to take your contractors to court, the written agreements will be your best ammunition.

Most contractors will ask you to give them a cash deposit when a contract is signed. It is typical for contractors to expect one-third of their money when the contract is signed, one-third when the rough work is complete, and the final third when the job is done. While this is common practice, it is not good business for you.

If you give contractors money they haven't earned, you are taking a big risk. What if the contractor goes out of business or skips town? You are out of luck and money. When possible, avoid giving advance deposits. If contractors need your money to get the job started, they are not very financially sound. On the other hand, contractors don't want to provide labor and materials and not get paid. It is understandable why they want the money, but it is in your best interest not to give it.

When you pay for your materials and contract labor, insist on having lien waivers signed. Lien waivers are simple pieces of paper that protect your home. Contractors and suppliers that provide labor or materials for a job have lien rights. If they don't get paid, they can place liens against the property. A lien causes a lot of trouble when you are trying to sell your house. By having the contractors and suppliers sign lien waivers when they are paid, you eliminate the risk of trouble down the road.

There are a number of other aspects about being your own general contractor that I would like to tell you, but that would require another book. The key is knowledge. Before you attempt these projects you should devour all the reading material you can. The more you know, the less trouble you will have. Now, let's see how your improvements will affect your tax consequences.

Chapter 9

Tax Effects of Your Improvements

The tax effects of your improvements are worth consideration. When you improve your home, its value should go up. When you increase your home's value and sell it, you may have to reinvest your proceeds in a more expensive home than you had previously planned to buy or pay additional taxes. It may be wise to consider putting off the closing of your sale until the next year, especially if you are selling near the end of a tax year. What you do with the gain of your sale could also have negative tax effects. This chapter is going to clear up some of the questions you may have on tax situations when selling your home.

I am not a tax expert, but I consulted with a man who is. The information in this chapter is a compilation of facts derived from a practicing certified public account (CPA) and various tax publications made available from the Internal Revenue Service. The information in this chapter is meant only as a broadbrush starting point for you. It is not intended to replace your need for current, professional tax advice. You should seek assistance from a local tax expert before relying on, or acting on, the information contained herein. I have done my best to interpret and translate the facts as they have been presented to me, but I may have stumbled here and there in my translation. Tax matters are serious business; please, talk with practicing professionals before making any tax-related decision. Now, with that said, let's get down to business.

Mr. Peter L. Chandler, a respected CPA with the prestigious firm of KPMG Peat Marwick, talked with me in his Portland, Maine, office. I asked him questions and he provided the answers. When I was done with my questioning, Mr. Chandler volunteered additional information on the tax ramifications of selling a home. He also provided me with various publications from the IRS that detail many aspects of home improvements, mortgage interest, points, and home sales. In examining the IRS documents and sifting through the notes of my consultation, I came to the conclusions that follow.

When you begin to dig into all the tax possibilities associated with home ownership, you can become overwhelmed quickly. Even though the words may be there in black and white, they can read like a cryptic foreign language. This chapter is going to give you a reader-friendly version of what you may experience when improving and selling your home.

This book and this chapter deal with what I call improvements. I use the word "improvements" to describe many facets of work in and around the home. While I have lumped all of the jobs discussed within this book under the heading of improvements, some are not true improvements—at least not by tax standards.

To my way of thinking, fixing holes in your wall is an improvement. Certainly, your home is improved to a better condition when the holes are repaired. However, when you start reading tax text, you will find there is a difference between an improvement and a repair. In the context of discussing ways to help sell your home, it doesn't make much difference if fixing holes in the wall is an improvement or a repair. But when it comes to tax time, it does make a difference. To explain this more thoroughly, let's look at how the IRS defines the two.

An Improvement

An improvement is considered work done to a home that can fulfill at least one of three goals. If the work will increase the home's value, it is an improvement. When the useful life of the home is extended by the work being done, the work is considered an improvement. Another way work qualifies as an improvement is by changing the use of the property. Let me give you quick examples of each of these types of criteria.

Increased Value

An improvement that adds increased value to your home could be one where a new bathroom is added or an attic is converted to living space. Building a new garage would also be an example of an increased-value improvement.

Extended Life

An improvement that gives extended life to your home could be the replacement of your existing roof shingles. Replacing your siding could be considered an extended-life improvement.

Change of Use

An improvement that could change the use of your property might be converting the garage into living quarters, for use as rental property. If you added a greenhouse to your home for the purpose of raising exotic plants that will be sold, you could be creating a change-of-use improvement.

A Repair

Under the tax explanations, a repair is a form of work that merely maintains the ordinary condition of your home. For example, replacing the washer in a dripping faucet would be considered a repair. Remember the holes in the wall? Fixing those holes would be a repair, not an improvement. Basically, repairs will not add value to your home, change its use, or extend its life; they will only maintain it.

On the surface the differences between repairs and improvements seem pretty easy to understand. But the distinction between the two can become confusing. What is the importance of establishing the difference? The importance is the deduction eligibility of the work.

Home repairs are not deductible for the average home. Unless the home is used as rental property or for business purposes, repairs are not allowable deductions. Now, since some of you may be selling rental property, this factor comes into play. If you are making repairs to property that provides rental income, you should be able to deduct the expenses. Home improvements, as defined by the tax authorities, may not be deducted from any of these properties. Ah, there's the importance: improvements are not deductible, but repairs might be, under special circumstances.

Repairs and improvements can bear a strong resemblance to each other. Would you consider painting the exterior of your home a repair or an improvement? If you don't paint the average frame home, time and weather will rot the wood. So, would it be safe to say that painting the siding is extending the useful life of the property? I would think so, but tax publications disagree. Painting is considered a repair, not an improvement. I suppose this ruling is made based on the paint merely replacing and maintaining the existing paint.

When is a repair an improvement? Repairs are considered to be improvements when they are done as a part of extensive remodeling or renovation. If improvements are made to your home, you must adjust the basis, or the tax value, of the home.

Increased Basis

Increased basis is going to alter your tax position when the home is sold. How much value will an improvement add to your house? The answer to this question depends upon which yardstick is used to measure value. For the purpose of basis, the amount of increased value will be equal to your actual cost. The actual cost will include all money spent, including borrowed money, for materials, and soft costs. Soft costs might be blueprints, permits, surveys, and so forth. The value of your personal labor is not a factor in increasing the basis of your home. You cannot increase the basis.

Basis Versus Appraised Value

When you look at basis versus appraised value, you are likely to arrive at two different numbers. Basis refers to the cost of your home in the eyes of taxing authorities. You have seen how improving your home affects its basis, but now let's look at some other ways your home's basis might affect your sale.

Gifts

Suppose the house you are about to sell was given to you as a gift by your parents, will the fact that the home was a gift have a bearing on its basis? Yes, the basis of a home given as a gift is determined by what the home cost while it was in the possession of the donor. What does this mean? To gain a better understanding, let's look at an example.

Assume your parents gave you a home ten years ago. At the time the property was deeded to you, it had a basis of $60,000. Since obtaining the home, you have invested $8,000 in home improvements. Having recently had your home appraised, you find it is worth $95,000 on the appraisal report. What figure will you use as the home's basis when calculating the taxes after the home is sold for $95,000?

To arrive at the proper basis, you must first take the figure for what the home's basis was when given to you. That number is $60,000. To the $60,000 you add $8,000, the value of your home improvements. The total amount is $68,000, and that is the basis for calculating your tax consequences. There are, however, many factors that may alter the determination of your basis.

Depending upon the year in which you were given the home, your circumstances may require a different method of calculation. There is a tax publication, number 551, that gives examples for figuring the basis on a home received as a gift. Even though there is a government guide to figuring basis, I recommend talking to a local tax expert when dealing with tax matters.

Inheritance

Inheritance is another way you may have come into possession of your home. If your home was inherited, you have to look at its basis through different eyes. This type of home is generally assigned a basis equal to its market value at the time of the decedent's death. As it seems to be with all tax questions, this matter has its share of exceptions and variations. There is a publication, number 559, available from the IRS for inheritance situations.

Trade

Some people trade properties. If your present home is the result of a real estate trade, the basis may not be what you think. If you own a home with a basis of $60,000 and a value of $100,000, you can trade it for another property valued at $100,000 and still maintain a basis of $60,000. As a reminder, always verify current requirements and seek professional assistance in tax matters.

Divorce Settlement

If you got your house from a divorce settlement, its basis should be the same as it was at the time of the transfer. You can refer to a government publication, number 504, for details on divorce transfers.

The Ups and Downs

There are many ups and downs possible in the basis of your home. Conditions that might raise the basis include capital expenses, additions, improvements, restoration, and so forth. Factors that could reduce the basis of your home might be casualty losses, easement agreements granted to others, and so on. There are additional considerations to this issue. Don't take anything for granted, check with tax professionals for your personal tax position.

What Difference Does Basis Make?

What difference does basis make? A lot, especially when you sell your home. Remember the house with a basis of $68,000 that sold for $95,000? If that seller thought basis was the same as appraised value, he or she may not have considered the fact that a profit was made from the sale. In reality, a strong gain was earned from the sale of the property, a gain that is taxable.

Basis has everything to do with the tax consequences of your sale. When you sell your home, or perhaps before, you should consult with a tax professional for advice on how to handle your personal situation.

Accurate Records

Accurate records are essential in tax matters. When you sell your home, you will have to compute the gain or loss of your sale. When doing this, you will need detailed records. These records should be maintained in an organized manner that will allow easy interpretation by the IRS. You can never be sure when your claims may be questioned and investigated.

The records you keep pertaining to your home and your improvements should include original acquisition documents, receipts, cancelled checks, contractor contracts, and any other documents that will support your claims. These records should be kept for at least three years after you have filed the tax return supported by the papers. Personally, I would recommend keeping the documents for a minimum of five years.

As a reminder, the receipts for expenditures on improvements will be subject to review from the time your home is sold; this can extend the time you should maintain your records. For example, let's say you made your home improvements five years prior to selling your home. These records should be kept for at least eight years. In other words, keep your improvement receipts for at least three years past the date of the sale of your home.

Home-Improvement Loans

Since some home improvements are quite expensive, it stands to reason that some people will rely on home-improvement loans to accomplish their improvement goals. The tax aspects of money borrowed for home improvements are worthy of consideration. Let's take a close look at how you may find some advantages in the financing of your improvements.

Points and Prepaid Interest

Points and prepaid interest can become factors in your home-improvement financing. Prepaid interest paid on your home mortgage is deductible, but there are limits to how much you can deduct in a given year. In any particular year you can usually deduct only the amount of prepaid interest that is relevant to the current tax year. Let me explain with an example.

Let's say that you paid $3,000 in prepaid interest in year one. For the sake of keeping this example simple, assume that the $3,000 payment is prepaid interest for three years. The mortgage interest is divided into three equal divisions of $1,000 for each of the three years.

When you file your taxes for year one, you cannot deduct the full $3,000. Since only $1,000 of the prepaid interest is being used for year one, you can only deduct $1,000 on the current tax return. In year two, you can deduct another $1,000, and in year three, you can deduct the last $1,000.

Points are often prepaid interest. Unlike the previous example for prepaid interest, points that are prepaid interest may, under certain circumstances, be deducted in full in the year they are paid. In other words, if you paid $3,000 in points when you arranged financing, you might be able to deduct the whole $3,000 on the current tax return.

As for certain circumstances, let me list them for you. First, the points must be prepaid interest; for tax purposes, points are generally represent prepaid interest, even though some points are labeled by lenders as origination fees. In addition to this first condition, your situation must meet all of the following criteria:

- You must itemize deductions on your tax return.
- The loan proceeds must be applied to improving or buying your primary home.
- The loan must be secured by your primary residence.
- The loan must meet all requirements as deductible mortgage interest.
- The practice of paying points for prepaid mortgage interest must be a common and normal practice in your area.
- The amount of money you paid in points must not exceed what would be considered a normal amount.
- When the loan proceeds are used to improve your primary home, you must have paid the points with money other than the funds dispersed from the loan.
- There are some additional exceptions and variations to these

rules, so always consult a tax expert before making tax decisions.

When you are refinancing your primary home for improvement money, the rules get a little more complicated. Points paid to refinance a home are not deductible in full in the year they are paid, unless the refinancing is being done to provide improvement money. The percentage of your deductible amount will relate directly to the percentage of the refinancing that applies to the home improvement. Let me give you a quick example of this.

Assume your loan meets the requirements for approved deductions. You pay $3,000 in points. When the refinancing is done, you use one-fourth of the proceeds to pay for a home improvement. In doing this, you can deduct 25 percent of your points in the current tax year. You will also be entitled to the standard prorated deduction on the remaining interest. Then, as the tax years roll by, you can continue your prorated deductions.

Defer the Closing

If you are selling your home near the end of a tax year, should you defer the closing until after the first of the new tax year? Probably. It is often considered wise to defer the gain from a property sale into a future tax year. However, there are times when it is best to close the sale before the end of the year. Much of the decision will depend on the anticipated tax rates for the coming year. Typically it is best to defer, but check with your accountant to be sure.

The Two-Year Rule

The two-year rule that applies to reinvesting the proceeds from your sale should not be overlooked. If after selling your primary home, you buy another home of equal or greater value, within two years from the closing of your sale, you do not have income tax consequences on the sale. Should you fail to reinvest your gain from the sale, you will be faced with potentially large tax repercussions. There are two exceptions to this rule worth mentioning here. Let me explain.

Military Personnel

Military personnel who are assigned to an active duty tour after selling a primary residence are entitled to some relief from the two-year rule. The two years allowed for reinvesting in another home may be extended by the length of time the individual is on active military duty. However, this extended time period may not exceed a total of four years: the two years allowed for everyone and two years for active duty. As always, there are some exceptions and variations to this ruling.

Once-in-a-Lifetime

There is also a once-in-a-lifetime exclusion to the two-year rule. If a home seller is 55 years of age or older, before selling the primary residence, he or she may exclude up to $125,000 of any gain realized from the sale of the property. If the home seller is married and filing a separate return, each spouse is allowed up to a $62,500 exclusion.

There are rules and regulations affecting this exception to the rule. One of the rules states that the home seller must have owned and occupied the home being sold for a minimum of at least three of the last five years prior to the sale. There are other factors affecting the once-in-a-lifetime exclusion, so check with your tax advisor for details that might pertain to you.

Home Equity

If you take out a home equity loan of up to $100,000, you should be able to deduct the interest paid on the loan. This can be a good way to finance your larger home improvements.

Can't Sell It? Rent It!

Sometimes no matter what you do trying to sell a home, you can't sell it. If you are being transferred or otherwise have to abandon the home, rent it out. By using your home as rental property, the losses you sustain from the venture may be deductible against your taxes, up to $25,000 a year.

The rental income you receive will be taxable income, but by taking an active interest in the management of your rental property, you should be able to generate some good deductions. If however, you cannot be actively involved in the rental management, you could lose your opportunity for deductions against your ordinary income. You can, however, write your losses off against any other passive income you may have.

Not only will renting the house allow you some breathing room, it will give the property a chance to appreciate in value. There are many factors about landlording that get complicated, so before you decide to rent your property, learn what you are getting into as a landlord.

The Alternative Minimum Tax

Did you know there is such a thing as an alternative minimum tax method to computing your tax liabilities? Well, there is, and it can cost you money. If you go to a CPA like Mr. Chandler, your tax situation will be analyzed under standard tax rules and under the rules for the alternative minimum tax method. You will be obligated to pay your taxes based on whichever of the two calculations is the higher.

According to Mr. Chandler, it is usually better to prepay state taxes on large gains in the same year the gains are realized. He cautions that this is not always the case, and that it takes careful scrutiny, on a case-by-case basis, to determine the ideal move to make. The point is this: if you make an unusually high income in any given year, check into your risks associated with the alternative minimum tax method.

Fixing-up Expenses

There is another tax angle you might be interested in. It is known as fixing-up expenses. The expenses incurred to fix up your home for sale may reduce the amount your are required to reinvest in a new residence, to avoid tax on the sale of the old home, if they meet certain criteria. What criteria must be met?

The first rule is that your fix-up expenses cannot be otherwise deductible, such as possibly in the case of a home used for business purposes or rental income. The expenses cannot be considered capital expenditures that result in permanent improvements or replacements, such as adding a garage or installing new replacement windows. In addition, the expenses must be paid within 30 days of the closing of your sale.

There is another rule that applies, and it can be the proverbial fly in the ointment. The fix-up expenses must have been incurred for work done during the 90 days prior to the signing of a purchase and sale agreement. How does all of this work?

Assume your house needs to be spruced up a bit on the exterior to make it attractive to buyers. Wanting a quick sale, you invest $1,000 in exterior painting and pay the bills upon receipt. The result of your efforts is a quicker sale: the house sell in 45 days. Your adjusted sales price would have been $83,000. However, since your fix-up expenses meet the tax criteria, your adjusted sales price is only $82,000, the $83,000 adjusted sales price minus the $1,000 fix-up expenses. In this example, to avoid tax on the sale of your home, you must acquire a new residence that costs at least $82,000, within 2 years of the sale of your property.

Tax Advice

The best tax advice I can give you is to consult a tax expert before you sell your home. Since houses are big-ticket items, you can afford the reasonable fees of a CPA. In fact, it has been my experience that good CPAs don't cost you money; they save you money.

This concludes our talk on tax matters. I hope my translation of otherwise complicated rhetoric has helped you in addressing your tax questions. Now, let's move on to Chapter 10 and learn about appraisals.

Chapter 10

Appraisal Facts about Your Improvements

There are many appraisal facts about your improvements that should be considered. Some improvements cost more than they are worth in the sale of your home. These improvements are not good moneymakers, but they can still help sell your home faster. The other type of improvements hold their own in a cash-on-cash comparison. In other words, if you spend $2,000 on the improvement, the appraised value of your home will increase by $2,000. These improvements, of course, are the most sought after.

We have talked about many improvements that you can make to your home in hopes of a quicker sale. As you have no doubt noticed, the majority of these projects can be done by average homeowners. When you provide the labor for an improvement, your chances for regaining your cash investment improve greatly.

This chapter is going to show you how to assess the cash-on-cash return for your improvement investment. I am a licensed real estate broker and general contractor. The experience I have gained working in these fields has shown me the difference between good and bad improvements as they relate to the sale of a home. However, for this chapter, I didn't want to rely on my own experiences. I wanted some expert

documentation to help you understand the different types of improvements and how they would affect the profit from the sale of your house.
For this purpose, I consulted with a licensed real estate appraiser.

The appraiser I talked with, Jane L. Furbeck-Owen, general partner
of Brunswick Real Estate Services, has years of experience in her field.
I have worked with Jane on various occasions and can attest to her
professionalism and expertise. Jane is approved by all the major banks
in Maine and is licensed as a general appraiser. Her help in dissecting
the value of various projects reinforced my opinions of value. What
follows is a compilation based on our combined experience.

There are many reasons to make improvements to your home. There
are also many ways to place a value on these improvements. As we
begin our exploration into values, we are going to look at all aspects of
residential improvements. We will study the market value of an improvement. The retail value of the improvement will be discussed, and
we will also look at the sales value—meaning the value to making a
quick sale. Let's start our journey with the issue of sales value.

Sales Value

Sales value is a term I use to describe improvements made with the
primary goal of invoking a quick sale. The person making these improvements may not expect to see the cost of the improvement
returned. The goal may be only to shorten the time the property is on
the market. This value is intangible. Its worth will vary among different
people. Some people would never consider spending money on an
improvement that they never expect to get back. Other people would
be happy to drop a $1,000 into their home if it would make the sale
come quicker. Let's look at two examples of different sellers to see how
these feelings might work.

In our first example, the sellers are empty-nesters. Their children
have moved away from home and their house is larger than they need.
This couple decides to sell the house and buy a condo on the golf
course. After talking with numerous real estate agents, they decide on
a price and list the house for sale.

The house is shown often in its first weeks on the market. Since the
couple chose a good broker, they have gotten a lot of feedback from the
people looking at their home. There are countless reasons why the
house hasn't sold, but there is a common denominator that continues to
pop up. Many of the prospective purchasers have told the broker they
were not interested in the house because the carpets were worn and the
roof looked like it would need replacing in the near future.

The broker sat down and talked with the couple about the recurring complaints. The broker advised the couple to replace the roof and the carpeting. The couple agreed to think about it. The sellers talked with their banker and an appraiser. They found that if they replaced their roof and their carpeting, the value of their home would not increase enough to offset the money they would be spending. Based on this, the couple refused to make the improvements. Their broker was disappointed, but accepted their decision.

The house stayed on the market for about six months before the sellers finally got an acceptable offer. The broker had worked hard and earned her commission. This couple didn't mind that the sale had taken half a year to make. They would much rather wait for just the right buyer than invest money that would not be returned.

In this example, the sellers were able to sell their house without making what they considered foolish improvements. Since they used a broker, they weren't paying for the advertising, at least not directly. The couple was under no pressure to sell the house quickly, and they could afford to wait. By waiting, they were able to allow the right buyer to find their home. The sale was made and everyone was happy. For these people, the sales value of a new roof and new floor coverings was nil. Now, lets see how similar sales circumstances worked out for our second couple.

Our second couple are moving due to a job relocation. The husband is a photographer and the wife is an executive with a major insurance company. The insurance company has offered the wife a good promotion, but she must relocate across the country. The couple has considered keeping their existing home as a rental-property investment, but they decide to sell it for money to use as a down payment on a home in their new location.

Since the wife has to move in 30 days, the husband will stay behind and handle the sale of the house with the help of a broker. The couple listed their house for sale and the wife transferred to her new job. She was 1,400 miles away from her husband. The couple missed each other and wanted a quick sale. Not only was being away from each other tough, paying rent for the wife's temporary apartment and the mortgage on the home was a struggle. The monthly mortgage payment was $1,200, and the wife's rent was $800. That extra $800 a month was a painful extra expense.

By the end of the third week, the broker came to the husband with the objections she had heard. She told the husband of the complaints about the carpeting and roof. The husband could understand the justified objections and said he would discuss the situation with his wife.

After a long-distance conference, the decision was made to get estimates for the improvements. When the bids were in, the cost to replace the roof and carpeting would be around $4,500.

When the husband talked to his broker, he found that the $4,500 improvement wouldn't pay for itself. The broker thought she could raise the price of the house by about $1,500, but that was it. This would mean eating $3,000 of the investment as a loss. The husband called the wife and they came to a conclusion. They decided to make the improvements.

The improvements were made and the price was raised $1,500. In less than two weeks, the house was placed under contract. The sales value of the improvements to this couple was considerable. However, did they really lose money? Under their circumstances, maybe not. Let's see what would have happened if they had waited six months for a sale.

This couple sold their house in less than two months. The first couple needed six months to sell their house. If the couple in this example had waited four extra months for the sale, they would have been making double payments for the entire time. Since the mortgage payment was $1,200 per month, the extra expense would have amounted to $4,800. The couple lost $3,000 on their improvement investment, but they saved $4,800 in double housing payments. The net result was a cash savings of $1,800, and they got to be reunited four months earlier.

These examples should make the identification of sales value clear. If you are in no hurry to sell your home, it is senseless to make improvements you don't believe will allow you to recover your money. If, on the other hand, you need a quick sale, improvements that first appear to be losers might be winners. There is definitely a place and a time for improvements made with the only hope being a faster sale.

Retail Value

The retail value of an improvement has little to do with what the improvement will command in the sales price of a home. In fact, retail prices are often higher than the improvement is worth on an appraisal report. If you hire a general contractor to make improvements for you, it is unlikely that you will recover your money in the sale of the home, especially if the home is sold shortly after the improvements are done.

General contractors try to sell their services at the maximum amount the market will bear. For the time they spend supervising and organizing work, general contractors often earn between 15 and 25 percent of the cost of the job. For example, if the cost of labor and materials to do a job is $1,000, a general contractor (GC) will try to sell the job for at least $1,200. This gives the GC a couple hundred bucks for the effort in selling, organizing, and supervising the job. When you consider all the time spent performing these functions, the general contractor isn't getting rich.

If, however, the improvement is a large one, like a room addition, an attic conversion, or building a garage, the GC does allright for himself. When you look at an addition that will have a wholesale cost of $15,000, the general is looking to make between $2,000 and $3,000 on the job. This is money you can save by being your own general contractor.

Let's look at an example of retail value and the sale of a home. You are the homeowner. The project is an attic conversion. You put the job out to bids and the best price you get from a general contractor is $12,000. The price includes converting the attic into two bedrooms and a bathroom. You are pleased, because you have talked to an appraiser and found that with the work completed, according to your plans and specifications, the improvement could add $15,000 to the value of your home.

Even though you are pleased with the quoted price, you decide to look into being your own general contractor and even doing some of the work yourself. You solicit bids from independent subcontractors. After looking at these bids, you see you can get the job done for around $10,000, if you act as the general contractor.

Upon further consideration, you decide to do your own painting and clean-up work. This saves you an additional $650. You undertake the job and invest a total of $9,350. After the job is complete, you hire an appraiser to give you a full-blown market appraisal of the house. The improvement has added $13,800 to the value of your home. You only spent $9,350 on the project, so you built an instant equity of $4,450.

At this point you have some options on what to do with your extra equity. You could raise the price of the house to its full value and pocket the extra equity. Another option would be to price the house a few thousand dollars below its appraised value in search of a quick sale. If you like, you could raise the price of the house and offer to pay some of the buyer's points or closing costs with your additional equity. Whichever option you choose, you benefit from your efforts.

Retail value is the value charged by contractors to complete an improvement. In the case of the attic conversion, the retail value was a good deal. However, the retail cost of finishing your buried basement or installing vinyl siding may not be such a good deal. There are many types of improvements where the retail value is more than the market value. Let's look at the issue of vinyl siding.

You see commercials on television all the time for vinyl siding. The announcers tell you what a great value vinyl siding is. They preach how it is a low-maintenance alternative to painting, and how it will improve the look of your home. Well, vinyl siding is not always maintenance free. It is true that you don't have to paint it, but in many parts of the country you have to have it power-washed. If the siding is not washed from time to time, it can discolor with mildew. This maintenance point is minor compared to the effect it might have on the sale of your home.

Vinyl siding is considered a cheap alternative to wood siding. No doubt, many people like the fact that it doesn't require painting. However, when it comes to your appraisal report, vinyl siding will not compare with wood siding. Why would anyone spend good money to cover up wood siding that only needs a coat of paint with vinyl siding? The cost of a paint job, even by professionals, is much less than the installation of vinyl siding. In addition, the completed paint job on the wood siding will maintain the home's value better than the installation of vinyl siding. You spend less money on the paint and get more for your house than if you spent big bucks on new siding.

Vinyl siding is a good product, and it certainly has its place in the construction of homes. There will be people who will buy your home quicker if it has vinyl siding. However, from a statistical approach, vinyl siding could be a major mistake for the well-meaning homeowner looking for a strong sale. This is a good example of where retail cost does not usually translate into realized profit.

Market Value

Market value is the value your improvement is worth on the open real estate market. This is the merit an appraiser will reward you with on an appraisal report. For some sellers, this is the value most often sought. Many sellers are not worried about how quickly their houses sell; they are more concerned with how much profit they will gain from the sale. If profit is your motivation, market value is the value you should be most interested in.

Sales value is the intangible value a seller places on an improvement intended to sell the house fast. Retail value is the price a contractor dictates for a job. Market value indicates how much money you will get for an improvement when you sell your house. These three values can be very different.

Appraisers work with several different types of values and formulas to assess the worth of a property. They will look at the replacement cost of the property, the cost of construction, and comparable sales. All of this investigation leads an appraiser to the market value of a home. To understand the basis behind market value fully, let's look at how an appraiser's research and your improvements can affect the market value of your home.

When appraisers look at the replacement cost of a home, they figure out what it would take to replace the home if it were destroyed. Since real estate generally appreciates in value, a deck that was built for $1,000 three years ago might be worth $1,200, if it had to be replaced at current construction costs. This doesn't mean the deck will rate a $1,200 value on the appraisal report. This is only one step in determining market value.

The cost of construction is another piece of the appraisal puzzle. How much did the deck cost to build? This is the question the appraiser must try to answer. Let's say the deck cost $1,000. Does that mean the deck is worth $1,000? No; the deck may have depreciated in value. If it has discolored or begun to rot, the value is surely less than it would have been when the deck was new. Again, this is only one piece of the puzzle.

Comparable sales are generally the best barometer for finding fair market value. When appraisers search for comparable values, they look for properties that have changed ownership recently, preferably within the last six months or less. The hunt is for properties that most closely resemble the property being appraised. It would be unusual for an appraiser to compare a one-level house with a two-level house. Generally, they will stick to the same basic styles and types of homes whenever possible.

Not only will appraisers try to match styles and types, they will search for properties in the same general location of the subject property. Location can mean everything when it comes to the value of real estate. To be fair, appraisers must use comparables that are in the same area as the house being assessed.

If an appraiser finds three homes that are very similar to the one being appraised, he or she can draw some strong conclusions on value. If two of the comparable homes didn't have decks and one did, the appraiser can get an idea what the public was willing to pay for a deck. If the house with the deck sold for $800 more than the two without decks, and everything else was comparable, it would be reasonable to assume the deck was worth $800. In light of this, the value assigned to the deck on the subject house would probably be close to $800. Adjustments might be made for size and condition, but the principles would apply.

Just as an appraiser arrives at improvement values, so can you. Finding construction costs is as simple as getting five bids for the work from five different contractors. The average of the five bids should represent the cost of construction.

Anyone can have access to the records of property transfers in the Town Hall or the Registry of Deeds. If you, as a home seller, investigate these current property transfers, you can begin to build your own list of comparable sales. By checking the identification cards used for tax assessments on the houses that have been sold, you can see how many bedrooms they had, how many bathrooms were in the homes, and so on. This information allows you to draw some of your own conclusions.

If you are thinking of converting one of your closets into a half-bath, you can check the public records to see how much more houses with half-baths sold for. This gives you pretty concrete numbers to base your improvement decision on. This is the same type of information an appraiser is going to use when appraising your house.

If you have more money than time, there is another way for you to determine what effect a given improvement will have on your home. You can hire an appraiser to put a value on your house as it stands, without the improvement. Then give the appraiser plans and specifications for your proposed improvement, and ask him or her to tell you approximately how much the improvement will add to your home's value. This before-and-after appraisal procedure is very accurate. You will know quickly if the improvement is justified as a cash-on-cash investment. The appraisal will probably cost you between $300 and $400, but it is money well spent when considering a major improvement.

Getting Carried Away

Getting carried away with improvement investments can be a costly lesson in what not to do. Some people just don't know when to stop. If you overimprove your home, you've got no chance of recovering your investment if the home is sold too soon. When too much improvement is done, you might have a chance to salvage your investment by holding the home and waiting for market conditions and the neighborhood to change, but even so you aren't likely to come out a winner. If you try to sell the house as soon as the improvements are complete, you will surely lose money.

What is overimproving? Overimproving is when you make your house too big or too fancy for the area. For example, if all the other homes on your street have three bedrooms and two bathrooms, you will probably be making a big mistake if you build an addition to give your house five bedrooms and three bathrooms. It rarely pays to have the largest, best, or most expensive house in the neighborhood.

There are many ways to fall into the trap of overimproving. You could get caught by building a three-car garage, when all the other homes either don't have garages or only have one-car garages. Installing a front door that has a price tag of $900 could be a regretful mistake. Room additions can get you in over your head very quickly. Installing a swimming pool or tennis court can be a big mistake, as I have indicated. In general, you must make sure the improvements you are making will be supported financially by comparable sales in the area.

Flash Improvements

Flash improvements made to help sell a house are done to impress people, but you can never be sure whether the impression will be favorable. When you are making home improvements to help sell your house, stick to dependable improvements, like the ones you've read about in this book. If you get too creative or too flashy, your efforts may backfire on you.

Let me give you examples of how some improvements that cost a lot of money may actually hurt the sale of your house. Assume that you are anxious to sell your home and that you are willing to invest serious money to do it. Now imagine that you have always wanted your own private swimming pool. In your mind a swimming pool would be one of the best amenities you could find with a home. The more you think about it, the more you become convinced to have an in-ground pool installed in your backyard. You are just sure buyers will stand in line to buy your house once the pool is built.

With your mind made up, you hire a company to build the pool and erect the fencing around it. By the time you are done, you have invested nearly $20,000 in the pool. The cement pond is not huge, but it is beautiful.

You raise the price of your house to reflect the investment in the pool and wait for the buyers to line up. Well, buyers do come to see your house, but they aren't signing any contracts. You can't understand it. You were sure the pool would make all the difference in the world.

After a few weeks of dull activity, you ask your broker what's going on. The broker sits down with you and tells you what the potential buyers are giving as feedback on the property. It turns out that many of the buyers aren't interested in the home because of the pool. What?

How could people not want the house because of the pool? The swimming pool was supposed to make people buy the house, not refuse it. According to the broker, the people don't want to pay extra for the pool. Some of the people don't want the house at any reasonable price, they don't want the maintenance headaches that go along with a pool. The families with small children see the pool as a safety hazard. You have just spent a lot of money on an improvement that is inhibiting the sale of your house. Now what do you do?

This example is not farfetched; it echoes the experiences of some distraught sellers. According to some statistics, swimming pools are unlikely to return more than 40 percent of their original costs. In other words, if you spent $20,000 on the pool, you will probably only see an extra $8,000 in the sale of your home. In some cases, again supported by statistics, you might not see any financial gain. A swimming pool is one improvement to avoid, unless you are buying it for your own personal pleasure.

Tennis courts can fall into the same category as swimming pools. If you build a tennis court in your backyard, you limit the list of potential buyers for your home to tennis players. Who else would want a tennis court in the backyard? Most people would much prefer grass.

Some of the Best

What are some of the best improvements you can make to help sell your home and return your investment? There are a number of solid improvements you can make. Before we look at them individually, let's make one point. Any improvement can be a bad improvement if it is done in amateur fashion or if the market won't support it. The examples I am about to give you are based on the assumption that the market will support the improvements. What works in one part of town might fail miserably in another section. You can't always go by averages. Averages are made from highs and lows. If you are unlucky, you might live in one of the areas where the improvement produced at the bottom end of the scale. Before you decide on any improvement, do your homework and prove the viability of the project. Now let's see what some of the most consistent improvements are.

Adding a Bathroom

Adding a bathroom, where the market supports it, is almost always a safe investment. It is, however, a high-dollar investment. If you are making the investment only to help sell your house, you must be careful not to price yourself out of the market.

A bathroom addition built by a general contractor could cost anywhere from $10,000 on up. A fancy one, with a whirlpool and all, might go for $25,000. In either case, this is a lot of money to add to the price of your home. You must be very careful to be sure the public can and will pay for the advantage of the extra bathroom.

Bathroom additions offer good potential for the return of your investment. Some people say you will get back at least half of your money and others say you can double your money. Typically, if you keep the improvement modest, you should recover all of your money. If you act as your own general contractor, you could see a profit for your efforts.

Complete Bath Remodeling

Complete bath remodeling is a pretty safe investment, most of the time. Again you are talking a lot of money. This type of job, done by a general contractor, can range from $4,000 to upward of $10,000. As with any improvement, acting as your own general contractor builds in a safety buffer. The money you save by coordinating your own work can be enough to keep you from losing any of your cash investment. A good bathroom remodeling job should return at least 75 percent of its retail value.

Complete Kitchen Remodeling

Complete kitchen remodeling is a lot like bathroom remodeling, except more expensive. Major overhaul of a kitchen can cost anywhere from $8,000 to $30,000. An average would probably fall between $12,000 and $15,000. Based on the price you would pay a general contractor, this type of work will probably return about 75 percent of its total cost. It could, however, return 100% of the expense; kitchen remodeling is popular, and people are willing to pay for it when they can.

Some Other Dependable Projects

Some other dependable projects include decks, interior cosmetics, additions, sunrooms, insulation, and closets. Closets can frequently be counted on to return 100 percent of their construction costs. The rest of the projects in this group should return around 75 percent of their retail values. Remember, doing the work yourself can give you, on average, a 20 to 30 percent head start on your savings. A project that returns

75 percent of its retail value will probably be returning 100 percent of your cash costs.

All You Can Get

When the sale of your home is being financed, the appraised value is all you can get out of your home. A lender isn't going to lend money to a borrower to buy a $100,000 house that will be appraised for only $85,000. Even if you show the banker receipts for the money spent on your improvement, you can bet the loan will be based on appraised value, not the cost of construction.

Since most homes are financed, appraisals are a very important part of the sale. You not only have to find a buyer willing to pay your asking price, you must find an appraiser who can justify the value of the home. Sometimes this is hard to do, and many sellers become irate at the appraisers. It is not the appraiser's fault that you overinvested in your house with the wrong improvements. If the appraiser has done a thorough job in seeking fair comparable sales, and most of the time they do, you will have to live with the stated value. You can arrange for a second opinion from another lender-approved appraiser, but the difference in value between the two appraisal reports will be minimal in most cases. If you are hoping to make a profit on your improvement, do your homework before you do your project. Make sure the improvement can carry its own weight.

If you are after a quick sale, you may need to do exhaustive searching through comparable sales. However, the work might well pay off in the end. If you research homes that have sold quickly, you should be able to decipher the amenities that these homes share. If all the fast sellers have decks, maybe you should build a deck. When all the quick sales have been made with houses having more than one bathroom, it might be wise to add a bathroom to your house. Research generally pays off.

All right, you now know a little about how the appraisal process works. Now let's see some examples of various improvements and how they might stack up on an appraisal report.

Window Treatments

We talked earlier about how window treatments can transform a house. There is no question that window treatments can help sell your house faster, but how will they fare on an appraisal? Poorly, I'm afraid. In the first place, window treatments are considered personal property, not real property. Appraisers typically base their evaluations on real property. Therefore, window treatments will not gain much consideration, at least not as window treatments. However, they can influence an appraisal.

Appraisers are human. If they walk into a house and are instantly depressed by darkness or ugly drapes, it is bound to have an effect on how they view the value of the property. Under such conditions, elements of the house that are a factor in the appraised value might not receive a maximum rating. Conversely, if an appraiser is taken aback by the beauty of a home, the appraised value is likely to be a little higher. For this reason, window treatments can lead to a better appraised value.

Appraised values are partly scientific and partly emotional. When a market value is being sought, an appraiser must determine what the property will be worth to the buying public. Obviously, a cheerful, pretty home should be worth more than a drab, dull one. While you aren't likely to see a cash-on-cash return for window treatments, they can still be advantageous in raising the value and sales potential of your home.

Landscaping

Will landscaping improve the appraised value of your home? Yes. Landscaping can raise the value of your home, but there is a point where the cost is not justified. From a value point of view, extensive landscaping, with exotic plantings and expensive accents, will not be recovered in the sale of your home. It can make the house sell much faster, but the increased price of the home will not cover the cost of the investment.

Moderate landscaping is a good value, and it is expected. By moderate landscaping, I mean a full lawn of grass, some foundation shrubs, and a tree or two. If you install a fish pond or an Oriental garden, I doubt you will see your appraised value rise to cover the cost.

If you don't install or maintain moderate landscaping, the value of your home will not reach its full potential. Not only will you not achieve maximum value, you may have difficulty finding a buyer for the house. The key to getting your money's worth out of landscaping is in keeping it simple and beautiful.

Little Touches

In the early chapters of the book we talked about numerous little touches you could do to improve the appeal of your home. These little jobs, like putting fresh caulking around your plumbing fixtures, are not going to show up on an appraisal in black and white. You will be hard pressed to find a category on the appraisal report for clean windows or fresh caulking. However, attention to detail on these small tasks will have a cumulative effect on the home's value.

Plumbing

Plumbing improvements are always appreciated. If all you do is stop a faucet from dripping, you will have smoothed out one rough spot in the sale of your home. If you replace a sink or a faucet, you will have improved the appearance of your home. Minor plumbing improvements are not going to show up on your appraisal report. However, major plumbing work will be noted by appraisers.

Heating

Most heating improvements will make a casual difference in your home. However, if you do a conversion from electric baseboard heat to a furnace or heat pump, the change should reflect a higher value for your home on the appraisal. This is especially true in areas with cold winter climates.

In Maine, houses with electric heat are very difficult to sell. Buyers know the high cost of heating the home will be a drain on their bank accounts. Oil heat is preferred in Maine. Sellers who are willing to convert from electric baseboard heat to an oil-fired system see higher resale values and faster sales.

Electrical

Small electrical improvements, like replacing wall plates or a ceiling light, are not going to do much for your home's appraised value. However, adding a post lamp or upgrading your electrical service should help to increase your home's value, but don't expect too much. Expensive chandeliers will not rate much higher than modest ones. In general, electrical improvements can help sell the house, but they are not going to make a major impact on the home's market value.

Specific Values

Let's get down to some specific values. When I talked to Jane, the appraiser, we discussed some specific projects. We talked about the cost of the improvements and how they would rate on an average appraisal in Maine. Here's what I found out.

All of the following guidelines are based on values in the mid-coast area of Maine. The assumptions and values are based on averages and general market conditions. As always, there are exceptions to rules, and there may be exceptions to the opinions and figures contained here. However, this information should be helpful to you in rating the improvements being considered for your home.

Fences

Fences, on the whole, are a bad investment. Many types of fencing detract from a home's exterior appearance. In this case you are paying for an improvement that will not allow you to recover its cost, and that, at the same time, is lowering the value of your home based on curb appeal. Accent fences are fine, but stay away from major fence installations.

Garages

Garages are generally a sound investment. Of course, market conditions and local houses play a role in determining how effective a garage improvement is. In Maine, a two-car garage, of average construction, will appraise, on average, for around $7,500. The value of a garage in another part of the country, say Virginia, might well be over $10,000. As we go through this list, remember that the opinions and values are based on a small section of Maine.

Paved Driveways

Paved driveways are popular everywhere. They are especially popular in Maine. Paved drives make plowing snow much easier than it would be with a gravel drive, and Mainers have to plow a lot of snow. Paved drives, depending on where they are located and how large they are, rate a value of between $1,500 and $2,500.

Storage Sheds

Storage sheds are a safe bet when they are built from modest materials and kept to a reasonable size. What is a reasonable size? A shed with dimensions of 10' x 12' or 10' x 14' is considered the most appealing in this part of Maine. Don't get me wrong, buyers might love a larger shed, but if the shed gets too big, it won't support its cost in increased value for the home.

Vaulted Ceilings

Vaulted ceilings are liked by a lot of people. The idea of a high ceiling, often with exposed beams and a ceiling fan, is a dream of many buyers. If you are going to build a room addition, you may be considering this type of ceiling. I don't doubt for a minute that this arrangement will be well received by the public or that it will help sell your home faster. But the appraiser says this type of ceiling won't pay for itself on the appraisal, at least not in this part of Maine.

Swimming Pools

We're back to swimming pools. You might think that people in Maine would have little use for swimming pools. It is a reasonable opinion to have, since Maine is very cold in winter and pretty cool all year. Even with the cool climate, many houses in Maine have swimming pools. Some of them are in-ground pools, and a lot of them are above-ground pools. According to Jane, these pools will recover no more than half of their initial value when the home is appraised.

Screen Porches

Screen porches should be very popular in Maine, when you consider the mosquitoes and black flies that thrive here. Even with the big bug problems, you won't find a lot of screen porches in the area. There are a number of tentlike screen houses, but not many screened-in porches. If sellers in Maine add screen porches to their home, they can expect to see appraised values ranging from $2,500 to $3,500.

Sunrooms

What are sunrooms worth in Maine? Jane says their value will run from a low of $3,500 to a high of $5,000. When you consider what a good sunroom costs to build, this is a losing proposition in Maine.

Spiral Stairs

A lot of people are enchanted with spiral stairs. When an attic or basement is being converted to living space, spiral stairs are often considered. There is a certain uniqueness about them. However, Jane warns that spiral stairs should not be used as the only means of access to a living area. Her point is a good one; she states that it is very difficult to get furniture up and down a spiral stairway. This is something most people do not consider until it is too late.

Decks

Decks are considered good home improvements, within reason. Jane's ballpark figure for decks worked out to be $10 per square foot, up to about 250 square feet. So if you build a 14' x 16' deck, you should recover most if not all of your investment. However, if you go overboard on intricate railings, seats, or high-dollar wood, you won't be so fortunate.

A Finished Buried Basement

A finished buried basement is going to be worth about $10 per square foot on Jane's appraisal reports. This means that if you do the work yourself and keep it simple, you might break even on this project. If you hire the job out to professionals or get fancy with your finishings, you are more than likely going to lose money.

Attic Conversion

Converting the attic of a Cape Cod into bedrooms, without adding a bathroom, will get you about $25 per square foot for the living space. There really is a big difference in value between buried basements and attics. This type of finished space doesn't cost a lot to do per square foot, so you should be safe in tackling this project, as long as the market and neighborhood will support your efforts.

Adding a Full Bath within the Home

Adding a full bath within the home should increase the appraised value by about $3,500. This is not the same as a bathroom addition. This is when you use an existing closet and convert it to a bathroom.

Now you have the rundown on how a Maine appraiser looks at various projects. Let's follow this with some examples of values.

Generic Values

When you read miscellaneous magazine articles and books that deal with home improvements, you run into a wide range of values. This is also true of books written to help estimate the costs of various projects. I've always found these generic values and costs to be somewhat high, when compared to my personal experiences.

I've been involved with real estate and construction for nearly 20 years. I'm licensed as a master plumber, general contractor, and real estate broker. I've owned several houses and I've done extensive building and remodeling, both for myself and for others. I've worked mostly in Maine and Virginia, but I've also worked in Maryland, Washington,

D.C., South Carolina, and Colorado. This is a pretty good cross-section of the county, so I don't think my experience has been derived from a pigeon hole in some remote, rural area. My experience contradicts many of the generic figures that pop up in articles and books. Let me give you some examples of what I'm talking about.

I've seen generic figures that indicate a skylight can cost up to $6,500 to install. Now I'm sure there must be some place and some way you can spend that much money on a skylight, but I can't believe it is a viable average. Even if you spent $2,000 on a super-fancy skylight, who is going to charge you $4,500 to install it? Skylights aren't the only areas where I question the generic figures.

Would you pay over $50,000 for a remodeled bedroom? I know places where you can buy a whole house, land and all, for less than $50,000. Yet I've seen published reports of bedroom remodeling with prices predicted on up and beyond $60,000. Well excuse me, but I can't imagine what a $60,000 bedroom would look like. Can you?

As a general contractor, I've built some pretty nice room additions for people on a budget of less than $25,000. I'm not talking about a bare bones, penny-pinching addition. I'm talking about a nice, big family room. Now if I've sold these room additions for $25,000 and made good money, why do some generic figures show the cost of a room addition hitting $75,000? I've built and sold brand-new homes, on 1 acre lots, for less than $75,000, and this wasn't 15 years ago, it was about 6 years ago. So why should a room addition cost as much as some houses?

I'm not trying to say that the numbers reported in these various books and magazines are fictitious. I'm simply curious where they are selling the jobs for that much; I might like to move my businesses to that area. The point of this section is not to attack generic values, it is to show you that you must sift through what you read, theirs and mine, to find the numbers that are right for you.

Local Conditions

Local conditions are a key element of real estate appraisal. An improvement that is worth $2,000 across town might be worth only $1,500 in another neighborhood. If you are going to make smart improvement investments, you will have to get to know your neighborhood.

We have already talked about the importance of researching comparable sales. What we haven't discussed is the buying climate. The buying climate refers to the type of buyers that are active and the competitive houses that are being offered for sale. These two factors should have a heavy influence on the improvements you decide to make and the value those improvements will have. Let's talk about the buyers first.

Active Buyers

What are the active buyers like in your area? Are they young couples, just starting out and looking for affordable housing. Will the buyers looking at your home have children, and if so, how old will they be? Does your neighborhood appeal to empty-nesters? If you can answer these questions, you have narrowed the field of the three most prevalent groups of buyers. Before you can predict the best improvements to make to your home, you must have an inkling of the type of buyers you will be attracting. It is sort of like fishing, you have to choose your bait to match the fish you are after. Crappies love minnows, and bluegill enjoy worms. Families with kids will appreciate practical floor and wall coverings. Empty-nesters may prefer delicate wallpaper and plush carpeting. Knowing what kind of bait to use makes all the difference in landing a fish and netting a sale.

If you have a good real estate agent, the broker should be able to read the market and tell you what type of fish you are trying to hook. If you are trying to sell your house without the assistance of a broker, you will have to determine what type of buyer will be interested in your home.

How can you make an educated guess at what type of buyer you are likely to attract? There is no sure way of knowing, but there are some factors that may point you in the right direction. The first factor we will cover is the market value of your home.

If you know about what your home is worth, you can plot a range of buyers that you might attract. If your price is near the low end of the housing scale, you will most likely pull first-time buyers or empty-nesters. This narrows the field of targets, but there is a big difference in the desires of empty-nesters and first-time buyers.

Most first-time buyers are not too choosy; they just want a house of their own. Empty-nesters, on the other hand, may have very definite plans for what they want in a house. So, how do you predict the future and decide what improvements to make? Look around your neighborhood. Are there any empty-nester types already in the community? Most empty-nesters will flock to an area inhabited by their peers. If there aren't any empty-nesters in the neighborhood, you will probably attract first-time buyers.

If your house is valued well above the low-end housing scale, say $20,000 over the upper limit of the low end, you will probably be attracting move-up buyers. These are buyers selling their present home and moving up in size, luxury, location, or all three. This group of buyers is likely to be discriminating in their tastes.

Each of these groups of buyers may want different types of improvements. Reading the market to determine which group to appeal to is paramount to your success.

Once you have targeted your market, you can home in on specific improvements. By tracking comparable sales and understanding your potential buyers, you can predict, with fair accuracy, what types of improvements will help sell your house faster.

Competitive Houses

Competitive houses can have a lot to do with your improvement decisions. Comparable sales are very good for historical data, but these houses are already sold. You will not be competing against comparable sales; you will be trying to win the battle of buyers against competitive properties. Before you can beat the enemy, in this case competitive houses, you must know your competition.

The best way to get to know the enemy is to visit his camp. In the battle of buyers, this is simple. Look for ads in the newspaper for houses in your area. Call and make an appointment to tour the houses. As you go through the homes, make mental notes of what these houses have that your house doesn't. If most of the competition has two bathrooms, and your house has only one, you should seriously consider adding another bathroom. If your competitors have paved driveways, and you don't, look into paving yours.

On-site inspections of competitive homes are a great way to get ideas. You can see, firsthand, what effect various improvements have. If you have trouble visualizing what a particular improvement will do for your home, look at other houses until you can draw a comparison. Once you know the competition, you can engage in a fair fight and win.

The buying climate is important in establishing the value of a property or improvement. Appraisers must assess public demand to define a value. Swimming pools are a great example. The pool that cost $20,000 to build might not be worth more than $5,000 to the buying public. Appraisers must get and maintain a feel for the ever-changing tides of the market. As the tides turn, so do values.

By far the safest approach to choosing wise improvements is to consult with a local appraiser. By talking directly to the person that may be appraising your improvements, you can decide what is and is not viable. Many appraisers will be happy to consult with you on an hourly basis. The fees for this type of consultation will probably run from $50 to $100 per hour. But if you get good information, this is a very small price to pay. Spending a few hundred dollars now is much better than losing several thousand dollars later.

Well, enough said on appraisals. Let's now turn to Chapter 11 and see what the best improvements are from a professional broker's perspective.

Chapter 11

A Broker's Opinion
of the Best Improvements

This chapter is going to give you the inside scoop on a broker's opinion of the best home improvements. Real estate brokers see and hear much more from buyers than sellers do. Buyers will normally be too polite to tell sellers what they really think, but they won't hesitate to make comments to their brokers. If sellers were privy to the inside scoop that brokers get, they could do much to make their house sell faster. Unfortunately, sellers seldom get the constructive criticism they need to remedy their problems. Even when a seller's broker has heard negative comments, the broker is often intimidated to reveal the objections to the seller. This is a shame and a shortcoming in a broker.

Most sellers are willing to address and correct a known defect or problem. But they can't fix what they don't know is broken. Too many brokers lack the confidence and experience to help their sellers by revealing the objections buyers lay out. The brokers are afraid they will alienate their sellers and lose the listing. This outcome is a possibility, but if the problem is corrected, a fast sale and a hefty commission check are more likely.

I have been buying and selling real estate for going on 20 years. During many of these transactions I was dealing with my own money and my own credit. When your own money is on the line, you sometimes play the game a little more seriously. As I grew into being a home builder, there were years my company was building and selling up to 60 single-family homes at a clip. Having 60 houses to sell in a year means you have to sell more than one a week, and we did. It wasn't easy and we made a lot of mistakes, but we also learned a great deal about selling homes.

In addition to my personal real estate activity, I am a licensed broker. In the beginning I became a broker to make selling my own houses easier. As time progressed I acquired licensed agents to work with my brokerage business. When I became surrounded by real estate agents, I quickly saw why so many homes stay on the market for six months or more. These agents didn't work to sell the houses. They showed them, but they didn't sell them.

Reflecting on the sales production of my team, I decided to try a different approach. As each new approach showed insignificant gains, I came to the conclusion that I was not like other brokers. I worked differently. I knew some other brokers who were also very successful, but they were happy where they were and wouldn't jump ship to join my brokerage. In time, I gave up on the brokerage idea and gradually downsized the brokerage to where I was again the only broker.

Much of my brokerage work has involved investment properties. I have specialized in filling out rental portfolios for investors. In addition to my investment activities, I have also catered strongly to first-time buyers. Many brokers turn their noses up at first-time buyers. They see these inexperienced buyers as being more trouble than they are worth. I see them as people needing guidance, but who are willing to be loyal to their broker.

In short, I've sold a lot of houses, both as an owner, a builder, and a broker. The houses have run the gamut from starter homes to mini-mansions. The buyers have been as diverse as the housing. During these years of experience, I have learned a lot about the sale of real estate. Now I'm going to share some of this valuable on-the-job experience with you. Not all of the situations will parallel yours, but I think you will learn from each and every account of my past experience.

Brokers

This chapter will deal primarily with my opinion on the best home improvements for selling your house quickly, but first I'd like to touch on the subject of brokers. A majority of home sellers depend on brokers to make the sale and close the transaction. There are also sellers who prefer to rely on their own initiatives and abilities to sell their homes. If you fall into the category of for-sale-by-owners (FSBOs), you can skip this small section of the chapter. This part of the chapter is written for sellers who will use brokers to effect the sale of their home.

If you are still reading in this section, I assume you plan to use a broker in the sale of your home. Before I start, let me say that I am a licensed broker, and I respect my license and field of endeavor. Further, I respect the real estate profession. But I have to tell you, there are a lot of agents and brokers out there who will not give you the service you deserve. That is what this section is all about: bad brokers.

If I wanted to stand on the stump long enough, I could give you countless accounts of bad brokers. Their failings run from misrepresentation to embezzlement. Generally, the bad brokers get all the attention from the media. If a broker takes advantage of a little old lady, you see it splashed in the headlines. When a broker helps a struggling couple find a way to buy their first home, the event is tucked away in the property-transfer section of the paper.

There are lots of good brokers available to help you. Finding them can be difficult, but I don't want to bog this chapter down with a how-to lesson in finding the best broker. What I want to stress is open communication between you and your broker. When you engage a broker to sell your house, you are taking on a partner in a manner of speaking. Would you go into business with a partner who didn't communicate with you? I don't think so.

Once you have chosen your broker, make sure you get your money's worth. Giving up 6 or 7 percent of the sales price of your home is no small token of gratitude. You are paying a fair price for your broker's best service, and you should get what you are paying for.

To speed this section up, I am going to assume you have chosen a good, successful broker. I will further assume that you have a reasonable understanding of what the broker is going to do for you. What I want to discuss is how you can get more out of your broker than you might if you didn't have this information.

Okay, you have a full-time professional broker. You've checked out references and confirmed a track record in sales. The brokerage is a high-profile, well-known company. It seems you have done everything right. What else do you have to do? You have to talk to your broker on an eye-to-eye basis.

Real estate brokers, even good ones, are reluctant to tell sellers what they may not want to hear. If this happens with your broker, the sale of your house can be delayed for months. When you sign the listing agreement with your broker, take the time to have a heart-to-heart talk. Tell the broker you want honesty out of your business relationship. Stress the fact that you want absolute honesty about the condition of your home and any improvements that may be involved in the sale. Insist that the broker keep a log of customer comments on your home. Listing agents are obligated to share the comments of buyers with their sellers. You can push this button by requiring a weekly report of objections and negative comments on your house.

At first the broker may feel uncomfortable telling you the bad aspects of your house. But if he or she is seasoned, he or she will jump at the chance to share honest comments and suggestions. The broker will know this type of criticism can result in a quicker sale. It is up to you to make your broker comfortable with telling you what you may not want to hear.

Once you've made this pact, don't blow up when the broker tells you your hunter-orange bedroom should be painted a more subtle color. You don't have to act on every suggestion the broker brings to the table, but you ought to listen and evaluate the opinion. Remember, the broker is a professional salesperson, who doesn't eat unless a sale is made. This fact should mean that the broker has some concept of how to sell your house. If you don't think the broker is right in the sales suggestions, you might be wise to find a new broker.

All right, we are going to close up this blip on brokers. The main thing for you to strive for with your broker is open communication. Don't settle for a broker who coddles you. Insist on knowing why buyers are not making offers on your home. If the broker honestly doesn't know, he or she isn't asking the right questions of the buyers. Good brokers don't let buyers get away without some type of objection. If your broker can't give you a list of complaints, he or she isn't doing a proper job. Listen to the objections, evaluate them, and decide if it is worthwhile to overcome them. Now let me tell you what I have found to be some of the most appreciated home improvements during my time as an active real estate broker.

Buyer Motivation

Buyer motivation is hard to understand, but it is not so difficult to predict. Buyers fall into certain categories and patterns. In addition to my business activities, I am a wildlife photographer. When I want close-up photos of wild animals, I must learn their habits, their terrain preferences, and their subtle signals. Hunting animals with a camera is not all that different from selling houses. When I am reading buyers, I must look for their habits, location preferences, and subtle signals. If I do a good job of sizing up the prospects, present myself as a caring professional, and execute my actions carefully, I'm going to get a sale.

As a home seller, you must learn to look for buyer motivation. The improvements you make to your home must appeal to potential buyers. Investing money in an improvement few if any buyers will want is an expensive lesson in life.

Once you own a home, there is nothing you can do about its location. If the location is desirable, you are in luck. When the location is not very good, you've got a serious obstacle to overcome. You can't move the house, at least not practically. However, there are improvements that will entice buyers to settle for a mediocre location to get the house of their dreams. To know what these important improvements will be, you must know what the buyers want.

How are you going to know what local buyers want? You are going to research comparable sale records and survey the interested parties who don't buy your house.

If you are working with a broker who has access to a multiple-listing service, you can get the information you need quickly. The books furnished to brokers by these services contain detailed information on all current sales made by various brokerages that are members of the service. The information provided includes the asking and selling price of the homes, how long the homes were on the market, and what amenities the homes and grounds offered.

With this type of information it is easy to plot a course for successful improvements. Look for the houses in your area that sold quickly. Compare the amenities of those houses with the features your house has to offer. Then look at the closed sales that took a long time to get under contract. Look at the offering prices, the selling prices, and the number of days the house was on the market. Compare the slow-moving houses with the ones that sold quickly. Establish what the differences were between these houses. For example, see how many bathrooms each type of house had. Did the house have a garage? Was it attached or detached? Compare the sizes of the rooms in each house; the listings in the broker's book will give all this information and a lot more.

If you don't have access to the services offering multiple-listing information, the job will take longer, but you can still compile much of the information you will need. Tax records are open to public inspection, and these records provide a depth of material on the houses being taxed. Comparing tax records will be more time consuming than using a comparable-sales book, but it will get the job done.

The other way to check the pulse of the current market is with a survey of your prospective buyers. When potential buyers look at your home, they will be impressed favorably with some features, and they will no doubt find aspects of the home unappealing. You need to know why these people are not willing to buy your home. To find out, you will probably have to ask. Most buyers don't throw out negative comments to sellers. To get truthful input, you are going to have to ask the buyers what you want to know. It may help to tell them you are asking so that you can improve the desirability of your home. People are flattered when they feel their opinion is valuable to someone else. If you approach the issue properly, you should be able to build a list of objections quickly.

Once you have received a number of rejections, study the list of complaints. Look for similarities in the list. Did three out of ten people complain about the bathroom? How many people didn't like the small master bedroom? As your list grows, so will your ability to narrow your improvements to include only the ones wanted by the buying public. This method of projection is very effective, but it takes time. If you can't afford the time needed for this approach, find a broker with a comparable-sales book or head to the tax office.

Using these methods will help you to avoid a costly mistake. You will know what is motivating buyers. Armed with this information, you can invest your money in the most productive improvements.

Exterior Improvements

Exterior improvements are what first catch the eye of a buyer. You cannot afford to underrate the importance of curb appeal. If a buyer drives up to the front of your house and is unimpressed, the interior of the home will have to work overtime to secure a sale. First impressions are very important. If buyers approach a home with a bad attitude, making the sale is all but impossible. You want buyers to arrive at your home and say, "Wow!" You can achieve this result with the proper exterior improvements.

We have talked about a number of exterior improvements in getting to this point in the book. All of the improvements listed should help to sell your home, but some are better than others. That is what we are going to look at now. We are not going to consider the return on your investment. The goal in this section is to establish the improvements that are most likely to trigger a fast sale. Sales power is the only factor being used in this assessment of potential improvements.

House Numbers

House numbers allow buyers and brokers to find your home. If the house is hard to find, seekers become frustrated. Frustrated buyers are not likely to buy. Avoid confusion and frustration by making your home easy to identify and locate.

Shrubbery

Shrubbery should be trimmed and neat at all times. If you don't have foundation shrubs, get some. Bare foundations tend to be ugly, unless they are brick. If your house doesn't have an attractive transition from the lawn to the siding, add landscaping to improve the appearance. This is especially important on the front of the home, but ideally, the landscaping should surround the house.

Flowers

Flowers have an almost magical effect on most people. When prospective buyers approach a house appointed with beautiful flowers, the buyers often stop to admire the beauty of the living landscape. Some people will not respond one way or the other to flowers, but most buyers will notice and appreciate them. I've heard many buyers comment on how lovely the flowers were at various homes. Some of these buyers took the time to carefully inspect the flower beds.

For a smart broker, this type of interest from a buyer is fuel for the fire. When I see buyers stop to smell the roses, I have something to talk to them about. A topic that will help lower their defensive shields and improve my odds for a sale. All of this advantage is created by seeing what the buyers are interested in. In many cases flowers are a starting point for breaking the ice with conversation that is not threatening to the buyers.

Exterior Lighting

Exterior lighting is valuable from two distinct standpoints. The first is the light it provides. The second is the decorative value it lends to the exterior of a home.

Many buyers are active during the late afternoon and evening hours. They are not available to attend showings until they are off from work. During the winter months, this usually means seeing homes in the dark. Most of these buyers will come back in daylight if they are interested in buying a home, but they won't come back if they aren't impressed with what they find on the first visit. Exterior lighting plays a role in making the good first impression that will bring the buyers back.

It is tough for a broker to show a house when a flashlight must be depended upon for illumination. Effective outdoor lighting helps to solve this problem. Accent lighting can make a home look better at night than it would during the day. Exterior lighting offers sellers the opportunity to capture the attention of more buyers, if they will only use it.

When you have exterior lighting, it should be in working order. Buyers won't be pleased to find floodlights and walkway lights that don't work. Remember that the light fixtures you choose will be a part of your home. Don't try to save a few dollars on a fixture that may blemish your expensive home.

The Lawn

The lawn can be the most impressive aspect of your home's exterior. Your lawn should be cared for frequently while your house is on the market. Don't let the grass get too long. Trim around the walkway and landscaping barriers. Call in a lawn-care company to spice up the grass with that deep green look that only seems to come from professional lawn-care companies. The lawn should be made beautiful and maintained.

Refinish Your Deck

Refinish your deck if it is showing the wear of weather. Decks that have turned gray and weathered will intimidate some buyers. This group of buyers will assume the deck has outlived its usefulness and must be repaired or replaced. They won't see a job that can be done over the weekend for a cost of less than $250. They will see a major project that will involve contractors and possibly thousands of dollars.

Not all home buyers have the skill or inclination to be handy homeowners. They want to buy a house that doesn't need fixing. If you put off refinishing your deck, you could lose the sale of your home or have to settle for a reduced offer.

Decks are regarded as strong selling points, but if a deck is in disrepair, it is a liability. Refinish or repaint the wood as needed and check the railings. Loose railings devalue a deck in the minds of many buyers. If you have a deck, shine it up and use it as one of your aces.

Walkways

Buyers like to see houses with walkways. They consider walkways to be an enhancement that saves wear and tear on the lawn while guiding visitors to the door. Many buyers will be looking for homes in all types of weather. If there has been a heavy dew or a recent rain, grass will hold the moisture. When buyers walk through the grass, their shoes will get wet, and they will be self-conscious about tracking through the home. Walkways eliminate this problem.

Make sure your walkway is even and solid. Having a buyer trip over a loose brick or dance around on a wobbly stepping stone is no way to start a showing. Keep in mind that many of the ladies may be wearing high heels. Avoid walkway cracks that may trap their heels.

If ice or snow is a problem when showing your home, keep the walkway cleared. Apply sand or some other substance to the walkway to provide sure traction. Don't let ice consume the walkway and discourage buyers. If you have had to use sand or some similar substance, provide a reliable doormat to collect the particles picked up on the soles of shoes.

Exterior Painting

Exterior painting can be a considerable factor in the sale of your home. If your home's paint is cracked and peeling, buyers will shy away. They may still offer to buy your home, but they will use the deteriorating paint as an excuse to justify a lower sales price. Smart buyers will associate the peeling paint with moisture problems.

You should be conscious of any repairs needed to keep your house looking good. If you allow buyers to see the home in poor condition, you cannot expect to garner your best price. Don't take the attitude that buyers will want to change the color of the house anyway, so why paint it? Most buyers don't repaint the homes they acquire just to change the colors. If you pick a traditional color and paint your home, you will have better luck with buyers.

If you repaint your home, don't overlook painting the trim. Further, don't put off painting the gable ends because your ladder won't reach them. You are much better off to do nothing than to do a halfway job of painting.

Another factor to keep in mind is the lawn and shrubbery. Before you paint your house, protect these assets from paint spillage and splattering. Cover the shrubbery and adjacent lawn with protective cloths. If you allow paint to drip into your mulch, shrubbery, or lawn, you are sending a signal that screams of an amateur paint job. Buyers will notice this and question the quality of the paint work.

Your Front Door

Your front door says a lot about your house. Buyers almost always see the front door up close and personal. As they stand there, waiting for it to be opened, buyers will examine the door carefully, especially if it is flawed. The few moments between the time the doorbell is rung and the door is answered can have an effect on what the buyers are thinking when they enter the home.

If the front door has seen too many sunny days, it will be faded and dull. When a door is peeling from the effects of moisture, concern will rise in the mind of consumers. Pieces of weatherstripping sticking out from the edges of the door will raise suspicions of a house that is hard to heat and cool. If the glazing around the glass in the door is cracked or missing, more questions will swirl around air infiltration. If buyers enter the home with built-in concerns, the odds for a quick sale worsen. Take these concerns away by replacing the old door with a new one.

I don't believe you need to invest a huge amount of money in your replacement door. People do like expensive doors, but they are generally content with a practical door that is in good condition.

Your Driveway

Keep your driveway in good shape. Whether this means sealing your paved drive or topping your gravel drive with a new layer of stone, do it. Buyers do pay attention to driveways and parking areas. If these surfaces are in bad shape, buyers will start their tour of your home with less than perfect thoughts.

Interior Improvements

Interior improvements pick up where exterior improvements leave off. Exterior improvements are needed to attract the attention of buyers and to get them inside. Interior improvements are meant to hold that attention and impress the buyers to the point where they must have your home. Let me share my experience of some of the most important interior improvements with you.

Neat and Orderly

Keeping your home neat and orderly should be a prime consideration. When you are trying to sell your home, you want it to look its best. Clutter is not only annoying to live with, it can kill a deal before the negotiations begin.

Don't leave dirty laundry in a pile on the floor, and don't hide it in a closet. Buyers open closet doors, and they don't like having dirty laundry jump out at them when they do. This may seem like common sense, but a lot of sellers fail the dirty laundry test. If you don't own a laundry hamper, buy one.

Avoid leaving dirty dishes in the kitchen sink. This is another fault many sellers suffer from. Even if you have an automatic dishwasher, don't leave it loaded with dirty dishes. The out-of-sight-out-of-mind approach will not work. Buyers will invariably open the dishwasher. When they do, they should see a clean appliance, not dirty dishes.

Keep the house free of clutter. Trying to walk over and around toys and unused exercise equipment takes all the fun out of house hunting. Clear and clean the rooms of your house to make them appear larger. Keeping your home organized doesn't require a cash investment, but it is a giant step in the fast sale of your home.

Patch Those Holes

Patch those holes you have been living with for years; you've put it off long enough. Holes in the walls and ceilings of homes, even small ones, scare some buyers. Even when they don't frighten a buyer, they lend justification for a low offer. If patching the holes will require you to paint the room, paint it. Get rid of the holes, and don't give buyers anything to complain about.

Clean, Clean, and Clean Some More

Before you open your house to buyers, clean, clean, and clean some more. A clean house that smells good will attract and hold buyers better than one that is grungy. You must make buyers feel at home if you expect them to buy your house. Having a clean home will help put buyers at ease.

If you looked in a bathroom and saw mildew growing on the shower curtain, caulking around the lavatory that was stained black with lack of attention, and an unremovable ring around the toilet bowl, would you want to spend hard-earned money to buy the bathroom? I doubt it, and neither will most other buyers. Bathrooms rank high on most buyers' priority lists. If you want to pass inspection, make sure the room is clean and bright.

Shampoo your carpets, wax your wood floors, and clean your vinyl floors. Pay attention to detail, the buyers will. Clean your kitchen appliances and wash your windows. Pretend you are living in rental property and will lose your security deposit if the place doesn't sparkle. There is a lot more money at stake than a security deposit, so take the job seriously.

Plumbing

Don't ignore any plumbing problems. Repair faulty faucets and replace them if necessary. Buyers are almost always concerned about the condition of the plumbing. They know plumbing repairs can be expensive, and many buyers don't have any desire to play plumber on weekends.

If your plumbing fixtures are stained and won't clean up, give some serious thought to replacing them. Plumbing fixtures are items associated with health and hygiene; if they are unattractive, buyers will be repelled.

Electrical

The electrical panel is usually on the list of questions brought with buyers. If your entrance panel is an old fuse box, give serious consideration to having it upgraded to circuit breakers. When buyers see old fuse boxes and small electrical services, they anticipate the costs required to replace them. You can expect the price you are offered to be lowered by enough to cover the cost of the conversion, if an offer is made at all.

Closets

Closets are critical in the sale of a home. Everyone wants more closet space than they need. If your home is restricted by minimal closet space, find a way to add some. Obviously, every bedroom should have a closet. Linen closets are nice, but if you don't have one, you can make up for it with add-on cabinetry in the bathroom. A closet near the main entrance to your home should be a standard feature. If it is not, look for a way to add this needed closet. There is usually enough wall space within the area to allow the construction of this type of closet.

Any additional closet space you can come up with will be appreciated. If you have a two-story home, you might be able to tuck a closet in under the steps. If this space is not being used for a powder room or for a stairway to a lower level, there should be plenty of opportunity for good storage space.

A pantry closet in the kitchen area will go over well with buyers. Framing up this type of closet is often possible and relatively inexpensive. The creative use of space and accessories can make the pantry one of the focal points of your home.

In general, the more closets you have, the more desirable your house will be. I know we are not supposed to be talking return on investment in this chapter, but closets will almost always return their cost in increased value and appeal.

Cabinets

Cabinets are much like closets. People like a lot of them. Adding a vanity to your bathroom will allow space for the new owners to store their personal effects and towels. Wall cabinets in the bathroom provide secure storage for medicines and toiletries.

In the kitchen, cabinets are the main feature. A kitchen without cabinets is like a lake without water. It's there, but it's not very usable. Buyers expect a kitchen to be fitted with both base and wall cabinets.

If your kitchen cabinets don't show well, you should either reface or replace them. The money will be well spent and the result should be a quicker sale.

When you have the space, adding cabinets in your kitchen will increase its attraction. Island cabinets are very popular, and so are broom and pantry cabinets. If you are going to remodel any room in your house, renovate the kitchen.

Shower Doors

Shower doors are not very expensive, but they do add to the value of a bathroom. There is no comparison between the effect of shower curtains and shower doors. Doors win the race hands down. Not many buyers will sit around and jot shower doors down on their have-to-have list, but the presence of the doors will be noted and appreciated.

Garage Door Openers

Garage door openers have become so common that buyers expect garages to be equipped with them. If you are still raising and lowering your garage door manually, it is time you bought a electric door opener. This is another improvement that most buyers won't have on the have-to-have list, but if you don't offer them a garage door opener, they may not offer to buy your house.

Dishwashers

Automatic dishwashers are to today's buyers what refrigerators were to buyers years ago. The dishwasher has become a standard feature in most homes. For many of today's buyers, a house without a dishwasher is like a house without a television: it just won't do. When conditions allow it, you should install a dishwasher. This is one appliance many buyers will no longer do without.

The Big Improvements

The big improvements are understandably the most difficult to decide upon. These projects require substantial money, and they can be a sizable risk. Sellers are naturally nervous about investing $10,000 in homes they hope to sell quickly. There is no question that the big-money improvements can be risky, and they should be dealt with in caution. However, the reward can be much greater than the risk.

You've been told how to reduce the risk of big improvements with thorough research. You know that the improvement that pays big dividends in one neighborhood may fail terribly in another. In my discussion here we are going to look at big improvements that buyers like. The improvements may not be right for your home, but they are very popular with a cross-section of generic buyers. Let's see what they are.

Decks

Decks are very popular with modern buyers. Decks are used for cooking out, lying in the sun, and socializing. A house doesn't have to have a deck to appeal to buyers, but adding a deck will swing some extra buyers in your direction.

How big should the deck be? Well, you learned earlier about the sizes that maximize your investment. As for sales power, the deck should have at least 150 square feet of space. Anything smaller will limit its use. If you have a large building lot, a bigger deck can be advantageous. Again, looking at it from a sales perspective, large decks with multiple levels and built-in seats will draw a lot of attention. Building a deck with multiple levels and unusual angles will run up the cost of construction, but it will also increase the interest of buyers.

Painted wood or pressure-treated lumber, which should you use? Most buyers will want the deck constructed of pressure-treated lumber. There will be a few people who will dislike the greenish tint of the pressure-treated wood, but by and large the longer-lasting wood will be favored.

What type of railing should you use? Railings that incorporate the use of vertical pickets and a drink rail are the most popular. Horizontal slat-type rails are acceptable, but the vertical pickets appeal to more people. The drink rail is almost mandatory. Having a deck with a narrow rail that will not support a drink is not good.

Most decks are built on pier foundations. Pier foundations are fine, but they should be enclosed with pressure-treated lattice. The lattice will conceal the piers and underside of the deck, giving a more finished and professional appearance. If the deck has enough height between its floor joists and the ground, you might want to build a door into the lattice work. This will allow for the storage of such items as a garden hose.

Decks can get very expensive. You will be wise to build only as much deck as you need to make your house desirable. If you have limited space in your yard, don't overpower it with a large deck. The deck size should compliment the home, not overshadow it.

Sunrooms

Sunrooms are a luxury many homeowners will not pay to add to their home, but if they can get it when they buy the home, they will love it. There are many ways to use sunrooms to make your house more salable.

Sunrooms don't have to be large to make a big impression. Let me give you an example of how a small sunroom can make a big difference in your home.

In our example assume you have a country kitchen where the kitchen flows into the informal dining area. The kitchen is well appointed with cabinets and space, but it tends to be dark. You have a single window in the kitchen and the dining area has a glass terrace door. The natural lighting is average, but not great.

The work space in the kitchen is large, but the breakfast bar between the kitchen and the dining area makes a table and chairs arrangement crowded. Having the exterior door in one wall of the dining area adds to the space restrictions for furniture. All in all, the setup is pleasant and functional, but it is not always comfortable. You want to improve the area, but you don't know what to do.

Consider this option. Suppose you removed most of the exterior wall holding the door in the dining area and expanding the room outward. This would certainly solve your space problem. Of course, you will still need the door, but it can be installed in one of the new side walls you will be building.

Now take the plan a step further. Consider making the back wall a wall of glass. Maybe you will even use the curved greenhouse sections that are so popular to give you a glass wall and a glass ceiling. Can you image what a difference this type of improvement would make to your home? Not only would your dining area be larger, the whole area would be filled with natural light, adding to the spacious feeling. All of a sudden, you would have a different house. A house where you could take your meals under the stars or with the rising sun. In summer, the extra ventilation would be welcome, and if the exposure is right, the warming rays of the sun will be comforting in winter.

This type of sunroom addition wouldn't be cheap, but it would probably be well worth the investment. The chances are that you could keep the additional space to a minimum. Adding 6' to the dining area with glass walls would make it feel immense. The cost would be manageable, and a quick sale would be more likely.

Even if all you did was rework the exterior wall to accommodate the glass panels, you would derive a new and desirable look, not to mention considerably more light. Sunrooms aren't always a solid investment in terms of their rate of return, but they are hard to beat as a sales feature.

Adding a Bathroom

Adding a bathroom when your home has less than two full baths is usually a good idea. One of the most effective places to put the extra bathroom is in or adjoining the master bedroom. Most production homes that have only one bathroom have them in the hallway. This makes sense; you wouldn't want guests and children running through your bedroom to get to the bathroom.

A lot of two-story homes have a full bath in the upstairs hallway and a half-bath on the main floor. The powder room is usually tucked under the stairs or placed to be convenient to the living room. Houses like this are functional, but having an extra bath to serve the master bedroom is very desirable. The need for this additional bathroom increases when both spouses work outside the home and when children share the primary bathroom.

Even if the bath added to the master suite is only a half-bath, it increases the usability of the home. Finding adequate space to install a full bath can be troublesome, but powder rooms don't require much space. If you've got a spot with dimensions of about 30" x 60", you've got potential for a powder room. Adding a bathroom is a major expense, but if your home needs it, it is a sound investment.

Garages

Garages are one amenity many buyers ask about before ever going to see a house. When a broker sits down in the office with clients, the broker prequalifies them and asks what type of homes they wish to see. Some buyers are in the early stage of their house hunting and don't know what they want. Serious buyers usually give specific details of what they want in a house. A good broker will do much of the sales work before ever leaving the office, and will know what the buyers want, where they want it, how much they can pay for it, and what turns them on.

When a buyer wants a house with a garage, it would be a stupid broker who would waste time showing houses without garages. Most brokers don't spend hours riding customers all over town in search of a house. They punch pertinent data into their computers and retrieve listing information on the houses for sale that meet the search criteria.

If one of the search requirements is a two-car garage, your house will never make it to the list of houses to be seen if it doesn't have a garage.

Not everyone demands a garage, but a lot of people do. If you have the space to accommodate a garage, it will give you an edge against homes without garages.

Room Additions

Room additions can be very expensive. It would not be unusual to pay a general contractor $25,000 for a modest room addition. The cost for these big improvements makes them a high risk. You could easily price your house right out of the market with a major addition.

Buyers want houses with enough space in them. But you may not be able to add space to your house without running the price up too high. If you are going to build a room addition, be careful to make your decision only after exhaustive research and a before-and-after appraisal.

Buyers don't look for houses with recent additions. They look for houses with certain features and rooms. For example, a buyer may specify a desire for a formal dining room, but won't care if you've just added the room or if it is the same age as the rest of the house. The buyer simply wants a formal dining room. However, this buyer isn't going to pay a lot more for your house just because it has a new dining room and the house down the street has an older dining room. To the buyer, a dining room is a dining room.

When you think of building an addition, think of what its specific purpose will be. Will it be an extra bedroom or an exercise room? Will the addition be a family room that allows you to dress your present living room up as a formal living room? Most important, be certain the neighborhood and market conditions will support your improvement.

Trigger Points

When you are thinking about home improvements that will help sell your house, think about trigger points. Trigger points are the features and benefits an experienced broker will use to sell your house. These key elements of your home are what will be advertised and pitched heavily to prospective buyers. When you are making home improvements, you want the improvements to make good trigger points. To make this a little clearer, let me expound on how trigger points will be used by an experienced broker.

Energy Issues

Energy issues are currently popular trigger points. Any improvements that increase the efficiency of your home's heating and cooling costs will be trigger points. Examples include storm windows, storm doors, extra insulation, replacement windows, new exterior doors, new heating and cooling systems, and so on.

The cost of heating and cooling a home will always have the potential to sway a buyer. If the buyer is looking at two similar houses where the only major difference is in the utility expenses, the house with the lowest utility costs will be favored.

Good brokers will play up the energy savings. They will tell the buyers how much the extra insulation is worth in the long run. They will point out the replacement windows and demonstrate their ease of operation and energy rating. The advertisements for the house will normally mention its energy efficiency.

Toys

Even grown-ups like their toys. In the case of real estate the toys might be spas, whirlpool tubs, saunas, or even a greenhouse. This type of improvement is often hard to justify in the sales price, but it could be the factor that prods a buyer into action.

Brokers know how much people want to have a little luxury in their lives. If you install a spa, you can bet the broker will use it as a trigger point.

Decorations

Decorations can become trigger points. Adding fake beams to a ceiling can give the broker a trigger point to work with. The ad will read: Large family room with exposed beams and ceiling fan. . . . This type of description in the advertising is what makes the phone ring.

People want four bedrooms and two and a half bathrooms, but that is rarely what makes them call. It is the colorful words describing the trigger points of a home that catch most of the attention. Take a moment to read the two mock advertisements below:

For Sale: Three-bedroom ranch in nice neighborhood. One and one-half baths, living room, eat-in kitchen, and sun deck. Large lot on the corner of a quiet street. Good schools, close to shopping, and motivated seller. Call Roger at 555-5555 to see this traditional home.

For Sale: Ranch-style home with fireplace in master bedroom. Hardwood floors, large country kitchen, vaulted ceiling in the dining area with exposed beams, skylights, and ceiling fan. The three bedrooms and one-and-a-half baths are tastefully decorated and recently remodeled. The energy package on this home is outstanding. Outside, the grounds are mesmerizing. There will be no need for a stroll in the park when you own this home; you will have your own private park in the backyard, complete with deck. Priced to sell. Call Roger at 555-5555 for details too numerous to mention in this limited space.

Well, which ad would you respond to? The first ad gives the facts needed to find a three-bedroom home with one-and-a-half baths. The second ad covers the necessary basics and is liberally sprinkled with trigger points. These ads show what a difference the right improvements can make in the sale of your home.

You can't sell your house without willing buyers, and you can't attract willing buyers without the right bait. When you plan your improvements, envision how they will look in your advertisements. Look for improvements that will stop readers in their tracks and make them call for a closer look at what you have to offer.

Once you've got the prospect in your home, you are way ahead of the competition. If you have chosen your improvements and broker wisely, you should get a sale very soon.

Chapter 12

Strategies for a Successful Showing

Experienced brokers know various strategies for a successful showing. They know the importance of furniture placement, how to showcase desirable features, and how to camouflage less desirable features. This knowledge serves them well in selling homes.

Inexperienced sales agents and homeowners don't have the years of experience to pull from in creating a highly successful showing. If they did, they would sell more houses in less time. Since you are probably one of these homeowners, you may need some help in staging a successful showing.

Even if you will be listing your home with a reputable brokerage, you may have to plan your own showing. No, I don't mean you will have to show your own home, but you may have to take care of the preliminary details that will make the showing go better. That's what this chapter is all about. You are going to learn the strategies used by top brokers to close more deals.

Showcase It

If you want to sell your house fast and for a good price, showcase it. At any given time there are a lot of houses available for purchase. There are also scads of people looking to buy them. The key is getting the right person interested in your home. To a large extent this is a numbers game. The more people you show your house to, the better your chances for a sale.

Inexperienced brokers often fall into the trap of the numbers game. They are taught how important it is to roll people through as many houses as possible, hoping they will stumble onto a sale. Since their trainers tell them to work by the numbers, they usually do, and they do have a sale fall into their lap now and then.

I know the real estate business is a numbers game, but I prefer to thin the numbers down. Inexperienced brokers, in my opinion, show houses, they don't sell them. They are little more than tour guides, waiting to take an offer from their customer, if the customer decides to make one. This behavior has always concerned me. I don't operate that way. It isn't fair to the sellers that the brokers are working for.

When you sign an exclusive listing with a broker to sell your house, the broker should try to sell your house, not just show it as one of 20 houses on the list for the weekend. A seasoned broker isn't going to want to waste time driving from house to house, but will want to limit the number of showings to keep from confusing the buyers. When buyers see too many homes, they lose track of which house had what feature. This means repeat showings and more time spent on the road.

Experienced brokers will try to make a sale before they have shown ten houses. In contrast, an inexperienced broker might show their buyers 30 homes and still never move in for a close. Sales is a tough business, and to be successful at it you have to be willing to take the lead. While you, as the homeowner, may not be selling your own home, you still may have to take the first steps toward getting a fast sale.

Not all brokers are going to have the knowledge to tell you how to make your house more appealing to buyers. These brokers probably will have a general idea of how to use trigger points, but they will not have learned how to stage a successful showing. Remember, they may be doing nothing more than running buyers through your house on their way to many others. If you have to deal with these circumstances, you must take action to stop the buyers from going to the next house.

The most effective way to make a sale without the benefit of a skilled salesperson is to showcase your home. Make buyers want to buy it. If the house is properly prepared, someone will ask their sales agent to stop and write up an offer. Even a rookie agent will understand if a buyer wants to make an offer on the home.

Assuming you have listed your house with a broker, you are not supposed to be involved directly with the selling of your home. You stay out of the way and let the broker do this job. This is the way it is supposed to work, and oftentimes it does. However, anything that you do to help the agent, short of talking to prospective buyers, will assist in getting the house sold quicker.

Your part of the job, while you are acting as the agent's silent partner, is to prepare the house. Give the agent as much to work with as possible. You've already read about the importance of keeping the house clean and organized. Now you are going to learn specifically how to showcase your home and your improvements.

Strategic Furniture Placement

Strategic furniture placement can go a long way toward achieving a successful showing. Most sellers and brokers don't give much thought to furniture placement. Sellers have lived in the home with the furniture where it is and have no plans to rearrange it. Average brokers come into the home to discuss listing it for sale and accept the listing under almost any terms. They are so concerned with getting an active listing that they don't worry about the furniture.

After the listing is signed and the sales effort begins, agents who are new to the business either don't know about the importance of furniture placement or are unsure of how to tell the seller their furniture should be moved. Consequently, the furniture doesn't get moved and the problem remains.

There are multiple reasons for paying attention to furniture placement. The first reason is confined movement. If buyers and brokers have to weave their way around furniture, they will spend more time watching their steps than admiring your home. If you have furniture placed in a way that doesn't allow freedom of movement, get rid of it. Either relocate it within the house, or if necessary, place it in storage.

Massive furniture can consume a room. If the furniture is too big or too numerous, it can visually shrink the size of the room. Let's take a bedroom as an example. The bedroom is on the small side, about 10' x 10'. There is a closet that takes a bite out of the room, and then there is the furniture.

The furniture consists of one queen-size bed, one dresser—with mirror, one chest of drawers, a fish aquarium—and its stand, two bedside tables, and a hope chest at the end of the bed.

When buyers come down the hall and stick their heads into this bedroom, they aren't going to go in; there won't be enough room to make them comfortable. People, in general, get nervous when walking through a stranger's home. They get particularly edgy when in the bathrooms and bedrooms. If these rooms are filled with furniture to the point where walking around is difficult, buyers will often take a quick look and move on. This gives the broker no chance to point out good features or to hold the buyers' interest.

In the case of this particular bedroom there are some ways to make it more inviting. Without major renovations, you can't make the room bigger, but you can make it feel more spacious. Let me tell you what I, as your broker, would advise you to do.

I would have you move the fish aquarium, one of the bedside tables, and the hope chest. None of these items are essential to the bedroom. Once the bedside table was removed, I would ask you to slide the bed into the space the table occupied, until the bed touched the wall. I would assess the placement of the drawers and dresser and have you put one of them on the wall with the door. That way, when someone looked through the door, they would see only the one piece of large furniture and the bed. They would, of course, see the other piece of furniture when they entered the room, but by that time I've at least got them in the room.

If you followed my suggestions, the room would open up and appear larger. As for the items being relocated, the fish tank could go in the family room, the table could go in the basement or attic, and the hope chest might be put into storage temporarily.

On the surface, it may not seem like such a minor rearrangement would make a difference but it will. There will be more wall space and flooring visible in the room. By removing the items suggested, there will be less to distract a buyer. All in all, you will be making the room look bigger and be giving the salesperson more to work with.

The Effects of Lighting

The effects of lighting play a big role in a successful showing. Walking up to a dark house after dark can be a little scary. Even though buyers are with a broker, they often become a little unsure of themselves when approaching a dark house. Give the house some light and the buyers are uninhibited.

Walkway lights and floodlights do a good job of getting people to the front door. Attractive lighting beside the door illuminates the steps and provides comfort while buyers are waiting for the door to be opened. Once inside the home, light can make the difference between feeling that you are in a dark, dreary box or a spacious, pretty home.

When your house is being shown at night or on cloudy days, turn on all the lights in the house. If the house is being toured during a sunny day, open the curtains and drapes to let natural light flood the home. Dark rooms hurt the sale of your home. Buyers want to see bright, cheerful space that they can call home.

If you have an accessible attic or basement, have those lights on as well. If buyers are interested in your home, they will want to see every aspect of it.

Having all the lights on will also make the showing easier for your sales agent. Since the agent may not know where all the switches are, you save time and possible embarrassment for the broker by having the lights already turned on. Further, the agent will not have to stop in the middle of a sales pitch or probing question to fumble for the light switch.

Mood Enhancement

You can use mood enhancement techniques to encourage buyers to stay in your home. Brokers want to keep buyers in the house as long as possible. They know that the longer the buyers are in the home, the better the chances are for a solid sale. Good brokers know the sales maneuvers to accomplish their goals, but you can help.

What is mood enhancement? Mood enhancement could be as simple as having the air conditioning on when it's a hot day outside. The cool, refreshing haven created by your home's air conditioning might be enough to encourage the buyers to sit down on the couch and talk with the broker. When good brokers get the opportunity to talk, they take the opportunity to sell.

There are many forms of mood enhancement. Remember earlier in the book when we talked about bird feeders? Bird feeders can contribute to mood enhancement. If the buying couple is standing in the kitchen admiring the birds and squirrels outside, they are more likely to linger in your home. The activity of the wildlife is a bit of a distraction, but it is a good distraction.

Can you remember how your first new car smelled? It smelled great, didn't it? Do you remember how, as a kid, you would come into the house and smell your grandmother's special recipes cooking? There was probably an unmistakable aroma to her cooking. Our noses tell us a lot about the world we live in. They tell us when we are around a comforting place, like our grandmother's. Our noses warn us of dangerous fumes, like gasoline. We depend on our sense of smell for many purposes. Knowing this, you can appeal to the sense of smell your buyers will be using.

Smells in the home can send different signals, some good—some bad. Nonsmokers who walk into a house that is smoked in daily will quickly distinguish the odor. People who walk into a house that contains a cat's litter box will have little trouble noticing the smell. Some people have very sensitive noses. They can walk through the front door and smell a dog's presence, last night's burned supper, and the contents of the garbage cans out in the garage. These are not the types of smells you want your buyers to associate your house with.

If it is cool weather, you might build a fire in the fireplace. This type of mood enhancement hits the sense of smell and has a visual impact. The faint aroma of wood smoke is very pleasing to most people, and seeing the flames flicker behind the glass doors of the fireplace can take a person to another time and place.

If you like to bake, consider making a pie on the day of a showing. The smell of a fresh apple pie radiating from the kitchen is sure to make people feel more at home.

There are many commercial scents and products available to help make your house smell better. Most of these are good sales tools, but avoid creating smells that are too thick, too sweet, or too strong. You should strive to create a faint, natural aroma, not an overpowering smell that might offend some sensitive noses.

Setting a bowl of potpourri on the table can give your house the smell of freshness. Placing cedar shavings in your closets can make the closets smell clean and outdoorsy. While we are on the subject of closets, if you use mothballs regularly, get rid of them while the house is being sold. Mothballs are not a favored smell, and they indicate pest problems that buyers don't want.

When you vacuum your carpets, and you should vacuum prior to each showing, use one of the many carpet deodorizers. These shake-on cleaners leave behind pleasant fragrances that rise from the carpeting.

Cats are neat pets, but their litter boxes often permeate the house with telltale odors. Buyers, even cat lovers, don't like the smell of a soiled litter box. I'm not suggesting that you get rid of Fluffy, but clean the box daily, and control the odor with air fresheners.

If you have pets in your home, check the furniture for hair. Not only is pet hair annoying when it gets on your good clothes, some people are allergic to it. Clean all the visible hair from the furniture, and try to limit the range of your animal while the house is for sale. Never, and I mean never, leave the pet loose with the run of the house when the home is being shown. The pet may be let out of the house accidentally, or it may sabotage the showing. Make arrangements with your broker for how and where you will confine the animal during the inspection.

Music can be a powerful mood enhancer. Choose a selection of music that is soft and relaxing, and have it playing during the showing. Stores use music to encourage people to spend money, you might as well do it, too.

Don't be washing or drying clothes or dishes in your automatic appliances when the house is shown. The noise from the appliances is not conducive to making a sale, and the buyers may want to inspect the appliances.

Keep you heating and cooling system set at comfortable temperatures for your showings. Many people conserve energy while they are at work by keeping the system at minimal operation. This is fine most of the time, but not when your house is being shown. The inside climate should be comfortable for the buyers. They may only be in the house 20 minutes, but it could be a very important 20 minutes.

Mood enhancement can mean the difference between a quick once-over and a lingering look. Give your broker all the help you can by creating an atmosphere that buyers will want to remain in.

Smart Traffic Patterns

Experienced brokers know the value of smart traffic patterns. They know that the order in which a house is shown can affect the way a buyer perceives it. As the homeowner, you should communicate with your broker and establish the showing pattern. You may have to relocate some furniture, and you might want to rearrange the art hanging on your walls, but make the traffic pattern perfect.

To get a real feel for what buyers will see, and the order they will see it in, ask your broker to walk you through the house, just as if you were a buyer. If you are selling your home, there is a good chance you have started looking at other homes. Take the time to look at your house with the same watchful eye you have applied to the homes you are considering purchasing. If you will do this, you may be surprised at the results.

Like anything you are around on a constant basis, you take your house for granted. You have become accustomed to things that strangers will notice. To show you what I mean, let's take a quick tour of a home that needs some work on its traffic pattern.

You are the buyer, and I am your broker. I've asked the home seller to make some changes, but these requests have been ignored. You are about to see the house for the first time. We ring the doorbell, and Mr. Seller opens the door.

We have just encountered our first showing mistake. Mr. Seller should have gone for a walk while we viewed the home, but he didn't. Now you will have to go through the house feeling as if the homeowner is watching over your shoulder. You won't feel comfortable making verbal comments to your spouse, so I won't be able to read your reactions to the house as well.

Mr. Seller greets us and then sits in his favorite reading chair while we tour the home. The front door opened into the living room, so we start the tour in the living room, with Mr. Sellers reading his book.

I point out the fireplace, the bay window, the textured ceiling, and the plush carpeting. Most of the showing is being done from where we stand at the slate entry. I would like to walk you over to the fireplace, but Mr. Seller's big chair and ottoman consume much of the open floor space, and the couch and coffee table take up the remaining floor area. To get you to the fireplace, we would have to weave through the furniture, pass in front of Mr. Seller, and huddle in the limited space available for walking and standing.

The mantle over the fireplace supports the trophies of Mr. Seller's daughter's athletic accomplishments. They are treasured trophies, but they clutter the mantle and hide the deep cherry wood that would be so pretty. Wanting to get away from the presence of the owner, I move you through the cased opening, into the hallway.

The hall has hardwood floors that I comment on. As you look down the hall, toward the bedrooms and bathroom, you notice that the hall is dark. There is only one light in the ceiling of the hall, and there is a dark, walnut washstand at the end of the hall. Your husband notices that there is no smoke detector in the hall ceiling.

I move you across the hall into the dining room. The room has a large table surrounded by big chairs. The china hutch is large enough that its sharp corner angles toward the corner of the table, creating a narrow passage for us to squeeze through. The area rug under the table is a dark brown, and the brown drapes covering the sliding glass door are closed. The dining room is dark and dismal.

As we move through the dining room and into the kitchen, you are pleased with the open design. There is plenty of counter space and the cabinets are abundant and in good condition. The appliances are not new, but they are clean and acceptable. The stainless-steel sink has two bowls and a single-handle faucet. So far the kitchen is making a good impression.

Your husband opens the doors beneath the sink to inspect the plumbing. Unfortunately, he can barely see the plumbing for all the cleaning solutions and clutter. You walk over to the kitchen window and notice it doesn't have a screen on the outside. This disappoints you, because you like to open your kitchen window when cooking, but without a screen, bugs will be a problem.

As you open the drawers and cabinet doors, Mr. Seller comes in to get a fresh cup of coffee. The moment is broken and you are ready to move on to the bedrooms. Mr. Seller doesn't realize it, but he has just destroyed the makings of a sale. We leave Mr. Seller at the coffee pot and squeeze back through the dining room.

As we start down the hall, we come to the bathroom. I reach in and cut on the light. It should have been on, but Mr. Seller doesn't like to waste electricity. The curtains are closed, and the bathroom is about as cheerful as a rainy day at a picnic. There is a roll of toilet paper sitting on the toilet tank. It has been kept there ever since the bar that fits in the standard holder was misplaced. The vanity is covered with a tube of toothpaste, a water glass, makeup, and miscellaneous personal items.

The shower curtain is pulled back and the toilet seat is up. The door on the linen closet has swollen with moisture and is hard to operate. There is a trace of mildew growing on the ceiling over the bathtub. You and your husband are quick to move on, and there isn't much I can say to change your mind.

We journey down the hall and inspect the three bedrooms. The inspection is little more than a glance. You've made up your mind this is not your dream home, and I can read it from your body language. Few words are exchanged in the house as we move for the exit. I thank Mr. Seller, and we all go out to my car.

This showing was a mild disaster. It got off on the wrong foot with the seller being in the house, and it continued to go downhill. The one bright spot was tarnished by the homeowner's interruption. The furniture placement was terrible, and the bathroom was appalling. The few good features to point out in the living room were all but inaccessible. I suppose it could have been worse. Mr. Seller could have been filling the house with a cloud of cigar smoke while his dog jumped on us for attention.

This type of showing isn't going to sell a house. When you do your mock walk-through with your broker, you will notice these types of problems. While the narrow passage at the dining room may not be a concern to you as an individual, when you, your spouse, and your broker try to get through the opening, you will realize quickly how difficult it can be.

Maybe you've been setting the toilet paper on the tank for so long you have grown accustomed to it. Having your broker put on the sales pitch and tour for you should open your eyes. How is the broker going to explain the missing tube on the toilet-paper holder? When the broker comments about the cultured marble top of your vanity, you are sure to see the clutter. When he or she starts making excuses for the mildew, you will recognize it and, hopefully, correct the problem.

This type of mock walk-through is good for both you and the broker. It gives the broker an opportunity to point out problems without being blunt about it. Instead of sitting at your dining room table and telling you that you should clean out the cabinet under your sink, the broker can open the cabinet to allow you to inspect the plumbing. You may never have thought buyers would be looking in the cabinet. By the broker opening the doors and commenting on the plumbing, you are sure to notice the problem.

The broker is going to want to control the customers. He or she will want them to see the rooms of your house in a specific order and may even want to position furniture in a way to turn buyers in the right direction at various points of the home.

Listen to your broker, the sales professional. If you are putting your house in a broker's hands to sell, let him or her do this job as the sales professional. Provide all the assistance you can, and then stay out of the way. Traffic patterns should be laid out and inspected in advance. If they are, your showing should go smoothly.

How to Highlight Desirable Features

Do you know how to highlight desirable features? If you don't, you should learn how to do it before putting your house up for sale. This is true for all sellers, but it is especially true if you have just spent money on new improvements.

You can be subtle in your highlighting or you can be aggressive. Usually, a little of each is a good approach. Let's talk about the aggressive method first.

Aggressive Highlighting

Aggressive highlighting of your home's special features is easy and effective. When your house is ready for showing, there should be property-data sheets made up. Usually, the broker will take care of this for you. But if your broker is a little slow in getting things done, do it yourself.

The property-data sheet is just a piece of paper that details the facts and features concerning your home. The sheet will list the number of bedrooms, the number of bathrooms, the dimensions of all rooms, and so on. The sheet should also include the address of the property, your broker's name and phone number, and a picture of your house.

Once the basic sheet is completed, you can add the list of goodies. The bottom of the sheet should have room for listing all of your home's best features. This is where you will write in items like ceiling fan in foyer, fireplace in master bedroom, whirlpool tub in master bath, and so on.

When you have the form finished, make several copies of it. These copies will be given to each prospect that tours your home. Before handing out the fact sheets, take a fluorescent marker and highlight the special features. Be selective, if you highlight all of the features, the sheet will lose some of its effectiveness. Only highlight the features that set your house apart from the competition. Place the sheets on a small table by the door the prospects will be entering your home through. A small index card propped up asking the visitors to "take one" will be helpful.

These data sheets will give the prospects something to remember your house by. Placing a few pencils on the table will enable the visitors to make notes as they tour your home. The highlighted features will stand out on the sheet and ensure that the potential buyers don't miss seeing them.

Have you ever gone to a model home where a builder was soliciting buyers? If you have, you have probably seen small signs providing information about various features in the home. For example, the kitchen sink may have had a card next to it saying, "Equipped with 1/2 hp garbage disposer." This sign told you in an instant that the sink had a disposer. Without the sign, you might not have noticed the disposer.

These little signs do a big job. They draw buyers' attention to special features and invite them to look further. For instance, there might be a sign on the garage door opener that says, "Try Me." This is an open invitation for you to flip the switch. Without the sign, a buyer might be hesitant to operate the automatic opener, but the sign tells the buyer it is all right.

These signs not only point out desirable features, they get the buyer involved in the house. When that buyer flips the switch, this is taking one step closer to an offer on the home.

While it is not common to find these prompter signs in older homes being offered for sale, there is no reason they shouldn't be used. They work for builders and they can work for you. You can use index cards to write your own messages to interested buyers. The cards will make the salesperson's job easier, and they will make the buyers more comfortable when trying out your home.

Subtle Highlighting

Subtle highlighting is not as easy as aggressive highlighting, but it is very effective, especially if you coordinate your plans with your broker. When you opt for subtle highlighting, you will have to be creative in drawing the attention of buyers to specific features. Some features require more creative thought than others. Let's look at some of the improvements we have discussed along the way and see how you might highlight them.

Bathroom Accessories

Bathroom accessories are not the type of improvement you are likely to list on a property-data sheet, but they can add to the overall impression of the bathroom. It's doubtful you will want to stick a sign on your towel rack to let buyers know it is new, but you do want them to notice it. How are you going to go about this job?

First, replace the original toilet paper tube with one of the tubes that freshen the air each time they are rolled around. Before you leave the house to allow for the showing, roll the paper around to activate the air freshener. Just the scent alone might draw attention to the richly grained oak paper holder. Choose a toilet paper with a colored design that blends with your room. The design on the paper could attract some subtle attention.

Hang a colorful towel on the towel rack or ring. Make it clear to all occupants of the home that this towel is for show only and is not to be used. The splash of color from the towel is likely to direct a buyer's eyes to your new towel holder.

If you recently installed glass doors on your shower, drape a pretty towel, maybe one with a duck or a goose on it, over the handle of the door. When buyers see the decorative towel, they will also notice the glass door. These are simple ways to get buyers to notice simple improvements, but they work.

Decks

Decks are pretty hard to miss if you are taking a close look at a house. However, there are ways you can draw attention to your new deck. If the door that leads to the deck has glass that is usually covered by curtains, open the curtains. Let buyers see the deck while they are still inside the home. If the house is being shown at night, have the deck lights turned on.

New Kitchen Counters

New kitchen counters will probably be noticed without any help. But if you want to make sure, set a bowl of fruit on the counter. The bowl of fruit will attract the buyers' attention to the counter.

There are many more ways to highlight your home in subtle ways. All you have to do is get a little creative, and the prompter signs don't hurt.

How to Camouflage Less Desirable Features

Learning how to camouflage less desirable features is another worthy lesson for home sellers. I am not suggesting that you deceive buyers, but on the other hand there is no need to spotlight a problem area for them to inspect on the initial visit. It would be wrong to conceal a damaged part of your flooring with an area rug, but it is not unethical to adjust your lighting to divert attention from a less than perfect job of drywall taping.

Hiding problem areas is a touchy issue. Sooner or later serious physical defects in the home are going to come to light. It might not happen until after the transaction is closed, but it is going to happen. And when it does, there are going to be consequences to face. You don't want the hassles that follow deceit; they won't be pleasant.

The real estate industry is plagued with horror stories of buyers being ripped off by greedy sellers and unethical brokers. Some of the stories are blown out of proportion and others are real. With the ever-present threat of fraud, modern buyers are becoming better educated on what to look for when buying a house. Most buyers hire professional inspectors to go through the property for assurance before the closing. In today's real estate market, people are more suspicious than ever.

Most sellers don't have any desire to con the public into a bad purchase. But the few bad sellers who attempt major coverups and get caught raise the awareness of everyone. These people make selling a house more of a chore than ever before.

While I would never suggest that you conceal material defects, I believe it is fine to highlight your strong points and keep a low profile on the areas you are not proud of. If your septic system needs to be replaced and you know it, tell the buyers about the problem early on. If you are annoyed by the noise in your wall when the toilet drains to the basement, don't flush the toilet during the showing.

Give buyers every opportunity to inspect any part of your home, but don't greet them at the door with a list of grievances you have compiled over the years spent in your house. If your house is in the proposed flight path of jets leaving the local airport, you will be wise to tell the buyers of the possibilities that exist for planes to come across the house. On the other hand, if an occasional military plane flies over your home and rattles the windows, you don't need to disclose it.

If your basement floods every spring, tell the buyers about it. If one of your water pipes broke and flooded the basement last year, don't worry about disclosing it. Are you getting the idea of what is and what is not acceptable? If you have any doubts, disclose what you know. You might lose a sale, but that's better than what could happen if you lost a lawsuit.

Now that we have established the ground rules, let's look at a few specific examples. In our first example let's assume that your upstairs bathtub had a leaky tub waste and it created a water spot on your hall ceiling. Is this a defect you must disclose? Not if you have repaired the leak and don't have a current problem. Okay, so this is a problem you can safely conceal. You can either apply a primer and a new coat of paint to the ceiling to hide the spot or you could cut out the bad section and replace it before painting. As long as there is no structural damage, painting over the spot is not only acceptable, it's smart.

The ceilings in many mass-produced homes lack in the quality of their finished workmanship. If you have ever looked up at a ceiling and seen the outline of drywall tape, you know what I mean. Seeing the impression of the tape doesn't mean the house is built poorly, but many buyers will get that impression. This certainly isn't a critical issue that you need to disclose. A few hours spent texturing the ceiling will hide the seams in the ceiling and solve your problem.

The strategic placement of a toaster can conceal a flaw where the drywall in your kitchen meets the backsplash of the counter. A wraparound mat in front of your toilet will hide the edges of the vinyl flooring that are just beginning to curl up around the base of the toilet. There are plenty of ways to camouflage your less desirable features.

I could go on and on, but I don't want to encourage hiding problems and potential problems. Concealing a problem until you have time to fix it is fine, as long as you fix it. But please, don't become one of the sellers that make the headlines for misrepresentation.

Reading the Room

Reading the room is a trait developed by brokers. They learn to look around a room and draw some pretty accurate conclusions. They can tell if children live in the home, approximately how old they are, and what sex they are. Savvy brokers can survey a room and tell what the owners like and how to strike up a good conversation. The skills they develop for reading a room are used in most of their sales presentations. Sometimes they are reading clothes and cars, but the principles remain the same.

As a seller, you might want to present a certain image to prospective buyers. You can send signals through your furniture, your decorations, and your apparent habits. For example, if buyers walk into your home and find the windows open, they will assume crime levels are low in the neighborhood. On the other hand, if they see double locks on the doors and screw-bolts holding the window sashes down, they are going to feel a little nervous about the criminal element.

A buyer who sees firewood stacked in the garage might move to thinking of termites and will wonder if the wood pile is allowing termites to infest the home. If the wood is stored under cover in the backyard, away from the house, this negative thought will never occur.

If you have stapled plastic over your windows in past winters to keep out the cold, the staple holes could be a quick tipoff to an astute buyer. If you have these staple holes, fill them with wood putty and paint over them.

If your floor covering is carpet, move your furniture a week or so before opening the house to showings. The indentations left in the carpet from the old furniture location may make a buyer suspicious of why the furniture was moved.

These are only some of the ways careful study can reveal little facts about a house. It will be difficult for you to read your own rooms. You are too close to the heat to see the flame. If you have a good broker, the broker will read the room for you. If you don't have a good broker, ask a few of your friends to come over and play the role of prospects. Let them go through the house making notes of items they notice that might deserve change. To make this exercise effective, your friends will have to take their time and be brutally honest in what they see. If you explain the importance of their help to you, they will comply with your request.

Regrouping

There comes a time in the sale of most homes when regrouping is necessary. If your home has been actively marketed and shown for more than a month without a reasonable offer, it is time to regroup. Call a meeting with your broker and find out what is going wrong. You can bet the problem won't fix itself. You may get lucky and have just the right buyer walk in the next day, but you can't afford to take that gamble. Instead, you must take action.

Sit down with your broker and be prepared for a lengthy session of playing "what-if." Start the meeting by going over the objections your broker has collected from past showings. See if there is any common ground between the complaints. If there is, target it for attention. When there is no apparent reason for the lack of interest in your house, start playing "what-if." This is when you brainstorm to see what would happen if you did this or that. You know: what if I had the carpets professionally cleaned, what if we left the car out of the garage to make it look bigger, what if . . . , and so on.

Write down all ideas, good and bad, during the meeting. When you are done, review your list of possibilities. If you feel comfortable with your new plans, put them into action. Should the list not be sufficient to provide the spark you need, call in the troops. Who are the troops? The troops are the other agents in your broker's agency.

Most large agencies have all of their agents view their new listings. They call the procedure going on a caravan. Your house is invaded by an army of agents looking to see what you have to offer. Comments will be made and suggestions will be offered. This open forum of professional salespeople can produce some excellent ideas. If your broker hasn't already conducted a caravan through your property, get it done now.

Try your new game plan for another month. If you still aren't getting results, go back over the comparable sales with your broker. Maybe prices have dropped since the first comparables you investigated. If the house hasn't sold in 90 days, you are going to have to pull out all the stops. This could mean reducing your price, offering bonuses to the brokers, giving special incentives to buyers, and any number of other major steps for getting a sale. If you've tried everything else, try another real estate brokerage.

If you decide to switch brokerages before your listing agreement expires, you could run into some trouble. The listing agreement is a contract that you have signed promising certain things to the brokerage. Technically, if you try to switch agencies, you could be in breach of your contract. This could get ugly.

A lot of brokers will tell you that you cannot terminate the listing early. If the broker won't support your decision to cancel the contract, talk to the sales manager, the designated broker, or the company's owner. If you raise a big enough stink and hold your ground on the lack of performance you have received, you will be able to cancel your listing agreement. You will probably get some sales pitch to continue the listing, but in the end, they will give in and void the agreement.

That brings us to the end of the line. All that is left for you to do now is to improve and sell your home. With the advice you have gained from this book, you should be much better prepared than you were. I appreciate your staying with me to the end, and I hope the sale of your home is fast and profitable. Good luck!

Index